Ocean County College

Student Resource Manual

for

Health and Physical Education
110 and 120

Ray Chatfield, Assistant Professor
Jill Gunther, Assistant Professor
Scott Heilman, Assistant Professor
William Middleton, Assistant Professor
Hyman Mittleberg, Professor
John Stauff, Professor, Assistant Dean

DEPARTMENT OF HEALTH AND PHYSICAL EDUCATION
OCEAN COUNTY COLLEGE

TABLE OF CONTENTS

Minimum Requirement for HPE 110

Obtain a locker assignment in the gym from the locker attendant. Buy texts assigned by your instructor and do assignments. All homework assignments must be handed in on time. Homework represents you. Be neat!

Obtain a 65 average on the three major tests. This is worth approximately 75 percent of your grade. Regular attendance at all classes is expected; absences affect the student's own academic achievement and detract from the value of the class for the instructor and for other students. The student should use mature judgment and consult with the instructor concerning unexcused absences from class. Students may be withdrawn from class if absences exceed 10% of the class meetings. You may make up an excused absence by attending another class with permission of the instructor.

Physical Requirements: One of the following must be accomplished (worth 25 percent of your grade).

A. Jogging Requirement: Under 30 years old

Men	1.5 miles (6 laps)	
Women	1.25 miles (5 laps)	

100	99	98	97	96	95	94	93	92	90	89	88	87	86
9:00	9:06	9:12	9:18	9:24	9:30	9:34	9:38	9:42	9:46	9:52	9:56	10:00	10:09

85	84	83	82	81	80	79	78	77	76	75	74
10:18	10:27	10:36	10:45	10:54	11:00	11:12	11:24	11:36	11:48	12:00	12:12

73	72	71	70	69	68	67	66	65	64	63	62
12:24	12:36	12:48	13:00	13:06	13:12	13:18	13:24	13:30	13:36	13:42	13:48

30-39 years old: Add 30 seconds (example: In order to get an 80 you have to run the distance in 11:30).
40-49 years old: Add 90 seconds (example: In order to get an 80 you have to run the distance in 12:30).
50 or more years old: Add 150 seconds (example: In order to get an 80 you have to run the distance in 786 seconds or 13:30).

B. Swimming Requirement: Under 30 years old

Men	400 yards (16 laps)	
Women	375 yards (15 laps)	

100	99	98	97	96	95	94	93	92	91	90	89	88	87	86	85	84	83
6:10	6:20	6:30	6:40	6:50	7:00	7:08	7:16	7:24	7:32	7:40	7:48	7:56	8:00	8:09	8:18	8:27	8:36

82	81	80	79	78	77	76	75	74	73	72	71	70	69	68	67	66
8:45	8:54	9:00	9:12	9:24	9:36	9:48	10:00	10:12	10:24	10:36	10:48	11:00	11:06	11:12	11:18	11:24

65	64	63	62	61	60	59	58	57	56	55	54	53	52	51	50
11:30	11:36	11:45	11:48	11:54	12:00	12:06	12:12	12:18	12:24	12:30	12:36	12:42	12:48	12:54	13:00

30-39 years old: Add 30 seconds (example: In order to get an 80 you have to swim the distance in 9:30).
40-49 years old: Add 60 seconds (example: In order to get an 80 you have to swim the distance in 10:00).
50 or more years old: Add 90 seconds (example: In order to get an 80 you have to swim the distance in 10:30).

Distance Option

Jog 2-1/2 miles (10 laps) with no time limit. Walking is not permitted.

Swim 800 yards (32 lengths) without stopping. Different strokes are permitted.

Prescribed Fitness Option: Walking Program

The Prescribed Physical Fitness Program is for students who identify themselves to their instructors and receive approval, and who qualify under the following criteria:

Criteria:

1. For students who are rehabilitating from accidents.
2. For students with a sedentary lifestyle over an extended period of time.
3. For students with a significant weight problem.
4. Medical waiver required.

Method of Evaluation:

Option I

A. Keep a written record (log) of physical activity using Ocean County College facilities as much as possible. (Pick up log sheets from instructor.)
B. Walk at least 50 miles within 8 weeks.
C. Complete a 2-1/4 mile walk on the track within 40 minutes.
D. Pass-fail grade assigned (not computed in academic average).

Option II

1 Mile Timed Walking Requirement

A. Keep a written record (log) of physical activity using Ocean County College facilities as much as possible. (Pick up log sheets from instructor.)
B. Walk at least 50 miles within 8 weeks.
C. Grade computed in academic average based upon the charts listed on page 3.

2

HPE 110
MEN 1 MILE
WALKING REQUIREMENT

100	99	98	97	96	95	94	93	92	91	90
10:00	10:10	10:19	10:29	10:38	10:48	10:57	11:07	11:16	11:26	11:35

89	88	87	86	85	84	83	82	81	80
11:45	11:54	12:04	12:13	12:23	12:32	12:42	12:51	13:01	13:10

79	78	77	76	75	74	73	72	71	69
13:20	13:29	13:39	13:48	13:58	14:07	14:17	14:26	14:36	14:45

69	68	67	66	65	64	63	62	61	60
14:55	15:04	15:14	15:23	15:33	15:42	15:52	16:01	16:11	16:20

59	58	57	56	55	54	53	52	51	50
16:30	16:39	16:49	16:58	17:08	17:17	17:27	17:37	17:46	17:56

HPE 110
WOMEN 1 MILE
WALKING REQUIREMENT

100	99	98	97	96	95	94	93	92	91	90
11:40	11:49	11:57	12:06	12:14	12:23	12:31	12:40	12:48	12:57	13:05

89	88	87	86	85	84	83	82	81	80
13:14	13:22	13:31	13:40	13:48	13:57	14:05	14:14	14:22	14:30

79	78	77	76	75	74	73	72	71	69
14:38	14:46	14:54	15:02	15:20	15:28	15:36	15:43	15:51	15:59

69	68	67	66	65	64	63	62	61	60
16:07	16:15	16:23	13:61	16:39	16:47	16:55	17:03	17:11	17:19

59	58	57	56	55	54	53	52	51	50
17:29	17:39	17:49	17:59	18:09	18:19	18:29	18:39	18:49	19:00

Minimum Requirements for HPE 120

Obtain a locker assignment in the gym from the locker attendant.

Purchase the *Student Resource Manual for Health and Physical Education 110 and 120* and *Understanding Your Health, 3/e* by Payne and Hahn.

All homework assignments must be handed in on time. Homework represents you. Be neat!

Regular attendance of *all* classes is expected, as absences affect a student's own academic achievement and detract from the value of the class for the instructor and other students. Students should use mature judgment and consult with the instructor concerning unexcused absences from class. Students may be withdrawn from class if absences exceed 10% of the class meetings. You may make up an excused absence by attending another class with permission of the instructor.

Examinations

Three lecture examinations will be given, with each examination worth 25 percent of the final grade—lecture examinations represent 75 percent of the total grade.

Two activity examinations will be given, with each worth 12.5 percent of the final grade for a total of 25 percent.

All examinations must be taken on the date they are scheduled. No make-up examinations are permitted for unexcused absences.

In written and/or oral form:

1. Explain three key concepts fundamental to the implementation of this program.

2. State five teaching and/or learning methods that will be used in implementing this program.

3. Report five of the lecture topics and five of the laboratory activities that make up the content of this course.

4. Define the concept of the Soft American.

5. Present three ways this course can help the Soft American become a happier and healthier person.

6. Explain the physiological benefits of regular exercise on the following functions of the body: circulatory, respiratory, neuromuscular, digestion, and metabolism and body composition.

7. Clearly describe five psychological benefits of regular exercise.

Ocean County College

Semester:_____ (FA, SP, or SU)

Year: 19____

HPE 110
HEALTH QUESTIONNAIRE

Section No: _____

Student I.D. No:_____ (1-30)

Sex:

Male_____ Female_____

Age: _____ years

Weight: _____ pounds

Skin Fold Measurement: _____

Life Expectancy: _____ years

Risk Factor Rating: _____

Resting Heart Range: _____

Vital Capacity: _____ Liters

Blood Pressure:
Systolic: _____
Diastolic: _____

<u>Waist</u>_____ Divided by <u>Hip</u>_____ = _____
   (in inches)   (in inches)   =   (measurement)

The Circulatory System

Self-Test and Instructional Objectives on the Circulatory System

In written and/or oral form:

1. Explain the function of the circulatory system.

2. Describe three functions of the bloodstream and four major components of blood.

3. Report three major parts of the vascular system and their primary functions.

4. Define pulse, blood pressure, systolic pressure, and diastolic pressure.

5. Explain the use of the sphygmomanometer.

6. Describe three factors influencing pulse rate and three factors influencing blood pressure.

7. Explain three benefits derived from a healthy and functionally efficient circulatory system.

8. Report what laboratory experiments have indicated about maintaining a functionally efficient circulatory system.

Self-Test and Instructional Objectives on the Heart

In written/or oral form:

1. Explain the primary function of the heart.

2. Describe the structure of the heart, including the functions of the following: atria, ventricles, septum, myocardium, valves, pulmonary vein, and aortic artery.

3. Demonstrate a knowledge and understanding of the course of blood as it flows through the heart.

4. Describe coronary circulation.

5. Explain the terms *systole* and *diastole*.

6. Summarize what controls the heartbeat, including definitions of the following: sinoatrial node, atrioventricular node, bundle of His, and Purkinje fibers.

7. Explain the effect of exercise on cardiac output (electrocardiogram).

8. Give three causes of heart acceleration during exercise.

Terms that Help Us Understand Heart Disease and Ways to Prevent It

Arteriosclerosis Commonly called "hardening of the arteries," arteriosclerosis includes a variety of conditions that cause the artery walls to become thick and hard and to lose elasticity. It is a common cause of high blood pressure and "heart attack."

Cholesterol A fatty substance present in blood and implicated experimentally in atherosclerosis, a form of arteriosclerosis.

Coronary occlusion Partial or total obstruction of a coronary artery.

Coronary thrombosis Blockage of a coronary artery by a thrombus (a clot that forms in a blood vessel and remains attached there), often causing sudden death.

Emotional storm A traumatic emotional experience which is likely to affect the human organism physiologically.

Fibrin The substance which forms a blood clot in combination with the blood cells.

Hypertension An unstable or persistent elevation of blood pressure above the normal range.

Lipid A term for all fats and fatty substances in the blood stream.

Myocardial infarction The process leading to the death of heart tissue due to diminished blood flow.

Obesity A condition of excessive body fat.

Parasympathetic nervous system A branch of the autonomic (existing independently) nervous system that slows the heart.

Risk factor Any condition that predisposes an individual to heart disease, including lack of exercise, smoking, stress and tension, heredity, and obesity.

Post mortem After death.

Sympathetic nervous system A branch of the autonomic (existing independently) nervous system which prepares the body for activity; it speeds up the heart.

Terms that Will Help Us to Know More About the Heart

Aorta The great trunk artery that carries the freshly oxygenated blood from the heart to be distributed by branch arteries throughout the body.

Atrium One of the upper chambers of the heart.

Blood pressure The pressure of blood in the blood vessels. Blood pressure when the heart contracts is called systolic; blood pressure when the heart relaxes between beats is called diastolic.

Cardiac output The total body blood flow (between heart beats).

Diastole Period of relaxation of the heart.

Pulmonary artery The carrier of spent or used blood to the lungs for oxygenation.

Pulmonary vein The carrier of oxygenated blood from the lungs to the heart.

Septum A dividing wall between left and right chambers of the heart.

Systole Period of contraction of the heart.

Valve An opening in the heart between chambers which allows forward flow of blood but prevents backward flow.

Ventricle One of the two lower chambers of the heart.

Notes on Heart Disorders and Related Diseases

Myocardial Failure

1. When the heart is unable to pump out all the blood that returns to it, blood backs up in the veins that lead to the heart.

2. The heart's failure to maintain good circulation may result in the accumulation of fluid in various parts of the body such as the abdomen, lungs, and legs.

Congenital Heart Abnormalities

1. Of the thirty-five known kinds of inborn heart defects, nearly twenty can be cured or improved by surgery.

2. "Blue babies" (cyanosis) have heart defects that prevent enough blood from getting to their lungs to pick up oxygen.

3. Heart murmur refers to abnormal or unusual sounds resulting from vibrations produced by the motion of blood within the heart.

Arrhythmia

1. This disorder is a change in the rhythm of the heart that may be caused by physiological or psychological disturbances.

2. Some arrhythmia is normal, especially during exertion, and a change in the heart rhythm is not necessarily indicative of this disorder.

Coronary Atherosclerosis

1. The coronary arteries supply the heart with its own rich blood supply.

2. Atherosclerosis leads to a thickening as well as a hardening of the walls of coronary arteries.

3. As the channel in the artery narrows, a blood clot (thrombus) may form in one of the branches of a coronary artery, thus blocking the blood supply to one part of the heart muscle.

4. Other arterial branches enlarge and new branches (collateral circulation) begin to form to bring a supply of blood to the area around the injury.

Angina Pectoris

1. Angina is not a disease. It occurs when some portion of the heart muscle is not furnished with enough blood and oxygen for the work being performed at that instant. It causes severe pain in the chest and often in the left arm and shoulder.

2. In most cases angina pain does not appear while a person is at rest, but only when the heart is asked to perform extra work.

Diseases of Blood Vessels of the Brain

1. A blood vessel may rupture or may become blocked, causing blood flow to the brain to be reduced or even stopped.

2. Causes for this disease include defects of the vessels which may develop before birth, as well as physical injuries, infections of the blood vessels, general infections, blood diseases, heart diseases, hardening of the arteries, and high blood pressure.

3. Headaches, vision difficulties, dizziness, fainting spells, numbness of hand or face, weakness, paralysis, difficulty in speaking, poor memory, difficulty in thinking, personality changes, and mental disturbances are among the common results of cerebral vascular disease.

Strokes or Cerebrovascular Accidents

1. A stroke usually occurs suddenly when an artery to a portion of the brain ruptures or is closed by thrombosis, embolism, or any other causes mentioned earlier.

2. High blood pressure is one of the major diseases associated with strokes.

3. A great deal of research is under way to learn more about hardening of the arteries (arteriosclerosis), the largest single cause of cerebral vascular disease.

4. Treatment should be started very soon after a stroke has occurred (often within 24 hours) to help restore use of the affected arm and leg.

Hypertension or High Blood Pressure

1. High blood pressure is often characterized by narrowing of the arterioles, through which the blood passes to feed the body tissues. The smaller the channel, the greater the pressure required to force the normal amount of blood through. Therefore, the heart works harder and blood pressure rises.

2. The important question is whether the blood pressure is normal, and what is normal depends on the individual.

3. Arteriosclerosis is a major cause of death among hypertensive patients. Cutting off the blood supply to vital tissues is as serious as depriving a plant of water.

Anemia

1. In this condition, the blood has too few red blood cells or too little hemoglobin.

2. Typical symptoms are fatigue, weakness, paleness, faintness, and shortness of breath.

3. Anemia can be brought about by improper diet, faulty absorption of food, loss of blood, injury to bone marrow, and certain infections and parasites.

4. When the number of red blood cells and amount of hemoglobin are reduced, the blood can no longer carry enough oxygen for the body's needs.

Burger's Disease

1. In this disease, a thickening, chronic inflammation (possibly blood clots) in the vessels interferes with the blood supply of the region, usually the legs.

2. This may result in swelling, ulceration, and gangrene.

3. Tobacco use is a major cause of the constriction of blood vessels in the extremities.

4. Smokers account for eighty percent of all cases.

Hemophilia

1. This disease is an inherited deficiency characterized by the lack of essential blood-clotting components.

2. Hemophilia is a sex-linked characteristic (carried on the X chromosome), usually inherited by males from mothers who carry the recessive trait but are themselves unaffected.

Leukemia

1. Sometimes called cancer of the blood, leukemia is a potentially fatal disease that affects blood-forming cells.

2. In this disease, there is overproduction of immature white blood cells that are not able to fight infection.

3. The number of red blood cells is reduced and the patient becomes anemic. The blood does not clot properly.

4. Symptoms resemble those in anemia, including enlargement of the lymph glands and the spleen. Recurrent fever is also common.

Phlebitis

1. Phlebitis is inflammation of a vein, usually caused by a blood clot. It most commonly occurs in veins in the legs.

2. The abnormally large amount of fluid in the intercellular spaces of the affected part causes pain and stiffness.

Varicose Veins

1. Any factor or combination of factors that cause increased pressure within the blood vessels in the legs will most likely lead to a thinning and weakening of the walls of the veins and finally result in varicose veins.

2. Varicose veins can bulge and cause irregularity in the contour of the skin. They are prevalent in people who stand for long periods of time.

3. Persons with varicose veins usually complain that their legs feel tired and heavy. There may be a burning, stinging sensation accompanied by aches and cramps in the calves.

PERSONAL ASSESSMENT

RISKO

Study each risk factor and its row. These are medical conditions and habits associated with an increased danger of heart attack. *Not all risk factors are measurable enough to be included.* Circle to number in the box applicable to you. For example, if you are 37, circle the number in the box labeled 31-40.

After checking all the rows, total the circled numbers. This score is an estimate of your chances of suffering a heart attack.

	1 10 to 20	2 21 to 30	3 31 to 40	4 41 to 50	6 51 to 60	8 61 and over
Age						
Heredity	1 No known history of heart disease	2 1 relative with cardio-vascular disease Over 60	3 2 relatives with cardio-vascular disease Over 60	4 1 relative with cardio-vascular disease Under 60	6 2 relatives with cardio-vascular disease Under 60	7 3 relatives with cardio-vascular disease Under 60
Weight	0 More than 5 lb below stan-dard weight	1 −5 to +5 lb standard weight	2 6 to 20 lb overweight	3 21 to 35 lb overweight	5 38 to 50 lb overweight	7 51 to 65 lb overweight
Tobacco smoking	0 Nonuser	1 Cigar and/or pipe	2 10 cigarettes or less a day	4 20 cigarettes a day	6 30 cigarettes a day	10 40 cigarettes a day or more
Exercise	1 Intense occu-pational and recreational exertion	2 Moderate oc-cupational and recre-ational exer-tion	3 Sedentary work and in-tense recre-ational exertion	5 Sedentary oc-cupational and moderate recreational exertion	6 Sedentary work and light recre-ational exer-tion	8 Complete lack of all exercise
Cholesterol or fat % in diet	1 Cholesterol below 100 mg/dl Diet contains no animal or solid fats	2 Cholesterol 181 to 205 mg/dl Diet contains 10% animal or solid fats	3 Cholesterol 206 to 230 mg/dl Diet contains 20% animal or solid fats	4 Cholesterol 231 to 255 mg/dl Diet contains 30% animal or solid fats	5 Cholesterol 256 to 280 mg/dl Diet contains 40% animal or solid fats	7 Cholesterol 281 to 305 mg/dl Diet contains 50% animal or solid fats
Blood pres-sure	1 100 upper reading	2 120 upper reading	3 140 upper reading	4 160 upper reading	6 180 upper reading	8 200 or over upper reading
Sex	1 Female under 40	2 Female 40 to 50	3 Female over 50	5 Male	6 Stocky male	7 Bald stocky male

For meaningful interpretation of RISKO only the official RISKO directions should be used.

Interpretation

6-11   Risk well below average

12-17   Risk below average

18-24   Risk generally average

25-31   Risk moderate

32-40   Risk at a dangerous level

41-62   Danger; see your doctor now

Heredity

Count parents, grandparents, brothers, sisters who have had a heart attack and/or stroke.

Tobacco Smoking

If you inhale deeply and smoke a cigarette down to the filter, add 1 to your classification. Do not subtract because you think you do not inhale or smoke only a half inch on a cigarette.

Exercise

Lower your score one point if you exercise regularly and frequently.

Cholesterol or Saturated Fat Intake Level

If you can't get your cholesterol blood level from your doctor, then estimate honestly the percentage of solid fats you eat. These are usually of animal origin—lard, cream, butter, and beef and lamb fat. If; you eat much of this, your cholesterol level probably will be high.

Blood Pressure

If you have no recent reading but have passed an insurance or industrial examination, chances are your blood pressure is 140 or less.

Gender

This takes into account the fact that men have from 6 to 10 times more heart attacks than do women of childbearing age.

Diagnostic Aids for the Heart and Circulatory System

Stethoscope

The stethoscope is used to listen to heart sounds. A physician may check to see whether:

1. the heart is beating rhythmically.
2. there is a rubbing sound against the pericardium which could indicate inflammation caused by a thrombus.
3. the valves are working properly. (Improper functioning of the valves of the heart will often be heard with a stethoscope as a "heart murmur.")
4. the heart recovers normally after exercise.

Sphygmomanometer

The phygmomanometer is used to measure blood pressure. Systolic pressure is the blood pressure when the heart contracts. Diastolic pressure is the blood pressure when the heart relaxes. Small changes in diastolic pressure during exercise are related to arterial blood flow dynamics and peripheral resistance.

Blood Pressure and Circulation

Blood pressure depends on the pumping action of the heart (cardiac output), peripheral resistance offered to the outflow of blood from the arteries (which varies with elasticity and vasoconstriction), and volume of circulating blood.

Cardiac output depends upon:

I. Venous return, which is
   A. Increased by:
      1. muscle contraction
      2. deep respiration
      3. duration of diastole
   B. Decreased by:
      1. ventricular chambers
      2. gravity of blood below heart level
      3. dilation of blood vessels over wide area
II. Force of heart beat, which is
   A. Increased by:
      1. epinephrine and norepinephrine
      2. reduction in size of heart
   B. Decreased by:
      1. shortening of diastole
   C. Maintained by
      1. adequate coronary circulation for proper nutrition
III. Heart rate, which is regulated by:
   A. cardiac nerves
   B. cardioaccleratory and cardioinhibitory impulses from higher brain centers
   C. carbon reflexes from pressure receptors
   D. carbon dioxide excess or oxygen decreases
   E. rise in body temperature
   F. epinephrine

Peripheral resistance depends upon:

I. Caliber of arterioles and capillaries
   A. vasodilator nerves and vasoconstrictor nerves
   B. epinephrine and norepinephrine
   C. temperature

ELECTROCARDIOGRAM (ECG)

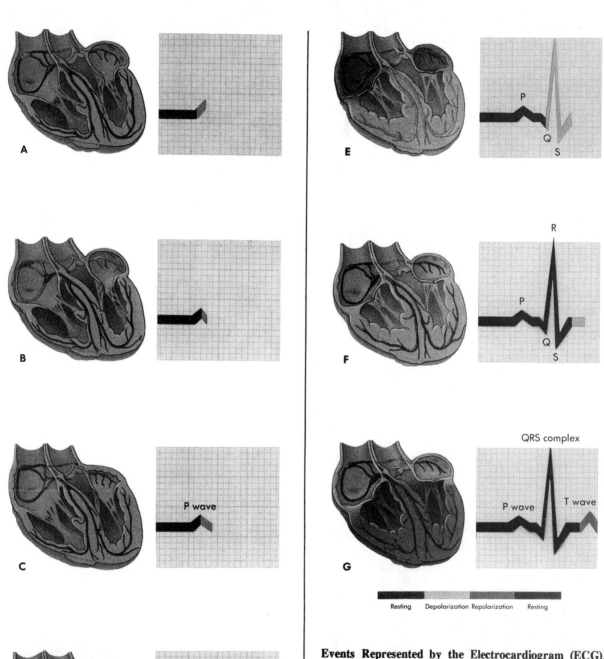

A

B

C

D

E

F

G

Resting   Depolarization Repolarization   Resting

Events Represented by the Electrocardiogram (ECG). A through C, The P wave represents the depolarization of cardiac muscle tissue in the SA node and atrial walls. **C and D,** Before the QRS complex is observed, the AV node and AV bundle depolarize. **E and F,** The QRS complex occurs as the atrial walls repolarize and the ventricular walls depolarize. **G,** the T wave is observed as the ventricular walls repolarize. Depolarization triggers contraction in the affected muscle tissue. Thus cardiac muscle contraction occurs *after* depolarization begins.

CARDIOVASCULAR FITNESS INVENTORY

Student name _____

Grading instructor _____

Sheet # _____ of (total #) _____

Time of class _____

Rest	Systolic	Pulse	Diastolic	Rest	Systolic	Pulse	Diastolic
1 min.				20			
2				21			
3				22			
4				23			
5				24			
6				25			
7				26			
8				27			
9				28			
10				29			
11				30			
12				REC			
13				1			
14				2			
15				3			
16				4			
17				5			
18				10			
19				15			

23

How Long Will You Live?

The following life-expectancy quiz is one of many health questionnaires now used by physicians, medical centers, and insurance groups. While quizzes can hardly be precise, they do give a more realistic picture of probable longevity than old-fashioned actuarial tables, which rely almost exclusively on heredity patterns and medical history. Current computations try to measure risk in relation to environment, stress, and general behavior, though statisticians and experts do not always agree on who to weigh the different components. A high salary (presumably indicative of competitive stress) may not be as detrimental to longevity as many quizzes suggest. On the other hand, marriage or cohabitation, usually assumed to increase one's chance of living longer, may actually increase stress.

PERSONAL AND FAMILY HISTORY

Start with 76.   76

If you are male, subtract 3   _____

If you are female, add 4.   _____

If you live in an urban area with a population over 2 million, subtract 2.   _____

If you live in a town with a population under 10,000 or on a farm, add 2.   _____

If any grandparent lived to age 85, add 2.   _____

If all four grandparents lived to age 80, add 6.   _____

If either parent died of a stroke or heart attack before the age of 50, subtract 4.   _____

If any parent, brother, or sister under 50 has (or had) cancer or a heart condition or has had diabetes since childhood, subtract 3.   _____

If you earn over $50,000 a year, subtract 2.   _____

If you finished college, add 1. If you have a graduate or professional degree, add 2 more.   _____

If you are 65 years or over and are still working, add 3.   _____

If you live with a spouse or friend, add 5. If not, subtract 1 for every ten years alone since age 25.   _____

Subtotal   _____

LIFESTYLE

If you work behind a desk, subtract 3.   _____

If your work requires heavy physical labor, add 3.   _____

If you exercise strenuously (tennis, running, swimming, etc.) five times a week for at least half an hour, add 4. Two or three times a week, add 2.   _____

If you sleep more than ten hours each night, subtract 4.   _____

If you are intense, aggressive, and easily angered, subtract 3.   _____

If you are a man over age 40 and have annual checkups, add 2.   _____

If you are a woman and see a gynecologist once a year, add 2.   _____

Subtotal   _____

AGE ADJUSTMENT

If you are between age 30 and age 40, add 2.   ————

If you are between age 40 and age 50, add 3.   ————

If you are between age 50 and age 60, add 4.   ————

If you are over the age of 70, add 5.   ————

ADD UP YOUR TOTAL TO GET YOUR LIFE EXPECTANCY   ————

Self-Test and Instructional Objectives on How Not to Have a Heart Attack

In written and/or oral form:

1. Discuss the theories about why men have more heart attacks than women.

2. Explain whether where one lives has any effect on heart disease.

3. Name the hereditary factors that can promote coronary disease.

4. State the effects of caloric intake (including lipids) on the occurrence of heart attacks.

5. Describe the relationship between diabetes and heart disease.

6. Describe the causes of high blood pressure.

7. Explain the effects smoking has on the heart and circulatory system.

8. Discuss the ways in which exercise may help prevent heart disease.

Self-Test and Instructional Objectives on the Role of Exercise in the Prevention of Cardiovascular Disease

In written and/or oral form:

1. State at least ten terms which help us better understand heart disease.

2. Report some of the statistical evidence gathered to support a link between heart disease and lack of exercise.

3. Report at least five factors which have been linked to susceptibility to heart disease.

4. Explain effects of increased physical activity on the body that may reduce the occurrence and/or severity of heart disease.

5. Describe two fitness effects exercise has on the circulatory system and two fitness effects exercise has on the respiratory system.

6. Present concise explanations of three theories about the causes of heart disease. State the role of exercise in each of these theories.

7. Describe coronary collateral circulation. State the effects of exercise on coronary collateral circulation.

LOG FOR PRESCRIBED PHYSICAL FITNESS PROGRAM

Date	Time of Day	Activity Type	Location	Pulse rate walking	Pulse rate at completion	Pulse rate (after recovery/5 min.)	Pulse rate (after recovery/10 min.)

LOG FOR PRESCRIBED PHYSICAL FITNESS PROGRAM

Sheet # _____ of (total #) _____

Time of class _____

Student name _____

Grading instructor _____

Date	Time	Activity type	Location	Duration of exercise (min.)	Option weight	Physical feeling (before and after)	Emotional state (before and after)	Options/thoughts/ attitudes, etc.

The Respiratory System

Self-Test and Instructional Objectives
on Respiration

In written and/or oral form:

1. Explain the process of respiration. Include at least five major functions.

2. Describe three important ways the respiratory tract is protected.

3. Present three necessary conditions in the process that provides oxygen for the cells of the body.

4. Define the following important aspects of respiration: vital capacity, oxygen debt, recovery period, working capacity, oxygen debt tolerance, and maximal oxygen intake.

5. State the three major effects of exercise on the respiratory system.

6. Define the following terms: trachea, bronchi, bronchioles, alveoli, aorta, mucus, sinuses, diaphragm, aerobic, anaerobic, internal respiration, external respiration, turbinate bones, and respiratory center.

7. Describe three major disorders of the respiratory system: asthma, chronic bronchitis, and emphysema.

THE RESPIRATORY SYSTEM

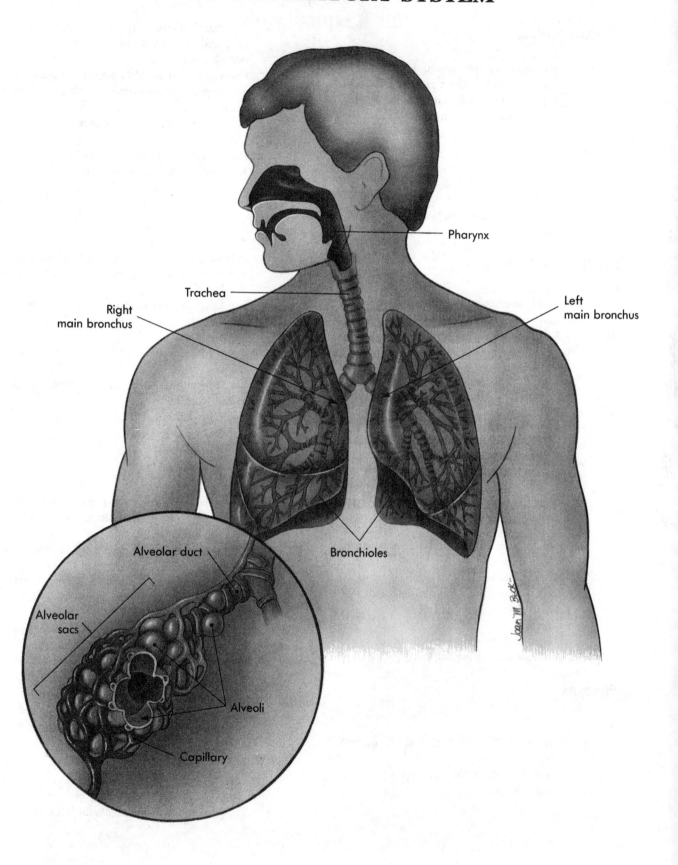

Pharynx

Trachea

Right
main bronchus

Left
main bronchus

Bronchioles

Alveolar duct

Alveolar
sacs

Alveoli

Capillary

Outline Summary on the Respiratory System

Structural Plan

Basic plan of respiratory system would be similar to an inverted tree if it were hollow; leaves of the tree would be comparable to alveoli, with the microscopic sacs enclosed by networks of capillaries.

Respiratory Tracts

A. Upper respiratory tract—nose, pharynx, and larynx
B. Lower respiratory tract—trachea, bronchial tree, and lungs

Respiratory Mucosa

A. Specialized membrane that lines the air distribution tubes in the respiratory tree
B. Over 125 ml of mucus produced each day forms a "mucous blanket" over much of the respiratory mucosa
C. Mucus serves as an air purification mechanism by trapping inspired irritants such as dust and pollen
D. Cilia on mucosal cells beat in only one direction, moving mucus upward to pharynx for removal

NOSE

A. Structure
1. Nasal septum separates interior of nose into two cavities
2. Mucous membrane lines nose
3. Frontal, maxillary, sphenoidal, and ethmoidal sinuses drain into nose
B. Functions
1. Warms and moistens inhaled air
2. Contains sense organs of smell

Pharynx

A. Structure
1. Pharynx (throat) about 12.5 cm (5 inches) long
2. Divided into nasopharynx, oropharynx, and laryngopharynx
3. Two nasal cavities, mouth, esophagus, larynx, and auditory tubes all have openings into pharynx
4. Pharyngeal tonsils and openings of auditory tubes open into nasopharynx; tonsils found in oropharynx
5. Mucous membrane lines pharynx
B. Functions
1. Passageway for food and liquids
2. Air distribution; passageway for air

Larynx

A. Structure
1. Several pieces of cartilage form framework
   a. Thyroid cartilage (Adam's apple) is largest
   b. Epiglottis partially covers opening into larynx
2. Mucous lining
3. Vocal cords stretch across interior of larynx
B. Functions
1. Air distribution; passageway for air to move to and from lungs
2. Voice production

Trachea (Windpipe)

A. Structure
1. Tube about 11 cm (4½ inches) long that extends from larynx into the thoracic cavity
2. Mucous lining
3. C-shaped rings of cartilage hold trachea open
B. Function—passageway for air to move to and from lungs
C. Obstruction
1. Blockage of trachea occludes the airway and if complete causes death in minutes
2. Tracheal obstruction causes over 4000 deaths annually in the United States
3. Heimlich maneuver (p. 287) is a lifesaving technique used to free the trachea of obstructions

Bronchi, Bronchioles, and Alveoli

A. Structure
1. Trachea branches into right and left bronchi

34

2. Each bronchus branches into smaller and smaller tubes eventually leading to bronchioles
3. Bronchioles end in clusters of microscopic alveolar sacs, the walls of which are made up of alveoli

B. Function
1. Bronchi and bronchioles—air distribution; passageway for air to move to and from alveoli
2. Alveoli—exchange of gases between air and blood

Lungs and Pleura

A. Structure
1. Size—large enough to fill the chest cavity, except for middle space occupied by heart and large blood vessels
2. Apex—narrow upper part of each lung, under collarbone
3. Base—broad lower part of each lung; rests on diaphragm
4. Pleura—moist, smooth, slipper membrane that lines chest cavity and covers outer surface of lungs; reduces friction between the lungs and chest wall during breathing

B. Function—breathing (pulmonary ventilation)

Respiration

A. Mechanics of breathing
1. Pulmonary ventilation includes two phases called *inspiration* (movement of air into lungs) and *expiration* (movement of air out of lungs
2. Changes in size and shape of thorax cause changes in air pressure within that cavity and in the lungs
3. Air pressure differences actually cause air to move into and out of the lungs

B. Inspiration
1. Active process—air moves into lungs
2. Inspiratory muscles include diaphragm and external intercostals
   a. Diaphragm flattens during inspiration—increases top to bottom length of thorax
   b. External intercostals—contraction elevates the ribs and increases the size of the thorax from the front to the back and from side to side

3. The increase in the size of the chest cavity reduces pressure within it, and air enters the lungs

C. Expiration
1. Quiet expiration is ordinarily a passive process
2. Inspiratory muscles include diaphragm and external intercostals
   a. Diaphragm flattens during inspiration—increases
   b. External intercostals—contraction elevates the ribs and increases the size of the thorax from the front to the back and from side to side
3. The increase in the size of the chest cavity reduces pressure within it, and air enters the lungs

C. Expiration
1. Quiet expiration is ordinarily a passive process
2. During expiration, thorax returns to its resting size and shape
3. Elastic recoil of lung tissues aids in expiration
4. Expiratory muscles used in forceful expiration are internal intercostals and abdominal muscles
   a. Internal intercostals—contraction depresses the rib cage and decreases the size of the thorax from the front to back
   b. Contraction of abdominal muscles elevates the diaphragm, thus decreasing size of the thoracic cavity from the top to bottom
5. Reduction in the size of the thoracic cavity increases its pressure and air leaves the lungs

D. Exchange of gases in lungs
1. Carbaminohemoglobin breaks down into carbon dioxide and hemoglobin
2. Carbon dioxide moves out of lung capillary blood into alveolar air and out of body in expired air
3. Oxygen moves from alveoli into lung capillaries
4. Hemoglobin combines with oxygen, producing oxyhemoglobin

E. Exchange of gases in tissues
1. Oxyhemoglobin breaks down into oxygen and hemoglobin
2. Oxygen moves out of tissue capillary blood into tissue cells
3. Carbon dioxide moves from tissue cells into tissue capillary blood

4. Hemoglobin combines with carbon dioxide, forming carbaminohemoglobin

F. Volumes of air exchanged in pulmonary ventilation
   1. Volumes of air exchanged in breathing can be measured with a spirometer
   2. Tidal volume (TV) amount normally breathed in or out with each breath
   3. Vital capacity (VC)—largest amount of air that one can breathe out in one expiration
   4. Expiratory reserve volume (ERV)—amount of air that can be forcibly exhaled after expiring the tidal volume
   5. Inspiratory reserve volume (IRV)—amount of air that can be forcibly inhaled after a normal inspiration
   6. Residual volume (RV)—air that remains in the lungs after the most forceful expiration
   7. Rate—usually about 12 to 18 breaths a minute; much faster during exercise

G. Regulation of respiration
   1. Regulation of respiration permits the body to adjust to varying demands for oxygen supply and carbon dioxide removal
   2. Most important central regulatory centers in medulla are called *respiratory control centers* (inspiratory and expiratory centers)
      a. Under resting conditions nervous activity in the respiratory control centers produces a normal rate and depth of respirations (12 to 18 per minute)
   3. Respiratory control centers in the medulla are influenced by "inputs" from receptors located in other body areas:
      a. Cerebral cortex—voluntary (but limited) voluntary control of respiratory activity
      b. Chemoreceptors—respond to changes in carbon dioxide, oxygen, and blood acid levels—located in carotid and aortic bodies
      c. Pulmonary stretch receptors—respond to the stretch in lungs, thus protecting respiratory organs from overinflation

Types of Breathing

A. Eupnea—normal breathing
B. Hyperventilation—rapid and deep respirations
C. Hypoventilation—slow and shallow respirations
D. Dyspnea—labored or difficult respirations
E. Apnea—stopped respiration
F. Respiratory arrest—failure to resume breathing after a period of apnea

36

Respiration Laboratory to Accompany
Vital Capacity Measurements

What is Vital Capacity and How Is It Measured?

Vital capacity (VC) is the greatest volume of air a person can exhale following as forceful and deep an inhalation as possible. Vital capacity can fall as much as 70 percent in certain diseases such as emphysema, left heart disease, chronic asthma and bronchitis, carcinoma, tuberculosis, and fibrotic pleurisy. A decrease of 20 percent could indicate pulmonary disease.

Vital capacity is measured by a spirometer. A spirometer records the volume of expired air. An average figure for a young man is 4.6 liters and for a young woman about 3.1 liters. VC's vary with the size of the body. Tidal volumes (the amount of air moving in and out during normal respiration) average around 500 ml. Residual volumes (air remaining in lungs after forceful exhalation) average around 1200 ml.

The tidal volume adjusts for changes in bodily activity: sleeping, sitting, walking, and running. The total air inhaled is automatically adjusted to maintain the interior atmosphere of the body.

The total amount of air taken in during one minute is called the minute volume. When physical exertion is steady, the minute volume will continue to increase for several minutes and then level off. When one has reached the stage of leveling off he or she is said to be in a steady state.

Other Factors Concerning the Respiratory System

1. The sensation of distress of breathing usually comes from the respiratory muscles themselves.

2. During intense exercise, the mouth, rather than the nasal passages, is the air pathway of choice.

3. A physically trained individual breathes more economically than an untrained individual. For the same task, trained individuals need less air because they can utilize a greater portion of oxygen than untrained individuals. (Utilization of air refers to the absorption of oxygen in the lung tissue.)

4. Deep breathing exercises done regularly will increase one's VC.

5. Research has indicated that those with higher VC's have a lower incidence of coronary heart disease.

The Digestive System

Outline Summary on the Digestive System

Wall of the Digestive Tract

The wall of the digestive tube is formed by four layers of tissue:

A. Mucosa—mucous epithelium
B. Submucosa—connective tissue
C. Muscularis—two or three layers of smooth muscle
D. Serosa—serous membrane that covers the outside of abdominal organs

Mouth

A. Roof—formed by hard palate (parts of maxillary and palatine bones) and soft palate, an arch-shaped muscle separating mouth from pharynx; uvula, a downward projection of soft palate
B. Floor—formed by tongue and its muscles; papillae, small elevations on mucosa of tongue; taste buds, found in many papillae; lingual frenulum, fold of mucous membrane that helps anchor tongue to floor of mouth

Teeth

A. Names of teeth—incisors, cuspids, bicuspids, and tricuspids
B. Twenty teeth in temporary set; average age for cutting first tooth about 6 months; set complete at about 2 years of age
C. Thirty-two teeth in permanent set; 6 years about average age for starting to cut first permanent tooth; set complete usually between ages 17 and 24 years
D. Structures of a typical tooth—crown, neck, and root

Salivary Glands

A. Parotid glands
B. Submandibular glands
C. Sublingual glands

Pharynx

Esophagus

Stomach

A. Size—expands after large meal; about size of large sausage when empty
B. Pylorus—lower part of stomach; pyloric sphincter muscle closes opening of pylorus into duodenum
C. Wall—many smooth muscle fibers; contractions produce churning movements (peristalsis)
D. Lining—mucous membrane; many microscopic glands that secrete gastric juice and hydrochloric acid into stomach; mucous membrane lies in folds (rugae) when stomach is empty

Small Intestine

A. Size—about 7 meters (20 feet) long but only 2 cm or so in diameter
B. Divisions
   1. Duodenum
   2. Jejunum
   3. Ileum
C. Wall—contains smooth muscle fibers that contract to produce peristalsis
D. Lining—mucous membrane; many microscopic glands (intestinal glands) secrete intestinal juice; villi (microscopic finger-shaped projects from surface of mucosa into intestinal cavity) contain blood and lymph capillaries

Liver and Gallbladder

A. Size and location—liver is largest gland; fills upper right section of abdominal cavity and extends over into left side
B. Liver secretes bile
C. Ducts
   1. Hepatic—drains bile from liver
   2. Cystic—duct by which bile enters and leaves gallbladder
   3. Common bile—formed by union of hepatic and cystic ducts; drains bile from hepatic or cystic ducts into duodenum
D. Gallbladder
   1. Location—undersurface of the liver
   2. Function—concentrates and stores bile produced in the liver

Pancreas

A. Location—behind stomach
B. Functions
    1. Pancreatic cells secrete pancreatic juice into pancreatic ducts; main duct empties into duodenum
    2. Pancreatic islets (of Langerhans)—cells not connected with pancreatic ducts; secrete hormones glucagon and insulin into the blood

Wall of the Digestive Tract

The wall of the digestive tube is formed by four layers of tissue:

A. Mucosa—mucous epithelium
B. Submucosa—connective tissue
C. Muscularis—two or three layers of smooth muscle
D. Serosa—serous membrane that covers the outside of abdominal organs

Mouth

A. Roof—formed by hard palate (parts of maxillary and palatine bones) and soft palate, an arch-shaped muscle separating mouth from pharynx; uvula, a downward projection of soft palate
B. Floor—formed by tongue and its muscles; papillae, small elevations on mucosa of tongue; taste buds, found in many papillae; lingual frenulum, fold of mucous membrane that helps anchor tongue to floor of mouth

Teeth

A. Names of teeth—incisors, cuspids, bicuspids, and tricuspids
B. Twenty teeth in temporary set; average age for cutting first tooth about 6 months; set complete at about 2 years of age
C. Thirty-two teeth in permanent set; 6 years about average age for starting to cut first permanent tooth; set complete usually between ages of 17 and 24 years
D. Structures of a typical tooth—crown neck and root

Small Intestine

A. Size—about 7 meters (20 feet) long but only 2 cm or so in diameter
B. Divisions
    1. Duodenum
    2. Jejunum
    3. Ileum
C. Wall—Wall—contains smooth muscle fibers that contract to produce peristalsis
D. Lining—mucous membrane; many microscopic glands (intestinal glands) secrete intestinal juice; villi (microscopic finger-shaped projections from surface of mucosa into intestinal cavity) contain blood and lymph capillaries

Liver and Gallbladder

A. Size and location—liver is largest gland; fills upper right section of abdominal cavity and extends over into left side
B. Liver secretes bile
C. Ducts
    1. Hepatic—drains bile from liver
    2. Cystic—duct by which bile enters and leaves gallbladder
    3. Common bile—formed by union of hepatic and cystic ducts; drains bile from hepatic or cystic ducts into duodenum

Nutrition and Weight Control

Self-Test and Instructional Objectives
on Nutrition

In written and/or oral form:

1. Define nutrition and give reasons for its importance.

2. Discuss five reasons why the body urgently needs water.

3. Define the following terms: kcalories, carbohydrates, fats, proteins, minerals, and vitamins.

4. State at least three reasons why the body needs the six substances listed in #3.

5. Define the following terms: metabolism, glycogen, glucose, saturated fatty acid, polyunsaturated fatty acid, cholesterol, essential amino acids, complete proteins, calcium, and phosphorus.

6. Define the following terms: hemoglobin, copper, iodine, sodium, potassium, fluorides, vitamin A, genitourinary system, energy intake, energy output, calorie balance, thiamine, riboflavin, niacin.

7. Explain five nutrition guidelines for athletes.

Nutrition Terminology

Amino acids They recombine inside the body to form the proteins that make up the body's main components (muscles, bones, and parts of blood, enzymes, some hormones, and cell membranes). Of the twenty common amino acids, eleven can be synthesized by the body; the other nine must be provided by the diet and are called essential amino acids.

Calcium A mineral important in the maintenance of bones and teeth, blood clotting, cell membranes, and the control of nerve impulses.

Carbohydrates Class of nutrients needed to supply energy, to furnish heat, and to serve proteins in the building and regulating of cells. Carbohydrates contain carbon, hydrogen, and oxygen.

Cholesterol A waxy substance found in the blood and implicated in heart disease.

Cooper A mineral essential for the metabolism of iron and the formation of red blood cells.

Energy intake The number of kcalories taken in by the body.

Energy output The number of calories used by the body.

Fiber Plant substances that are difficult or impossible for humans to digest. Diets low in fiber have been linked to hemorrhoids, diverticulitis, and a higher incidence of colon cancer.

Fluoride A mineral that stabilizes bone and makes teeth resistant to decay; it has not been proven an essential nutrient.

Glucose A simple sugar that is the body's basic fuel.

Glycogen An animal starch that is the storage form of glucose in the liver and muscles.

Iodine A mineral that is an essential part of thyroid hormones and used in the regulation of body metabolism.

Iron A mineral that is a component of hemoglobin (carries oxygen to the tissues), myoglobin (in muscle fibers), and enzymes.

Kcalorie A unit of fuel potential in a diet, 1 kcalorie represents the amount of heat needed to raise the temperature of 1 liter of water 1° C. A kcalorie is what people often refer to as a calorie.

Lecithin A phospholipid (contains fatty acids, glycerol, and a phosphorus-containing acid) that is a major constituent of cell membranes. It is manufactured by the liver and also found in many foods.

Metabolism The sum of biochemical activities within the body.

Minerals Inorganic compounds needed in relatively small amounts for regulation, growth, and maintenance of body tissues and functions.

Nutrition The sum of the processes by which the body takes in and utilizes food.

Phosphorus A mineral important in bone growth and maintenance and energy transfer in cells.

Polyunsaturated fatty acids Fatty acids that have two or more places where additional hydrogen atoms can be added. Examples include sunflower, corn, soybean, safflower, and fish oils.

Proteins Essential nutrients, made up of amino acids, that form important parts of muscles, bones, blood, enzymes, some hormones, and cell membranes.

Saturated fatty acids Fatty acids that carry the maximum possible number of hydrogen atoms. Sources of saturated fatty acids include animal flesh, whole milk, cheese, butter and shortening, and lunch meats. Limiting saturated fat intake is important in controlling blood cholesterol levels.

Sodium and potassium Electrolytes that maintain normal fluid balance inside and outside cells and a proper balance of acids and bases in the body.

Vitamins Noncaloric essential nutrients that are vital to life and indispensable to body functions. They are organic compounds.

Chapter 5
Nutrition: The Role of Diet in Your Health

Learning Objectives: Review of the Content

Directions: After reading Chapter 5 of the textbook, you should be able to complete the learning objectives below. The number(s) in parentheses at the end of each objective is (are) the page number(s) in the textbook on which the information appears.

1.   List the six categories of nutrients and their contribution to the diet. (109-120)

2.   State which of the nutrient categories provides Calories. (109)

3.   Distinguish between monosaccharides, disaccharides, and polysaccharides. (109-111)

4.   Identify the nutrient category that yields the greatest number of Calories per gram consumed. (111)

5.   Briefly describe the major categories of fats. (111-114)

6.   Explain the difference between water soluble and fat soluble vitamins and provide a list of each. (115)

7. Identify the three nutrient categories that do not contribute Calories in our diet and explain the role of each. (115-120)

8. Describe the difference between micronutrients and macronutrients. (118)

9. Summarize how the nonnutritive food element fiber aids in the digestion process and helps maintain good physical health. (100-101)

10. List the five food groups, the contribution of each to our diet, and the recommended minimum number of servings needed per day for an adult. (124-128)

11. Describe the nutritional value of fast foods and the efforts of fast food restaurants to provide meals with less fat. (129)

12. List the most recent dietary guidelines. (137)

13. Differentiate between the ovolactovegetarian, the lactovegetarian, and the vegan vegetarian diets. (138-139)

14. Summarize the potential difficulties of consuming a vegan vegetarian diet. (139)

15. Explain why a macrobiotic diet and unbalanced and fad diets are considered high risk dietary practices. (139-142)

16. Describe nutrition concerns for third world countries. (142)

17. List the six categories of recommended dietary modifications young adults should consider and briefly state the reason for the modifications. (142-145)

18. Identify three factors that impact the nutrition of the older adult. (145)

Terms: Review of New Vocabulary

Directions: Match the appropriate term with its definition by writing the term next to the definition. so that you can check your answers, the page number on which the term appears in the textbook is presented in parentheses.

amino acids	folacin	proteins
balanced diet	food additives	satiety value
Calories	food supplements	saturated fats
carbohydrates	hypervitaminosis	trace elements
cellulose	lactating	unbalanced diet
cholesterol	macrocytic	macrobiotic
complete protein	nutrients	vegan vegetarian diet
dehydration	osteoporosis	vitamins
enriched	ovolactovegetarian	water soluble
fat soluble		

1. _____   elements in foods that are required for the growth, repair, and regulation of body processes. (109)

2. _____   units of heat (energy); the amount of heat required to raise one kilogram of water one degree C. (109)

3. _____   chemical compounds comprising sugar or saccharide units; the body's primary source of energy. (109)

4. _____   the feeling of fullness. (111)

5. _____   fats found in animal products (112)

6. _____   fat-related substance in alcohol form; lipid material manufactured within the body as well as derived through dietary sources. (113)

49

7. _____ compounds composed of chains of amino acids; primary components of muscle and connective tissue. (114)

8. _____ chief components of protein; synthesized by the body or obtained from dietary sources. (114)

9. _____ a food that contains all nine essential amino acids. (114)

10. _____ organic compounds that facilitate the action of enzymes. (115)

11. _____ capable of being dissolved in water. (115)

12. _____ capable of being dissolved in fat or lipid tissue. (115)

13. _____ excessive accumulation of vitamins within the body; associated with fat-soluble vitamins. (115)

14. _____ minerals whose presence in the body occurs in very small amounts; micronutrient elements. (118)

15. _____ abnormal depletion of fluids from the body (118)

16. _____ the indigestible portion of vegetables, fruits, and cereals. (120)

17. _____ a diet that includes selections from several food groups. (124)

18. _____ the result of the process of returning to foods some of the nutritional elements (b vitamins and iron) removed during processing. (128)

19. _____ chemical compounds that are intentionally or unintentionally added to our food supply. (131)

20. _____ diet that excludes the use of all meat but does allow the consumption of eggs and dairy products. (138)

21. _____ nutrients taken in addition to those obtained through the diet; powdered protein, vitamins, mineral extracts, etc. (138)

22. _____ vegetarian diet that excludes the use of all animal products, including eggs and dairy products. (139)

23. _____ breastfeeding; nursing. (139)

24. _____ diet lacking adequate representation from each of the four food groups. (142)

25. _____ a loss in bone density. (142)

26. _____ folic acid; a vitamin of the B-complex group; used in the treatment of nutritional anemia. (144)

27. _____ form of anemia in which large red blood cells predominate, but in which total red blood cell count is depressed. (144)

28. _____ a diet characterized by almost total dependence in brown rice as the source of nutrients (139-140)

Quiz: A Self-Check on Mastery of Content

Directions: Place your answer in the space provided to the left of each question. So that you can check your responses, the correct answers to the questions are provided in Appendix A. If you want to go back to the textbook to read more about an answer, the page number(s) on which the answer appears in the textbook is (are) presented in parentheses after the question.

A. Multiple Choice Questions

_____ 1. The six major nutrient categories are: (109-120)
   a. vitamins, minerals, carbohydrates, protein, fat, and water.
   b. Calories, breads and cereals, milk products, energy, fuel, and fat.
   c. cholesterol, meat, minerals, water, glucose, and protein.
   d. fruits, fat, carbohydrates, minerals, vitamins, and bread.

_____ 2. Monosaccharides, disaccharides, and polysaccharides are all forms of: (109-110)
   a. vitamins.   c. carbohydrates
   b. fats.   d. fiber

_____ 3. Vitamins A, D, E, and K are all _____-soluble. (115)
a. fat
b. fiber
c. water
d. non

_____ 4. Fats which are found in abundance in animal products are: (112)
a. monounsaturated
b. saturated
c. unsaturated
d. polyunsaturated

_____ 5. The nutrient which is composed of chains of amino acids is: (114)
a. protein
b. carbohydrates
c. fats
d. vitamins

_____ 6. An example of a micronutrient element or trace element is: (118)
a. water.
b. calcium.
c. iron.
d. vitamin C.

_____ 7. The average adult requires how many glasses of water per day? (120)
a. 2
b. 6
c. 12
d. 18

_____ 8. The substance that consists of plant materials and is not digestible is: (120)
a. water.
b. fiber.
c. calcium
d. muscle.

_____ 9. What food group includes cookies, corn chips, and pastries? (128)
a. breads and cereals
b. protein rich foods
c. fats, oils and sweets
d. none of the above

_____ 10. The one food group that stipulates a different number of recommended daily servings for adults and children is: (125)
a. milk and milk products.
b. meat, poultry, fish, and eggs.
c. junk food.
d. fruits and vegetables

Chapter 6
Weight Management: A Question of Calories

Learning Objectives: Review of the Content

Directions: After reading Chapter 6 of the textbook, you should be able to complete the learning objectives below. The number(s) in parentheses at the end of each objective is (are) the page numbers(s) in the textbook on which the information appears.

1. Briefly describe the different between overweight and obesity. (149)

2. Explain what is meant by healthy body weight. (150)

3. Explain how to determine a healthy body weight using hip and waist measurements. (151-152)

4. Compute your Body Mass Index (BMI) using the formula on page 152 of the textbook. (152)

5. List and briefly explain the theories that describe the origins of obesity. (158-162)

6. Describe the role inactivity in obesity. (162)

7. Explain the difference between caloric balance and caloric imbalance and how they affect a person's weight. (163)

8. List the three factors that determine the energy needs of the body and briefly describe each. (164-166)

9. Identify the five major categories of alternative diet plans and provide a one sentence explanation of each. (167-171)

10. List and briefly describe four different physical interventions for weight management. (171-177)

11. Identify the components of what the authors of the textbook see as the best approach to weight reduction. (177)

12. Identify those weight management techniques that individuals can do themselves without the help of a health professional to lose weight. (167-177)

13. Identify those weight management techniques which necessitate the aid of a health professional for a person to lose weight. (167-177)

14. List the characteristics of a reputable weight loss program. (179)

Calisthenic Exercise, Circuit Training, and Weight Training

Calisthenics and Circuit Training

Calisthenics is a series of rhythmic exercises usually performed without apparatus to develop muscular strength, muscular endurance, and flexibility.

Facts about Calisthenics

Calisthenic exercises:

- Are easy to learn and easy to perform.
- Require no special equipment and a minimal amount of space to perform.
- Allow you to get a vigorous workout in a short time.
- Allow you to develop all the major muscle groups by performing carefully selected exercises.
- Can be made more enjoyable by doing them to music.
- Can be part of a circuit training program.
- Can become monotonous if done exclusively for a long period of time.
- Do not involve much overload; they can be supplemented with other types of exercises to increase the amount of overload and further the development of muscular strength and endurance.

Calisthenic Exercises

Calisthenic exercises that can be done without special equipment include:

For abdominals:
a. sit-ups
b. leg lifts in supine position (keeping back flat)
c. head and shoulder curl
d. hump back (bring knee to nose and then extend back)

For upper arms and chest area:
a. push-ups
b. two person pull-ups
c. squat-push-ups

For upper and lower back:
a. prone back lift (upper back and lower back)
b. flutter kick in prone position

For legs:
a. stride squat
b. leg lift (dog position)
c. knee bends
d. leg lifts (front, side, back)
e. ankle stretch

For coordination:
a. toe-knee-chest-stomach
b. toe rotation (front, side, front, return)

Doing Calisthenic Exercises

- To start, move very slowly to the cadence or rhythm count. Be sure to perform each exercise correctly (maximum benefit can only be achieved if you use correct form).

- For all-around development, use a variety of exercises. You should use between ten and fifteen different exercises in your program.

- Increase the work load regularly by increasing the number of steps in each exercise count. Begin with five or six repetitions of each exercise and increase to about twenty or more.

- Overload can be achieved by increasing the speed and/or the number of repetitions of each exercise and by decreasing the rest period between each exercise.

- Perform the exercises in a sequence that works different parts of the body in turn.

- Individuals with physical limitations should avoid doing exercises that force movement of damaged joints beyond the limits of safety.

Sample Calisthenics Program

This program does not emphasize cardiovascular endurance; you should supplement the exercises described here with some sport or activity that develops cardiovascular endurance.

Description of Exercises

Toe touch Stand at attention with legs straight and feet together. Bend the trunk forward, touching the fingers to the ankles, to the top of the feet, and to the toes. Return to the starting position. This counts as one repetition.

Sprinter Squat with hands on the floor and fingers pointing forward; extend the left leg to the rear. With a bounding movement, reverse the position of the feat by bringing the left foot level with the hands and extending the right foot backward. Return to the starting position by bouncing and reversing the feet again. This counts as one repetition.

Sitting stretch Assume a sitting position on the floor with legs spread apart and hands on the knees. Bend forward at the waist, extending your arms as far forward as possible. Return to the starting position. This counts as one repetition.

Push-up Depending on your level of muscular strength, perform regular or modified push-ups.

Sit-up Perform sit-ups with fingers interlocked behind the neck.

Leg raise Lie on your right side on the floor with right arm fully extended above the head, which is resting on it. Lift the left leg approximately 24 inches off the floor, keeping it straight, and then lower it again. When the required number of repetitions are completed on one side, the position is reversed, and the exercise is repeated with the other leg.

Flutter kick Lie facedown with your hands tucked under your thighs. Arch your back by lifting your chest and head off the floor. Kick your legs, moving them 8 to 10 inches apart. Perform these kicks from the hips. Each kick counts as one repetition.

Circuit Training

Circuit training is a system of organizing a series of exercises arranged for consecutive performance. You should choose a variety of exercises to develop muscular strength, muscular endurance, flexibility, and cardiovascular endurance. Each different exercise within a circuit is called a station. You move from station to station, performing a set number of repetitions of each exercise, until the entire circuit is complete. Then repeat the circuit two more times, for a total of three complete circuits.

Terminology

Repetitions The number of times you perform an exercise. To begin with, the number of repetitions should be half of your maximum effort; that is, half the number of repetitions you can perform (when completely rested) in one minute. Performing your exercises at one-half of your maximum effort for three trips around the circuit provides progressive overload. Your maximum effort (and the number of repetitions you perform at each station) will increase as you become more fit.

Target time The time within which you hope to complete three complete circuits. When you hit your target time, you should increase the number of repetitions of each exercise.

Choosing Exercises

Exercises for different muscle groups follow each other to help delay the onset of fatigue. Circuit training exercises that require no equipment include: step-ups (using a bench or chair), isometric arm exercises, squat thrusts, body rotations, isometric back exercise, push-ups, sit-ups, and running in place or shuttle running.

Weight Training

To increase muscular strength and endurance, you must do resistive exercises: exercises in which your muscles must exert force against a significant resistance. Your muscles become stronger when you subject them to overload, an exercise stress that is more severe than what they are used to. If you use heavy resistance with few repetitions, you build strength; if you use lighter resistance and do more repetitions, you improve muscular endurance.

Terminology

Bar A steel bar or pipe 4, 5, or 6 feet long. The middle section of the bar may have a knurled surface to provide friction for gripping.

Barbell A bar with plates and collars attached.

Bench A bench 12 to 16 inches high, 10 to 16 inches wide, and 4 to 6 feet long, preferably padded; used for performing certain exercises.

Collars Metal rings with set screws used to hold the plates in place on the bar.

Load The total number of pounds lifted during each movement of an exercise, including the weight of the bar, the plates, and the collars.

Plates Iron or sand-filled plastic discs with a center hole. These are slipped into the ends of the bar and secured with collars. Plates are usually available in weights of 1¼, 2½, 5, 10, 20 pounds and up.

Resistance A force tending to prevent motion. When you increase the resistance (by adding weight to the equipment), your muscles work harder; the harder they work, the stronger they become. Regular increase in resistance provides overload.

Repetitions The number of times you perform an exercise. Set a series of repetitions for a specific exercise.

Putting Together a Weight Training Program

Intensity and Duration

1. Start with a load you can easily handle.

2. Do as many repetitions as you can, but not less than 8.

3. Perform three sets of each exercise, with a rest between each set.

4. When you can do three sets of 15 repetitions of an exercise, increase the load by adding weight (five pounds for arm exercises and ten pounds for leg exercises).

5. After each increase in load, return to performing as many repetitions as you can (but not less than 8).

Skeletal Muscles (Anterior View)

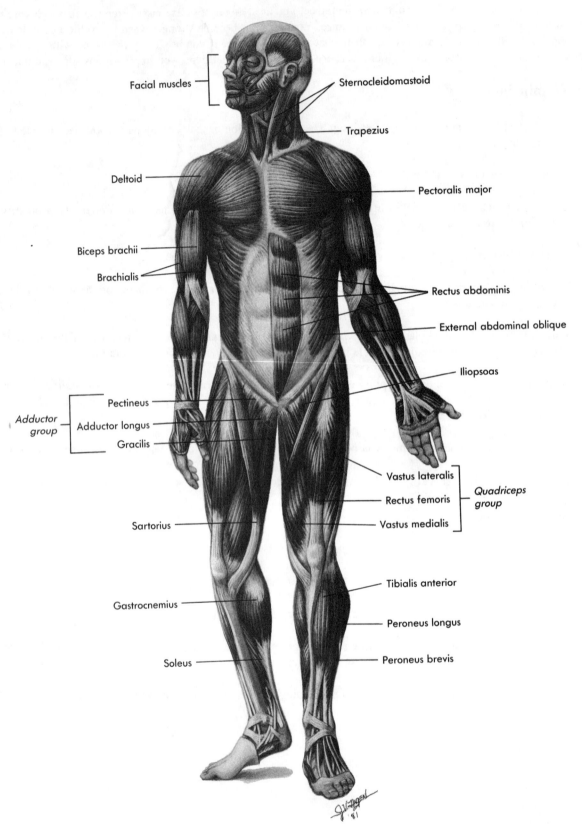

Facial muscles

Sternocleidomastoid

Trapezius

Deltoid

Pectoralis major

Biceps brachii

Brachialis

Rectus abdominis

External abdominal oblique

Iliopsoas

Pectineus

Adductor longus

Gracilis

Adductor group

Vastus lateralis

Rectus femoris

Vastus medialis

Quadriceps group

Sartorius

Tibialis anterior

Gastrocnemius

Peroneus longus

Peroneus brevis

Soleus

60

Skeletal Muscles (Posterior View)

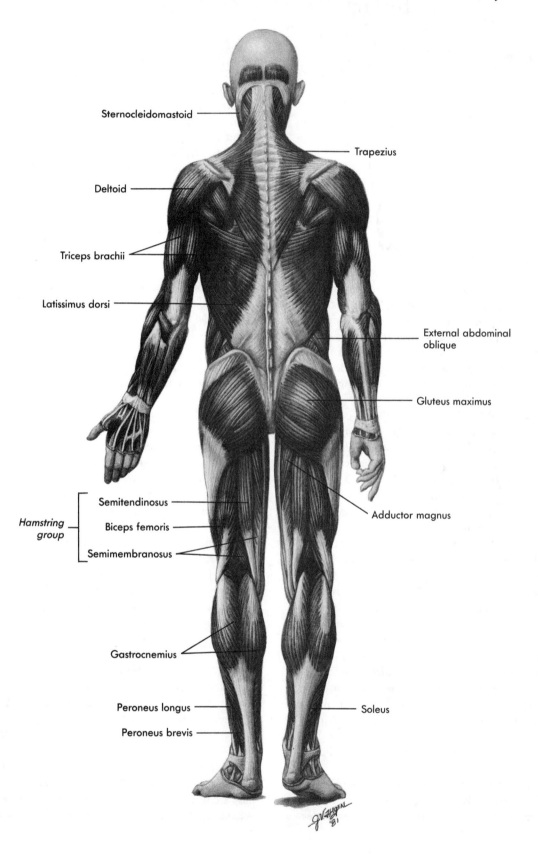

Sternocleidomastoid

Trapezius

Deltoid

Triceps brachii

Latissimus dorsi

External abdominal oblique

Gluteus maximus

Adductor magnus

Hamstring group

Semitendinosus

Biceps femoris

Semimembranosus

Gastrocnemius

Peroneus longus

Soleus

Peroneus brevis

Improvement of Muscular Strength and Endurance through Weight Training

KEY TERMS

strength
muscular endurance
power
hypertrophy
atrophy
isometric exercise

concentric contraction
eccentric contraction
isokinetic exercise
circuit training
plyometric training

OBJECTIVES

After completing this chapter you will be able to:

✓ Define strength and indicate its significance to health and skill of performance.
✓ Discuss the anatomy and physiology of skeletal muscle.
✓ Discuss the physiology of strength development and factors that determine strength.
✓ Describe specific methods for improving muscular strength.
✓ Differentiate between muscle strength and muscle endurance.
✓ Identify strength-training exercises for developing specific muscle groups.
✓ Demonstrate proper techniques for using weights to develop strength and muscular endurance.

The development of muscular strength is an essential component of fitness for anyone involved in a physical activity program. By definition, **strength** is the maximal force that can be applied by a muscle during a single maximal contraction.

The development of muscular strength may best be considered as both a skill-related and a health-related component of physical fitness. Maintenance of at least a normal level of strength in a given muscle or muscle group is important for normal healthy living. Muscle weakness or imbalance can result in abnormal movement or gait and can impair normal functional movement. Muscle weakness can also produce poor posture, which can affect your appearance. One of the most common health ailments in the United States is lower back pain, which is related in the large majority of cases to lack of muscular fitness, especially lack of muscular strength in the abdominals and loss of flexibility of the hamstrings. Thus strength training may play a critical role not only in training programs but also in injury rehabilitation.

Muscular strength is also related to agility, or the ability of the body to change direction rapidly in a coordinated manner. Agility not only enhances athletic performance but also may allow the performer to avoid potentially injurious situations.

Muscular strength is closely associated with muscular endurance. **Muscular endurance** is the ability to perform repetitive muscular contractions against some resistance. As we will see later, as muscular strength increases, there tends to be a corresponding increase in endurance. For example, a person can lift a weight 25 times. If muscular strength is increased by 10% through weight training, it is very likely that the maximal number of repetitions would be increased because it is easier for the person to lift the weight.

For most people, developing muscular endurance is more important than developing muscular strength, since muscular endurance is probably more critical in carrying out the everyday activities of living. This becomes increasingly true with age. However, a tremendous amount of strength is necessary for anyone involved in some type of competition.

Most movements in sports are explosive and must include elements of both strength and speed if they are to be effective. If a large amount of force is generated quickly, the movement can be referred to as a **power** movement. Without the ability to generate power, an athlete will be limited in his or her performance capabilities.

ANATOMY AND PHYSIOLOGY OF SKELETAL MUSCLE CONTRACTION

Skeletal muscle consists of two portions: (1) the muscle belly and (2) its tendons, which are collectively referred to as a *musculotendinous unit*. The muscle belly is composed of separate, parallel elastic fibers. Muscle fibers are composed of thousands of small protein fibers called *myofibrils*, within which the contractile elements are found, as well as of a substantial amount of connective tissue that holds the fibers together. The skeletal musculotendinous unit attaches two bones across a joint. When a muscle contracts, the small contractile elements or *myofilaments* within the myofibrils are stimulated to move closer together, thus producing a shortening of the muscles and movement at the joint that the muscle crosses.

The muscle tendon attaches muscle directly to bone. The muscle tendon is composed primarily of connective tissue and is relatively inelastic when compared with muscle fibers.

All skeletal muscles exhibit four characteristics: (1) the ability to change in length or stretch, which is elasticity; (2) the ability to shorten and return to normal length, which is extensibility; (3) the ability to respond to stimulation from the nervous system, which is excitability; and (4) the ability to shorten and contract in response to some neural command, which is contractility.

Skeletal muscles show considerable variation in size and shape. Large muscles generally produce gross motor movements at large joints, such as knee flexion produced by contraction of the large, bulky hamstring muscles. Smaller skeletal muscles, such as the long flexors of the fingers, produce fine motor movements. Muscles producing movements that are powerful in nature are usually thicker and long, whereas those producing finer movements requiring coordination are thin and relatively shorter., Other muscles may be flat, round, or fan shaped.

Muscles may be connected to bone by a single tendon or by two or three separate tendons at either end. Those muscles that have two separate muscle and tendon attachments are called biceps, and those with three separate muscle and tendon attachments are called triceps.

Muscles contract in response to stimulation by the central nervous system. An electrical impulse transmitted from the central nervous system through a single motor nerve to a group of muscle fibers will cause a depolarization of those fibers. The motor nerve and the group of muscle fibers that it innervates is referred to collectively as a *motor unit*. An impulse coming from the central nervous system and traveling to a group of fibers through a particular motor nerve causes all the muscle fibers in that motor unit to depolarize and contract. This is referred to as the *all-or-none* response and applies to all skeletal muscles in the body.

Fast Twitch versus Slow-Twitch Fibers

All fibers in a particular motor unit are either *slow-twitch or fast-twitch fibers*, each of which has distinctive metabolic as well as contractile capabilities. Slow-twitch fibers are reddish. They are more resistant to fatigue than are fast-twitch fibers; however, the time required to generate force is much greater in slow-twitch fibers.

Fast twitch fibers are white. They are capable of producing quick, forceful contractions but have a tendency to fatigue more rapidly than slow twitch fibers do. Fast twitch fibers are capable of producing powerful contractions, whereas slow-twitch fibers produce a long-endurance type of force.

Slow-twitch fibers are relatively fatigue resistant and are associated primarily with long-duration, aerobic-type activities. Fast twitch fibers are useful in short-term, high-intensity activities, which mainly involve the anaerobic system.

Within a particular muscle are both types of fibers, and the ratio varies with each person. The average is about 50% slow-twitch and 50% fast-twitch fibers. However, tremendous variations have been demonstrated in various athletes.

Because this ratio is genetically determined, it may play a large role in determining ability for a given sport activity. Sprinters, for example, have a large percentage of fast-twitch fibers in relation to slow-twitch fibers. One study has shown that they may have as much as 95% fast-twitch fibers in certain muscles. Conversely, marathon runners generally have a higher percentage of slow-twitch fibers.

FACTORS THAT DETERMINE MUSCULAR STRENGTH

Muscular strength is closely related to the cross-sectional diameter of a muscle. The bigger a particular muscle, the stronger it is, and thus the more force it is capable of generating. The size of a muscle tends to increase in cross-sectional diameter with weight training. This increase in muscle size is referred to as **hypertrophy.** Conversely, a decrease in the size of a muscle is referred to as **atrophy.**

Strength is a function of the number and diameter of muscle fibers composing a given muscle. The number of fibers is an inherited characteristics; thus a person with a large number of muscle fibers to begin with has the potential to hypertrophy to a much greater degree than does someone with relatively fewer fibers.

Strength is also directly related to the efficiency of the neuromuscular system and the function of the motor unit in producing muscular force. As will be indicated later in this chapter, initial increases in strength during a weight-training program can be attributed primarily to increased neuromuscular efficiency.

Strength in a given muscle is determined not only by the physical properties of the muscle itself but also by mechanical factors that dictate how much force can be generated through a system of levers to an external object.

If we think of the elbow joint as one of these lever systems, we would have the biceps muscle producing flexion of this joint. The position of attachment of the biceps muscle on the lever arm, in this case the forearm, will largely determine how much force this muscle is capable of generating. If there are two persons, *A* and *B*, and *A* has a biceps attachment that is closer to the fulcrum (the elbow joint) than *B*, then *A* must produce a greater force with the biceps muscle to hold the weight at a right angle because the length of the lever arm will be greater than with *B*.

When the weight is held at an angle of 45° or 150°, the contracting force of the biceps muscle required to hold the weight stationary is considerably less than it would be at 90°. Thus if we move this weight through a full range of motion from extension to flexion, the amount of strength, or force, required to move the weight varies at different angles, forming a strength curve for that movement.

A third critical factor in determining muscle strength is muscle length. A muscle is capable of generating its maximal force when it is in its fully stretched or extended position. If the muscle is stretched beyond its normal length, it may be incapable of producing any muscular force, and it is likely that injury will occur. In fact, the initial stretch of a muscle will evoke a reflex called the stretch reflex, which will not allow the muscle to be lengthened. This stretch reflex is discussed in detail in Chapter 6.

The shorter a muscle becomes, the less force it is capable of generating. A muscle that is fully contracted is incapable of producing additional muscular force past this point.

The ability to generate muscular force is also related to age. Both men and women seem to be able to increase strength throughout puberty and adolescence, reaching a peak around 20 to 25 years of age, at which time this ability begins to level off and in some cases decline. After about age 25 a person generally loses an average of 1% of his or her maximal remaining strength each year. Thus at age 65 a person would have only about 60% of the strength he or she had at age 25.

This loss in muscle strength is definitely related to individual levels of physical activity. Those people who are more active, or perhaps those who continue to strength train, considerably decrease this tendency toward declining muscle strength. In addition to retarding this decrease in muscular strength, exercise may also have an effect in slowing the decrease in cardiorespiratory endurance, flexibility, and so on. Thus strength maintenance is important for all individuals regardless of age or the level of competition if total wellness and health is an ultimate goal.

PHYSIOLOGY OF STRENGTH DEVELOPMENT

There is no question that weight training to improve muscular strength results in an increased size, or hypertrophy, of a muscle. What causes a muscle to hypertrophy? A number of theories have been proposed to explain this increase in muscle size.

Some evidence exists that there is an increase in the number of muscle fibers due to fibers' splitting in response to training. However, this research has been conducted in animals and should not be generalized to humans. It is generally accepted that the number of fibers is genetically determined and does not seem to increase with training.

It has been hypothesized that because the muscle is working harder in weight training, more blood is required to supply that muscle with oxygen and other nutrients. Thus it is thought that the number of capillaries is increased. This hypothesis is only partially correct; no new capillaries are formed during strength training; however, a number of dormant capillaries may well become patent to meet this increased demand for blood supply.

A third theory to explain this increase in muscle size seems the most credible. It was mentioned earlier that muscle fibers are composed primarily of small protein filaments, called myofilaments, which are the contractile elements in muscle. These myofilaments increase in both size and number as a result of strength training, causing the individual muscle fibers themselves to increase in cross-sectional diameter. This is particularly true in men, although women will also see some increase in muscle size.

METHODS OF IMPROVING STRENGTH

There are three different methods of training for strength improvement: isometric training, isotonic training, and isokinetic training. Regardless of which of these three methods is used, one basic principle of training is extremely important. For muscle to improve in strength, it must be forced to work at a higher level than that to which it is accustomed. In other words, the muscle must be *overloaded*. Without overload the muscle will be able to maintain strength as long as training is continued against a resistance the muscle is accustomed to. However, no additional strength gains will be realized. This maintenance of existing levels of muscular strength may be more important in weight training programs that emphasize muscular endurance rather than strength gains. It is certainly true that many individuals can benefit more in terms of overall health by concentrating on improving muscular endurance. However, to most effectively build muscular strength, weight training requires a consistent, increasing effort against progressively increasing resistance. If this principle of overload is applied, all three training methods will produce improvement of muscular strength over a period of time. Table 5-1 summarizes the three different methods for improving muscular strength.

Isometric Exercise

An **isometric exercise** involves a muscle contraction in which the length of the muscle remains constant while tension develops toward a maximal force against an immovable resistance. The muscle should generate a maximal force for 5 seconds at a time, and this contraction should be repeated five to ten times per day.

Isometric exercises were popular in the late 1960s and early 1970s. Several books were published that discussed a series of isometric exercises that could be done while sitting at a desk. The exercises included techniques such as putting your arms underneath the middle desk drawer and pushing up as hard as you can, or pushing out on the inside of the chair space with your knees. It was claimed that these brief maximal isometric contractions were capable of producing some rather dramatic increases in muscular strength. And indeed these isometric exercises are capable of increasing muscular strength; unfortunate-

ly, strength gains are specific to the joint angle at which training is performed. At other angles, the strength curve drops off dramatically because of a lack of motor activity at that angle. Thus arm strength is increased at the specific angle pressed against the desk drawer, but there is no corresponding increase in strength at other positions in the range of motion.

Another major disadvantage of these isometric "sit at your desk" exercises is that they tend to produce a spike in blood pressure that can result in potentially life-threatening cardiovascular accidents. This sharp increase in blood pressure results from holding your breath and increasing intrathoracic pressure. Consequently, the blood pressure experienced by the heart is increased significantly. This has been referred to as the Valsalva effect. To avoid or minimize this effect, it is recommended that breathing be done during the maximal contraction to prevent this increase in pressure.

We do not mean to imply that isometric exercises have no place in a training program. There are certain instances in which an isometric contraction can greatly enhance a particular movement. For example, one of the exercises in power weight-lifting is a squat. A squat is an exercise in which the weight is supported on the shoulders in a standing position. The knees are then flexed and the weight is lowered to a three-quarter squat position, from which the lifter must stand completely straight once again.

It is not uncommon for there to be one particular angle in the range of motion at which smooth movement through that specific angle is difficult because of insufficient strength. This joint angle is referred to as a "sticking point." A power lifter will typically employ an isometric contraction against some immovable resistance to increase strength at this sticking point. If strength can be improved at this joint angle, then a smooth, coordinated power lift can be performed through a full range of movement.

A more common use for isometric exercises would be for injury rehabilitation or reconditioning. There are a number of conditions or ailments resulting either from trauma or overuse that must be treated with strengthening exercises. Unfortunately, these problems may be exacerbated with full range-of-motion strengthening exercises. It may be more desirable to make use of isometric exercises until the injury has healed to the point that full-range activities can be performed.

Isotonic Exercise

A second method of weight training is more commonly used in improving muscular strength. **Isotonic exercise** involves a muscle contraction in which force is generated while the muscle is changing in length.

There are two types of isotonic contractions. Suppose you are going to perform a biceps curl. To lift the weight from the starting position, the biceps muscle must contract and shorten in length. This shortening contraction is referred to as a **concentric (positive) contraction.** If the biceps muscle does not remain contracted when the weight is being lowered, gravity would cause this weight to simply fall back to the starting position. Thus to control the weight as it is being lowered, the biceps muscle must continue to contract while at the same time gradually lengthening. A contraction in which the muscle is lengthening while still applying force is called an **eccentric (negative) contraction.** Eccentric or negative contractions are less resistant to fatigue than are concentric contractions. In addition, it is possible to generate greater amounts of force eccentrically than concentrically.

It is essential when training isotonically to utilize both concentric and eccentric contractions. Research has clearly demonstrated that the muscle must be overloaded and fatigued both concentrically and eccentrically for the greatest strength improvement to occur. Both types of contractions can be done using any type of isotonic equipment.

There are various devices and machines that can be classified as isotonic devices. Free weights, barbells, and dumbbells are the most common forms of isotonic equipment. Universal and Nautilus machines are also considered to be isotonic machines. Free weights and barbells require the use of iron plates of varying weights that can be easily changed by adding or subtracting equal amounts of weight to both sides of the bar. The Universal and Nautilus machines both have a stack of weights that are lifted through a series of levers or pulleys. The stack of weights slides up and down on a pair of bars that restrict the movement to only one plane. Weight can be increased or decreased simply by changing the position of a weight key.

There are advantages and disadvantages to each type of isotonic device. The Nautilus and Universal machines are both relatively safe to use in comparison with free weights. For example, it is essential to have someone "spot" you (help you lift the weights back onto the support racks if you don't have enough strength to complete the lift); otherwise you may end up dropping the weight on your chest. With the Nautilus and Universal equipment you can easily and safely drop the weight without fear of injury.

It is also a simple process to increase or decrease the weight by moving a single weight key with Nautilus and Universal equipment, although changes can generally be made only in increments of 10 or 15 pounds. With free weights, iron plates must be added or removed from each side of the barbell.

Regardless of which type of equipment is used, the same principles of isotonic training may be applied.

When training specifically for the development of muscular strength, the concentric, or positive, contraction should be an explosive power movement, with the weight being lifted against gravity at maximal speed and force. Conversely, when lowering the weight, the eccentric contraction should be relatively slow and gradually. Physiologically the muscle will fatigue much more rapidly concentrically than eccentrically. Arthur Jones, the inventor of the Nautilus equipment, stresses the use of these positive and negative contractions in his training program, although this principle should be applied regardless of which brand of equipment is being used.

Persons who have strength-trained using both free weights and either the Nautilus or Universal machine realize the difference in the amount of weight that can be lifted. Unlike the machines, free weights have no restricted motion and can thus move in many different directions, depending on the forces applied. With free weights, an element of muscular control on the part of the lifter to prevent the weight from moving in any other direction other than vertical will usually decrease the amount of weight that can be lifted.

One problem often mentioned in relation to isotonic training involves changes that occur in the muscles' capabilities of moving the resistance throughout the range of motion. In discussing mechanical factors that determine levels of strength, it was indicated that the amount of force necessary to move a weight through a range of motion changes according to the joint angle and is greatest when the joint angle is approximately 90°. In addition, once the inertia of the weight has been overcome and momentum has been established, the force required to move the resistance varies according to the force that muscle can produce through the range of motion. Thus it has been argued that a disadvantage of any type of isotonic equipment is that force required to move the resistance is constantly changing throughout the range of movement.

Nautilus has attempted to alleviate this problem of changing force capabilities by using a cam in its pulley system. The cam has been individually designed for each piece of equipment so that the resistance is variable throughout the movement. It attempts to alter resistance so that the muscle can handle a greater load, but at the points where the joint angle or muscle length is mechanically disadvantageous, it reduces the resistance to muscle movement. Whether this design does what it claims is debatable. This change in resistance at different points in the range has been labeled *accommodating resistance,* or *variable resistance.*

Isokinetic Exercise

The third method of strength training takes a little different approach to the problem of changing force capabilities. An **isokinetic exercise** is one in which the length of the muscle is changing while the contraction is performed at a constant velocity. In theory, maximal resistance is provided throughout the range of motion, since the resistance will move only at some preset speed regardless of the force applied to it. Thus the key to isokinetic exercise is not the resistance, but the speed at which resistance can be moved.

Several isokinetic devices are available commercially; Cybex, Orthotron, Biodex, KinCom, and Mini-gym are among the more common isokinetic devices. In general, they rely on hydraulic, pneumatic, and mechanical pressure systems to produce this constant velocity of motion.

A major disadvantage of these units is their cost. Many of them come with a computer and printing device and are used primarily as diagnostic and rehabilitative tools in the treatment of various injuries.

Isokinetic devices are designed so that regardless of the amount of force applied against a resistance, it can only be moved at a certain speed. That speed will be the same whether maximal force or only half the maximal force is applied. consequently, when training isokinetically, it is absolutely necessary to exert as much force against the resistance as possible (maximal effort) for maximal strength gains to occur. This is one of the major problems with an isokinetic strength-training program.

Anyone who has been involved in a weight-training program knows that on some days it is difficult to find the motivation to work out. Because isokinetic training requires a maximal effort, it is very easy to "cheat" and not go through the workout at a high level of intensity. In an isotonic program, you know how much weight has to be lifted with how many repetitions. Thus isokinetic training is often

more effective if a partner system is used primarily as a means of motivation toward a maximal effort.

When isokinetic training is done properly with a maximal effort, it is theoretically possible that maximal strength gains are best achieved through the isokinetic training method in which the velocity and force of the resistance are equal throughout the range of motion.

Whether this changing force capability is in fact a deterrent to improving the ability to generate force against some resistance is debatable. It must be remembered that in real life it does not matter whether the resistance is changing; what is important is that you develop enough strength to move objects from one place to another. The amount of strength necessary for each person is largely dependent on his or her life-style and occupation.

Name _____ Age _____ Class _____

School _____ Coach _____

Chest Press	Wide																	
	Reg																	
Leg Press	4																	
	3																	
	2																	
	1																	
Shoulder Press	Back																	
	Front																	
Pully Chins	Back																	
	Front																	
Toe Raises																		
Posture Row	Two Arms																	
	One Arm																	
Arm Curles																		
Tri Extension																		
Chinning																		
Hip Flex																		
Dipping																		
Sit Ups																		
Leg Extension																		
Leg Curls																		

Name _____ Age _____ Class _____

School _____ Coach _____

Chest Press	Wide																			
	Reg																			
Leg Press	4																			
	3																			
	2																			
	1																			
Shoulder Press	Back																			
	Front																			
Pully Chins	Back																			
	Front																			
Toe Raises																				
Posture Row	Two Arms																			
	One Arm																			
Arm Curles																				
Tri Extension																				
Chinning																				
Hip Flex																				
Dipping																				
Sit Ups																				
Leg Extension																				
Leg Curls																				

Human Sexuality

Self-Test and Instructional Objectives
on Human Sexuality

In written and/or oral form:

1. Present the names and functions of principal male sex structures.

2. Describe how the male sperm cells are expelled during ejaculation.

3. Present the names and functions of the principal external female sex structures.

4. Name and describe the principal internal female sex structures, including the major functions of each structure.

5. Describe the functions of the glands in the lining of the uterus and the cervix.

6. Describe the structure and functions of the female breasts.

7. Explain how conception occurs.

8. Explain the four major phases of the sexual response cycles of women and men.

9. Name and describe current abortion techniques.

10. Describe the role of the pituitary and hypothalamus glands in the reproductive systems of the male and female.

Self-Test and Instructional Objectives on Birth Control Methods

In written and/or oral form:

1. List and define ten important terms which helps us to better understand contraception.

2. Present five advantages of oral contraceptives.

3. Present at least three disadvantages of oral contraceptives.

4. Report five advantages of intrauterine devices (IUD).

5. Present at least five disadvantages of IUDs.

6. State three purposes of the Planned Parenthood Federation of America.

7. Explain five advantages of condoms.

8. Present three warnings for condom use.

9. Describe the diaphragm and give three advantages and three disadvantages of its use.

10. Explain what vaginal spermicides are and how they are used.

11. Describe the rhythm method of contraception and give three disadvantages in its use.

12. State at least one way to improve the use effectiveness of the following: oral contraceptives, IUD, condom, diaphragm and jelly, and vaginal spermicides.

13. Explain at least five important facts concerning sterilization of the male and five facts concerning the female.

Self-Test and Instructional Objectives
on Abortion

In written and/or oral form:

1. Describe at least three political and/or legal aspects concerning abortion.

2. Describe the process of vacuum aspiration.

3. Describe the process of dilation and curettage.

4. List three techniques used in the saline method of abortion.

5. Define the role prostaglandins play in abortion.

6. State three important facts about hysterotomy.

7. Describe three complications that may occur after an abortion.

8. Review three statements made by the Supreme Court in *Roe vs. Wade.*

Self-Test and Instructional Objectives on Genetic Abnormalities

In written and/or oral form:

1. Give four significant facts about the basic unit of life (the cell).

2. Define chromosome.

3. Explain how biological sex is determined.

4. Demonstrate a basic knowledge of the relationship between heredity and environment.

5. Define the following: gametes, somatic, X chromosome, Y chromosome, mitosis, meiosis, homozygous.

6. Describe sickle-cell anemia and explain how the disease is inherited.

7. Explain the major function of the genes, the actions of undesirable genes, and the dominant and recessive effect.

8. Describe several environmental conditions that are capable of affecting the developing fetus.

9. Define PKU, Tay-Sachs, Cystic fibrosis, and the Rh factor.

10. Define meiotic non-disjunction, translocation, deletion, Down's syndrome, Turner's syndrome, Klinefelter's syndrome, and the XYY syndrome.

11. Describe amniocentesis and chorionic villus sampling.

12. Explain the mechanism involved in the development of sex-linked disorders and be able to list at least two.

13. Describe the relationship between rubella, diabetes, and the Rh factor and genetic abnormalities.

14. Describe the role of genetic counseling and its accuracy in making objective assessments.

Throughout history people have been interested in what factors determine whether an offspring is male or female. Attempts to predetermine the sex of offspring have taken place since antiquity. The ancient Greeks thought that having intercourse in a north wind would produce a boy and intercourse in a south wind would produce a female child. Other ideas involved the phase of the moon, on what side the male lay during coitus, and if the male had his shoes on or off during coitus.

At the present time two approaches can be used to choose the sex of an infant. One is selective termination of pregnancy;p that is, the woman could have an abortion if the fetus is not the desired sex. This approach is fraught with legal, moral, medical, and religious considerations. The other method is to influence the probability that an X-bearing or a Y-bearing sperm call will do the fertilization, which determines the sex of the child.

Since the male ejaculate contains approximately equal numbers of X- and Y-bearing sperm, normally the probability or a boy or girl is 50%. Any consistent change in this proportion would mean success. Two techniques are used to alter the X and Y chromosomal balance. The first involves separating the ejaculate into two portions before insemination. One portion contains the X-bearing sperm and the other the Y-bearing sperm. A method using columns made of cattle albumin (one of a group of protein substances) of increasing densities indicates that human Y-bearing sperm swim and diffuse downward into the densest albumin portion. When these Y-enriched sperm were used to artificially inseminate a small number of women, it was found that 72% of the offspring were male. However, the yield of Y-bearing sperm portions was very low. This loss of sperm count led to low conception rates, and even the fractions of sperm with 80% Y-bearing sperm produced female offspring. AT the present time this technique cannot be used on a large scale.

A second technique to influence the probability that an X-bearing or Y-bearing sperm will do the fertilization involves altering the vaginal environment to favor either X- or Y-bearing sperm. Early work on humans and other species indicated that more males were conceived when intercourse took place before or at the time of ovulation. Other researchers have shown that for both natural and artificial insemination, the human sex ratio changed significantly during the menstrual cycle (Guerrero, 1975; Harlap, 1979). A high proportion of male infants was observed among couples in whom intercourse with ejaculation occurred several days before ovulation. The proportion of males then dropped to a minimum on the day of ovulation, and then the proportion of females rose steeply for infants conceived 2 to 3 days after ovulation. Researchers believe that changes in the vaginal pH (whether acidic or alkaline) are responsible for the alterations in the sex ratio over the menstrual cycle. In 1970 Shettles and Rorvik published a book instructing couples on how to produce male or female offspring. They argued that human sperm could be divided into androsperm (Y-bearing) or gynosperm (X-bearing) based on the form and speed of movement of the sperm. These characteristics would influence survival of the sperm in the vagina. The ideas proposed by Shettles and Rorvik have not been replicated by other researchers and clinicians.

ProCare Industries markets a product called Gender Choice, which the company claims can increase the chances of having a boy or a girl. Many ideas used in the development and method of the Gender Choice kit are similar to the theories of Shettles and Rorvik. As previously mentioned, the theories proposed by Shettles and Rorvik have not been proved and some have been disproved (Harlap, 1979).

Self-Test and Instruction Objectives
on AIDS

In written and/or oral form:

1. Explain how the AIDS virus causes opportunistic diseases.

2. Explain the importance of *Pneumocystic carinii*, Kaposi's sarcoma, and dementia as they relate to AIDS.

3. Describe five major ways that AIDS is spread.

4. State the advantage and disadvantages of the screening test to detect HIV infection.

5. Describe at least eight ways AIDS may be prevented.

6. Explain whether or not AIDS can be treated effectively.

7. State how you can tell if you have the AIDS virus.

8. Explain five to ten of the most important symptoms of AIDS.

9. Describe the special problems of AIDS during pregnancy.

10. Describe prospects for the immediate future concerning AIDS.

The Nervous System

Self-Test and Instructional Objectives on the Nervous System

In written and/or oral form:

1. State the function of the nervous system.

2. Explain the general structure of the nervous system, including its protective devices.

3. Describe the components of the neuron and their functions.

4. Explain the neuron classifications.

5. Describe the mechanism of the nerve impulse including the sodium pump mechanism.

6. Explain the condition in which a nerve can regenerate.

7. Describe the "reflex arc."

8. List the main components of the central nervous system and explain their functions.

9. Describe the CNS's control of volitional movement.

10. Describe proprioception and give an example of a proprioreceptor.

11. Describe the major diseases of the nervous system, their causes, and their treatments (if any).

Nervous System Terminology

Acetylcholine The dominant chemical neurotransmitter released by axons in the peripheral nervous system; also released by some axons in the brain.

Adrenocorticotrophic hormone (ACTH) A hormone released by the anterior pituitary that stimulates the release of steroid hormones by the adrenal glands.

Axon Elongated extension of a neuron that conducts the impulse away from the cell body toward the end of the neuron.

Autonomic nervous system Branch of the nervous system that controls all involuntary functions.

Brain stem The brain minus the cerebrum and cerebellum; site of cardiac and respiratory reflex centers.

Central nervous system (CNS) The spinal cord and the brain.

Cerebellum Midbrain structure responsible for smooth muscle action and coordination.

Cerebral cortex Area of the brain responsible for learning, memory, and conscious behavior.

Cerebrospinal fluid A fluid lubricating and protecting the brain and spinal cord.

Dendrite Nerve fiber that conducts nerve impulses toward the cell body.

End brush Attached to very end of nerve cell.

Hypothalamus Brain region that plays a role in temperature regulation, metabolic and heart rates, sleep activities and emotions such as fear and rage.

Interneurons (association neurons) Neurons within the CNS that form links between other neurons. They transfer incoming sensory nerve impulses to motor neurons or to other parts of the CNS.

Motor neurons (efferent neurons) Carry impulses from the brain and spinal cord to muscles and glands.

Myelin sheath Insulating covering of many axons; may be constricted at sites to form nodes of Ranvier.

Neurilemma Thin outer covering on some neurons that can allow a severed nerve to regenerate.

Neuron One of the individual cells that makes up nervous tissue; the basic unit of nervous system.

Nodes of Ranvier Constrictions at regular intervals on myelinated nerve fibers. Nerve impulses can jump from node to node, resulting in a large increase in impulse velocity.

Parasympathetic nervous system Counteracts the effects of the sympathetic nervous system by returning body functions to normal after an emergency.

Peripheral nervous system The sum total of sensory and motor nerves.

Pons Brain structure connecting the hemispheres of the cerebellum; important in controlling posture.

Reaction time Time between stimulus and response.

Reflex time Time between the response of an efferent neuron and the response of a corresponding efferent neuron.

Sensory neuron (afferent neuron) Neuron capable of detecting and carrying environmental stimuli to appropriate CNS centers.

Sympathetic nervous system Portion of the CNS that prepares the body for emergency.

Vertebrae Bony structures that protect the spinal cord.

Brain Structures and Some of Their Functions

Brain Structure	Function(s)
Amygdala	Fear and anxiety responses
Basal ganglia	Control of equilibrium
Cerebellum	Control of smooth muscle coordination
Cerebral cortex	Control of higher mental functions
Frontal lobe	Ability to plan
Hippocampus	Site of short-term memory and ability to learn
Hypothalamus	Control of emotions, body temperature, and hunger
Medulla oblongata	Center for cardiac and respiratory reflexes
Olfactory bulb	Sense of smell
Parietal lobe	Sense of touch and spatial information
Pons	Control of posture
Temporal lobe	Center for hearing and storage site of permanent memories
Thalamus	Relays information from the senses to the cerebral cortex
Visual cortex	Receives and processes information from the eyes

Stress

Self-Test and Instructional Objectives on
the Concept of Stress

In written and/or oral form:

1. State three significant facts about stress.

2. Indicate three reasons why stress is considered important.

3. Present three controversial questions about stress that scholars have not yet been able to answer.

4. Describe the conflict between biological and cultural evolution. Give examples.

5. Explain why the interaction between you and your environment is so important. Give examples.

6. Describe the three stages of the general adaptation syndrome. Why are they important?

7. Describe three major symptoms of stress.

8. List three common cause of stress.

9. Comment on the role of stress in disease. Include a discussion of Type A and Type B personalities.

10. Describe social support systems and their effects on social stressors.

11. Describe several strategies and techniques for combating stress.

12. Explain the role of nutrition in combating stress.

13. Describe the role of humor in helping to combat stress.

Stress

Dr. Hans Selye of the University of Montreal on the nature of stress and distress and what to do about them.

Stress is the non-specific response of the body to any demand made on it. From the point of view of its stress-producing or stressor activity, it is immaterial whether the agent or situation we face is pleasant or unpleasant; all that counts is the intensity of the demand for readjustment or adaptation. The mother who is suddenly told that her only son died in battle suffers a terrible mental shock; if years later it turns out that the news was false, and the son unexpectedly walks into the room alive and well, she experiences extreme joy. Her sorrow and joy are opposites, yet their effects as stressors may be the same.

The businessman who is under constant pressure from his clients and employees alike, the air-traffic controller who knows that a moment of distraction may mean death for hundreds of people, the athlete who desperately wants to win a race, and the husband who helplessly watches his wife slowly and painfully dying from cancer all suffer from stress. The problems they face are totally different, but in certain respects the body responds in a stereotyped manner.

It is difficult to see how such different things as cold, heat, drugs, hormones, sorrow, and joy could provide an identical biochemical reaction in the body. Nevertheless, it can now be shown, by highly objective, biochemical determinations, that certain reactions are non-specific and common to all stress. Stress, then, is not merely "nervous tension."

Stress is not always the non-specific result of damage. We have seen that it is immaterial whether a stressor is pleasant or unpleasant; its stressor effect depends merely on the intensity of the demand upon the adaptive capacity of the body. Any kind of normal activity—a game of chess or even a passionate embrace—can produce considerable stress without causing harmful effects. Damaging or unpleasant stress is "distress."

The word "stress" allegedly came into common English usage, via Old French and Middle English, as "distress." The first syllable was eventually lost through slurring, just as children turn "because" into cause. In the light of our investigations, the true meaning of the two words became totally different despite their common ancestry. Activity associated with stress may be pleasant or unpleasant; distress is always disagreeable.

Stress is not something to be avoided. In common parlance, when we say someone is under stress, we actually mean under excessive stress or distress—just as the statement "he is running a temperature" refers to an abnormally high temperature. Some heat production is essential for life.

Similarly, no matter what you do or what happens to you, there arises a demand for the necessary energy required to maintain life, to resist aggression, or to adapt to constantly changing external influences. Even while fully relaxed and asleep, you are under some stress. Your heart must continue to pump blood, your intestines to digest last night's dinner and your muscles to move your chest for respiration. Your brain is not at rest while you are dreaming. And complete freedom from stress is death.

Stress is the spice of life. Since it is associated with all types of activity, we could avoid it only by never doing anything. Who would enjoy a life consisting of "no hits, no runs, no errors?"

Each of us has an optimal stress level. To keep stress from becoming distress, we must not only have the right amount but the right kind for the right duration. Distress often results from prolonged or unvaried stress or from frustration.

Even the greatest experts in the field do not know why the stress of frustration rather than that of excessive muscular work is much more likely to produce disease—peptic ulcers, migraine, high blood pressure, or even a simple "pain in the neck." In fact, physical exercise can even relax us and help us withstand mental frustration.

Often a voluntary change of activity is as good as or even better than rest when completion of a particular task becomes impossible. For example, when either fatigue or enforce interruption prevents us from finishing a mathematical problem, it is better to go for a swim than just to sit around. Substituting demands on our musculature for those previously made on the intellect not only gives our brain a rest but helps us avoid worrying about the frustrating interruption. Stress on one system helps relax another.

The best way to avoid harmful stress is to select an environment (wife, boss, friends) that is in line with your innate preferences and to find an activity you like and respect. Only thus can you eliminate the need for frustrating, constant readaptation that is a major cause of distress.

Frustration and variation aside, it remains true that man must work. It is biological necessity. Just as our muscles become flabby and degenerate if not used, our brain slips into chaos unless we constantly use it for some work that seems worthwhile to us.

Do not listen to the tempting slogans of those who keep repeating that "there is more to life than just work" or "you should work to live, not live to work." This sounds pretty convincing, but is it really? Of course, in themselves, these statements are true, but your original aim should be not to avoid work but to find the kind of occupation that, for you, is play.

The continuous leisure of enforced retirement or of solitary confinement even if the food and bed were the best in the world—is certainly not an attractive way of life. It is now a generally accepted principle in medicine not to require complete rest for a long time after an operation.

On the endless journeys of the old sailing ships, when there was often nothing to do for weeks, the sailors had to be kept busy washing the deck or painting the ship just to avoid mutiny as the only relief from boredom.

Since work is a basic need of man, the question is not whether we should work but what kind of work suits us best. Stress is associated with every kind of work, but distress is not. To function normally, man needs work just as he needs air, food, sleep, social contacts, and sex.

The art is to find, among the jobs ;you are capable of doing, the one you really like best and that people appreciate. Man must have recognition; he cannot tolerate constant censure, for that is what more than any other stress makes work frustrating and harmful for him.

Many of those who spend much time on things other than their "official duty" or occupation often feel righteous about their secondary endeavors. They consider it their obligation to devote time to "civic duties" or to live a "cultural life."

It is self-deceit to elevate any "extracurricular activity" sanctimoniously. Indeed, as Shaw put it, "When a stupid man is doing something he is ashamed of, he always declares that it is his duty."

But this needn't be so. As Friedrich Nietzsche said in a more poetic tone:
I slept and I dreamed that life is pleasure;
I woke and I saw that life is duty;
I worked and I noticed that duty is pleasure.
But what is work and what is leisure?

I agree with George Bernard Shaw's definition. "Labor is doing what we must; leisure is doing what we like." Even reading the best prose or poetry is work for the professional literary critic, as tennis or golf is work for the paid pro. Yet, the athlete may read for relaxation, and the man of letters may engage in sports to relax.

What scares us most? Not work but failure.

If man has no more incentive to work, he is likely to seek destructive, revolutionary outlets to relieve his basic need for self-assertive activity. Man may be able to solve his age-old problem of having to live by the sweat of his brown, but the fatal enemy of all utopias is boredom. What we shall have to do after technology makes most "useful work" redundant is to invent new occupations. It will require a full-scale effort to teach "play professions"—the arts, philosophy, crafts, science—to the public at large; there is no limit to how much man can work on the perfection of his own self.

There exists a close relationship between work, stress, and aging. Aging results from the sum of all the stresses to which the body has been exposed during a lifetime. Each period of stress—especially if it derives from frustrating, unsuccessful struggles—leaves some irreversible chemical scars which accumulate to constitute the signs of tissue aging. But successful activity, no matter how intense, leaves you with comparatively few such scars. On the contrary, it provides you with the exhilarating feeling of youthful strength, even at a very advanced age. Work wears you out mainly through the frustration of failure. Many of the most eminent among the hard workers in almost any field have lived a long life. Think of Pablo Casals, Winston Churchill, Henry Ford, Charles de Gaulle, Eamon De Valera, Bertrand Russell, Queen Victoria, Titian, Voltaire, Bismarck, Michelangelo, Picasso, Matisse, Rubinstein, Toscanini. And in my own profession of medical research, the Nobel Prize winners Szent-Györgyi, Otto Loewi, Huggins, Waksman, Rous, Warburg. All these people continued or are continuing to be successful, and what is more important, on the whole happy well into their seventies, eighties, or even late nineties. They lived or are living a life of constant leisure by always doing what they like to do.

Few people belong to this group of the creative elite; admittedly, their success in meeting the challenge of stress cannot serve as a basis for a general code of behavior. But you can live long and happily by working hard along more modest lines if you have found the proper job and are reasonably successful at it.

There will still remain many tasks that require no particular craft or artistic talent and yet offer the satisfaction of a job well done. Whenever I take taxis, I like to converse with the drivers, many of whom tel me that they like their job, despite the frustrations of traffic tie-ups. Some of the older ones claim that they could afford to retire but prefer to do something useful, especially because they enjoy talking to their customers; and they get pleasure from earning a grateful smile for having been efficient and courteous. (No, I am quite sure it is not always only the tip that counts.)

Pride in excellence is again a primeval biological feeling; it is not limited to our species. Even a hunting dog is proud to bring in this quarry unscathed; just look at his face and you will see that his work has made him happy. A performing seal is manifestly pleased by earning applause. Only the stress of frustration, a lack of purpose, can spoil the satisfaction of performance. Friction and constant aimless changes in direction are as prone to cause wear and tear and the accumulation of wastes in living machines as in inanimate ones.

Personal Assessment

How Vulnerable Are You to Stress?

A wide variety of situations can function as stressors that influence us physically and psychologically. This assessment will help to identify situations that could be stressful and to determine your overall vulnerability to stress. Use the following scoring system for each situation below.

1 = Always (yes)
2 = Almost always
3 = Most of the time
4 = Some of the time
5 = Never (no)

Situation	Score
I get the appropriate amount of sleep my body needs to function.	_____
I exercise to the point of perspiration at least twice a week.	_____
I do not smoke, or I smoke less than half a pack of cigarettes a day.	_____
I regularly attend club or social activities.	_____
I have one or more friends to confide in about personal matters.	_____
I am able to vent my feelings when angry or worried.	_____
I am able to organize my time effectively.	_____
I drink fewer than three cups of coffee (or tea or cola drinks) a day.	_____
I take quiet time for myself during the day.	_____
I do not procrastinate; I get things done right away.	_____
Before a test I got to bed the same time I normally would.	_____
I live at home (with my family or spouse) while attending school.	_____
I try not to let other people's problems become my own.	_____
(If sexually active) I practice safer sex.	_____
The people closest to me are supportive of my goals.	_____
I have money to meet recreational expenses.	_____
I am attending college by choice.	_____
I rarely compare myself with my friends.	_____
I do not hold a job and go to school full time.	_____
My grade point average is set only for personal satisfaction.	_____
I do not plan on going on to higher levels of education.	_____

Scoring

Your Total Point _____ - 20 = ░░░░░░░ **Final Score**

Interpretation

30-49 Points = Vulnerable to stress
50-75 Points = Seriously vulnerable to stress
76-105 Points = Extremely vulnerable to stress

To carry this further:

Having completed this Personal Assessment and the interpretation based on your responses, is the "stress status" indicated by your score compatible with your own feelings regarding your vulnerability to stress? Have you identified the specific behaviors that needed alteration to reduce your level of vulnerability to stress?

Personal Assessment

Life Stressors

Which of the following events have you experienced in the past 12 months?

	Life Event	Point Values
_____	Death of a close family member	100
_____	Jail term	80
_____	Final year or first year in college	63
_____	Pregnancy (yours or caused by you)	60
_____	Severe personal illness or injury	53
_____	Marriage	50
_____	Any interpersonal problems	45
_____	Financial difficulties	40
_____	Death of a close friend	40
_____	Arguments with your roommate (more than every other day)	40
_____	Major disagreements with your family	40
_____	Major change in personal habits	30
_____	Change in living environment	30
_____	Beginning or ending a job	30
_____	Problems with your boss or professor	25
_____	Outstanding personal achievement	25
_____	Failure in some course	25
_____	Final exams	20
_____	Increased or decreased dating	20
_____	Change in working conditions	20
_____	Change in your major	20
_____	Change in your sleeping habits	18
_____	Several day vacation	15
_____	Change in eating habits	15
_____	Family reunion	15
_____	Change in recreational activities	15
_____	Minor illness or injury	15
_____	Minor violations of the law	11

Score: _____

Interpretation

Life events can function as stressors that influence the body through activation of the stress response. It has been suggested that an accumulation of 150 or more points in a 1-year period may predispose a person to increased physical illness within the coming year. Of course you must remember that for a given person, certain events may be more or less stressful than the point values indicated.

To carry this further . . .

Having completed this Personal Assessment and evaluated your responses based on the interpretation, were you surprised by the number of stress points that you generated? Are there stressors listed ont eh instrument that you have not encountered either in your own experiences or in those of your close friends? Have you experienced a stressor that should be added to this list? Would attending a different college or switching majors change your present level of stress?

Name_____
Section_____
Instructor_____
Class Time_____

Personal Assessment

Life Stressors

Which of the following events have you experienced within the last year?

Life Events	Points
1. Death of a spouse	100
2. Death of a close family member	95
3. Divorce from spouse	90
4. Diagnosis of serious illness	85
5. Divorce of parents	80
6. Dismissal from university	75
7. Broken engagement	73
8. Difficulty in parenting	70
9. Getting married	70
10. Loss of job	60
11. Marital reconciliation	45
12. Change in health of a family member	44
13. Pregnancy	40
14. Beginning a new dating relationship	39
15. Lessened harmony in a marital relationship	39
16. Change in financial status	38
17. Death of a close friend	37
18. Lessened harmony in a dating relationship	35
19. Assumption of a large loan	30
20. Outstanding personal achievement	29
21. Relocation of family	28
22. Completion of degree	25
23. Change in living conditions	25
24. Change in personal habits	24
25. Conflict with a faculty member	23
26. Scheduling conflicts	20
27. Change in residence	20
28. Change in religious practices	19
29. Change in school (transfer)	19
30. Change in level of social involvement	18
31. Assumption of small loan	17
32. Change in sleeping patterns	16
33. Being at home for school holidays	15
34. Change in eating habits	13
35. Change in activity patterns	13
36. Minor violations of the law	11

Your total points _____

Interpretation

Life events can function as stressors that influence the body through activation of the stress response. It has been suggested that an accumulation of 150 or more points in a 1-year period may predispose a person to increased physical illness within the coming year. Of course you must remember that for a given person, certain events may be more or less stressful than the point values indicated.

Drug and Alcohol Use
and Abuse

Self-Test and Instructional Objectives on Drug Use and Abuse Part I and Part II

In written and/or oral form:

1. Present six general facts that help us to understand drug use and abuse.

2. Define narcotics and give five of their general effects on the human body.

3. Describe four of the major narcotics abused throughout the world.

4. Define volatile solvents, indicate four sources, and explain how volatile solvents are abused.

5. Describe two major groups of CNS depressants and indicate two effects of each group.

6. Define tranquilizers and explain how they are used.

7. Describe hallucinogenic compounds and list two effects of each of three different types.

8. State three facts about cocaine and its effects on the human body.

9. State three facts about amphetamines and list three common types.

10. Describe five major causes of drug addiction.

11. Discuss five legal provisions designed to help in the treatment of drug abusers.

12. Describe five of the major treatments used to help drug abusers.

Self-Test and Instructional Objectives on Alcohol
Part I and Part II

In written and/or oral form:

1. Define alcohol and list three of its major effects on the human body.

2. Explain the causes of a hangover.

3. Describe the effects of alcohol on the following: body weight, sexual activity, ability to drive an automobile, muscle tissue, circulation of the blood, respiration, digestion, the central nervous system, and the sense organs.

4. Define intoxication and alcoholism.

5. Describe how drinking contributes to the development of five diseases other than alcoholism.

6. Discuss three reasons why people drink alcohol.

7. Describe five effects of excessive drinking of alcohol on society as a whole.

8. Explain methods used in the treatment of alcoholism.

9. Define the following: detoxication, oxidation, alcohol oxidation rate, rate of alcoholic absorption, peristaltic action, cirrhosis of the liver, escape mechanism, Al-Anon, Alateens.

10. Describe three common effects of alcohol on behavior.

Personal Assessment

Do You Recognize Drug Use?

To assess whether you may be experiencing the symptoms of drug use, circle **Y** for yes and **N** for no.

1.	A sudden increase or loss of appetite, or sudden weight loss or gain.	Y	N
2.	Moodiness, depression, Irritability, or withdrawal.	Y	N
3.	Disorientation, lack of concentration, or forgetfulness.	Y	N
4.	Frequent use of eye drops or inappropriate wearing of sunglasses.	Y	N
5.	Disruption or change in sleep patterns, or a lack of energy	Y	N
6.	Borrowing money more and more, working excessive hours, selling personal items, or an incident of stealing or shoplifting.	Y	N
7.	Persistent and frequent nosebleeds, sniffles, coughs, and other signs of upper respiratory infection.	Y	N
8.	Change in speech patterns or vocabulary, or a deterioration in academic performance.	Y	N
9.	Feeling ill-at-ease with family members and other adults.	Y	N
10.	Neglect of personal appearance.	Y	N

Interpretation:

A yes response to more than three questions indicates that there may be drug-dependence, and professional help should be obtained.

Personal Assessment

Nonchemical High Challenge

Experts agree that drug use provides only short-term, ineffective, and often destructive solutions to problems. We hope that you have found (or will find) innovative, invigorating nondrug experiences that will make your life more exciting. Circle the number for each activity that reflects your intention to try that activity. Use the following guide:

1 No intention of trying this activity
2 Intend to try this within 2 years
3 Intend to try this within 6 months
4 Already tried this activity
5 Regularly do this activity

1	Learn to juggle	1	2	3	4	5
2	Go backpacking	1	2	3	4	5
3	Complete a marathon race	1	2	3	4	5
4	Start a vegetable garden	1	2	3	4	5
5	Ride in a hot air balloon	1	2	3	4	5
6	Snow ski or water ski	1	2	3	4	5
7	Donate blood	1	2	3	4	5
8	Go river rafting	1	2	3	4	5
9	Learn to play a musical instrument	1	2	3	4	5
10	Cycle 100 miles	1	2	3	4	5
11	Parachute from a plane	1	2	3	4	5
12	Go rockclimbing	1	2	3	4	5
13	Take a role in a theater production	1	2	3	4	5
14	Build a piece of furniture	1	2	3	4	5
15	Solicit funds for a worthy cause	1	2	3	4	5
16	Learn to swim	1	2	3	4	5
17	Overhaul your car engine	1	2	3	4	5
18	Compose a song	1	2	3	4	5
19	Travel to a foreign country	1	2	3	4	5
20	Write a first chapter of a book	1	2	3	4	5

Your total points _____

Interpretation

61-100   You participate in many challenging experiences
41-60   You are willing to try some challenging experiences
20-40   You take few challenging risks described here

To carry this further . . .

Looking at your point total, were you surprised at the degree to which you are aware of alternative activities? What are the top five activities, and can you understand their importance? What activities would you add to our list?

Name_____

Section_____

Instructor_____

Class Time_____

Personal Assessment

How Do You Use Alcohol Beverages

Answer the following questions in terms of your own alcohol use. Record your number of YES and NO responses in the box at the end of the questionnaire.

Do you: **Yes**   **No**

1   Drink more frequently than you did a year ago?   _____ _____

2   Drink more heavily than you did a year ago?   _____ _____

3   Plan to drink, sometimes days in advance?   _____ _____

4   Gulp or "chug" your drinks, perhaps in a contest?   _____ _____

5   Set personal limits on the amount you plan to drink but then _____ _____
     consistently disregard these limits?

6   Drink at a rate greater than two drinks per hour?   _____ _____

7   Encourage or even pressure others to drink with you?   _____ _____

8   Frequently want a nonalcohol beverage but then end up drinking an _____ _____
     alcohol drink?

9   Drive your car while under the influence of alcohol or ride with _____ _____
     another person who has been drinking?

10   Use alcohol beverages while taking prescription or OPTC medications? _____ _____

11   Forget what happened while you were drinking?   _____ _____

12   Have a tendency to disregard information about the effects of drinking? _____ _____

13   Find your reputation fading because of alcohol use?   _____ _____

                                                          Total   _____ _____

Interpretation

If you indicate a "yes" response on any of these questions, you may be demonstrating aspects of irresponsible alcohol use. Two or more "yes" responses indicates an unacceptable pattern of alcohol use and may reflect problem drinking behavior.

To carry this further . . .

Ask your friends or roommates to take this assessment. Are they willing to take this assessment and then talk about their results with you? Be prepared to discuss any follow-up questions they might have about their (or your) alcohol consumption patterns. Your willingness to talk about drinking behaviors might help someone to realize that this topic can and should be discussed openly. Finally, be aware of how people in your area can get professional help with drinking or other drug concerns.

Personal Assessment

One for the Road?

Test your knowledge about alcohol use and safe driving. Circle **T** for true and **F** for false; then check your response against the answers at right. Knowing the right answers may save your life or the life of a friend.

T F	1	Alcohol is a factor in one half of all highway fatalities.	True	1	Just over 46,000 persons were killed in U.S. traffic accidents in 1987. About half of these deaths were alcohol-related.
T F	2	One and one-half ounces of 86-proof whiskey contains as much alcohol as 12 ounces of beer or 5 ounces of wine.	True	2	Many alcohol beverages are of the same approximate strength.
T F	3	A blood alcohol concentration (BAC) of 0.10% is considered legal evidence of intoxication while operating a motor vehicle in most states.	True	3	Even more important, art 0.10% BAC the chances of your having an accident are seven and one-half times greater than when you are sober. These chances increase to 25 times if your BAC reaches 0.15%.
T F	4	A 150-pound drinker (male or female) having four drinks per hour would be considered legally drunk if stopped while operating a motor vehicle.	True	4	Using the blood alcohol chart, you can determine your own safe drinking-driving blood alcohol concentration.
T F	5	Having one to two drinks per hour will cause intoxication within a 4-hour period.	False	5	The body metabolizes one to two drinks per hour. Therefore if you have only one to two drinks per hour you will not become intoxicated.
T F	6	Drinking large amounts of coffee or taking a cold shower will "sober up" a drinker.	False	6	Absolutely nothing but time will "sober up" an intoxicated person.
T F	7	If your friend has been drinking heavily, your kindest act may be to hide his or her car keys.	True	7	A friend who drives while intoxicated may not be a friend for long. Hide your friend's car keys if he or she drinks too much.

T F 8 Eating before drinking or while drinking is a good idea.

True 8 Alcohol enters the bloodstream rapidly because it requires no digestion. Eating slows the absorption of alcohol; also, providing high-protein snacks at a drinking party may prevent a friend from becoming intoxicated.

To carry this further . . .

Do you think any of these questions could be answered differently? If so, which ones? Can you think of other important information regarding drinking and driving that college students should know?

Friends Don't Let Friends Drive Drunk!

Personal Assessment

Test Your Knowledge About Cigarette Smoking

Assumption		**Discussion**	
1	There are now safe cigarettes on the market.	F	Depending on the brand, some cigarettes contain less tar and nicotine; none are safe, however.
2	A small number of cigarettes can be smoked without risk.	F	Even a low level of smoking exposes the body to harmful substances in tobacco smoke.
3	Most early changers in the body resulting from cigarette smoking are temporary.	T	Some, however, cannot be reversed—particularly changes associated with emphysema.
4	Filters provide a measure of safety to cigarette smokers.	T	However, the protection is far from adequate.
5	Low tar-low nicotine cigarettes are safer than high tar-high nicotine brands.	T	Many persons, however, smoke low tar-low nicotine cigarettes in a manner that makes them just as dangerous as stronger cigarettes.
6	Mentholated cigarettes are better for the smoker than are nonmentholated brands.	F	Menthol simply makes cigarette smoke feel cooler. The smoke contains all of the harmful agents found in the smoke from regular cigarettes.
7	It has been scientifically proved that cigarette smoking causes cancer.	T	Particularly lung cancer and cancers of the larynx, esophagus, oral cavity, and urinary bladder.
8	No specific agent capable of causing cancer has ever been identified in the tobacco used in smokeless tobacco.	F	Unfortunately, smokeless tobacco is no safer than the tobacco that is burned. The user of smokeless tobacco swallows much of what the smoker inhales.
9	The cure rate for lung cancer is so good that no one should fear developing this form of cancer.	F	Approximately 10% of those persons having lung cancer will live the 5 years required to meet the medical definition of "cured."
10	Smoking is not harmful as long as the smoke is not inhaled.	F	Because of the toxic material in smoke, even its contact with the tissue of the oral cavity introduces a measure of risk in this form of cigarette use.

Assumption   **Discussion**

11	The "smoker's cough" reflects under-lying damage to the tissue of the airways.	T	The "cough" occurs in response to an inability to clear the airway of mucus as a result of changes in the cells that normally keep the air passages clear.
12	Cigarette smoking does not appear to be associated with damage of the heart and blood vessels.	F	Cigarette smoking is, in fact, the single most important risk factor in the development of cardiovascular disease.
13	Because of the design of the placenta, smoking does not present a major risk to the developing fetus.	F	Children born to women who smoked during pregnancy show a variety of health impairments, including smaller birth size, premature birth, and more illnesses during the first year of life. Smoking women also have more still-births.
14	Women who smoke cigarettes and use an oral contraceptive should decide which they which to continue, because there is a risk in using both.	T	Women over 35 years of age, in particular, are at risk of experiencing serious heart disease should they continue using both cigarettes and an oral contraceptive.
15	Air pollution is a greater risk to our respiratory health than is cigarette smoking.	F	Although air pollution does expose the body to potentially serious problems, the risk is considerably less than that associated with smoking.
16	Addiction, in the sense of physical addiction, is found in conjunction with cigarette smoking.	T	Dependence, including true physical addiction, is widely recognized in cigarette smokers.
17	The best "teachers" a young smoker has are his or her parents.	T	There is a strong correlation between cigarette smoking of parents and the subsequent smoking of their children. Parents who do not want their children to smoke should not smoke.
18	Nonsmoking and higher levels of education are directly related.	T	The higher one's level of education, the less likely one is to smoke.
19	About as many women smoke cigarettes as do men.	T	Although in the past more men smoked than did women, the trend is changing. In the future cigarette smoking could become a woman's pastime.
20	Fortunately, for those who now smoke, stopping is relatively easy.	F	Unfortunately, relatively few smokers can quit. The best advice is never to begin smoking.

To carry this further . . .

Were you surprised at the number of items that you answered correctly? In what areas did you hold misconceptions regarding cigarette smoking? Do you think that most university students are as knowledgeable as you? Where do you see the general public in terms of their understanding of cigarette smoking? How can the health care community do a better job in educating the public about tobacco use?

Mental Health

Self-Test and Instructional Objectives on Mental Health

In written and/or oral form:

1. Explain three basic emotional needs.

2. State at least two psychological reactions and two physiological reactions to anxiety.

3. Describe the difference between a normal individual and a neurotic individual.

4. List three types of neuroses.

5. Explain the difference between a neurotic and a psychotic.

6. Describe three types of psychosis.

7. Describe the causes of organic psychosis and list three types.

8. Define community psychiatry, symptomatic treatment, behavior therapy, and psychotherapy.

9. Describe the advantages of family therapy and group therapy.

10. List two injustices of involuntary commitment.

Personal Assessment

Mental Health

<u>Directions:</u> This assessment is based on the National Mental Health Association's characteristics of mentally healthy people. In the left column, a characteristic is listed. In the middle column, mark an "X" if you think you possess that characteristic. In the column on the far right make a list of those behaviors you exhibit which are indicative of that characteristic.

<u>Characteristic</u>	<u>Do You Possess</u>	<u>Indicative Behaviors</u>
1. Feels comfortable about oneself		
2. Feels right about others		
3. Able to meet the demands of life		

Consider this . . .

1. What criteria did you use to decide whether or not you possessed each of these characteristics?

2. Would others agree with your assessment? Why or why not?

3. How did you decide what behaviors exemplified each of these characteristics?

Personal Assesment

Your Range of Emotions

<u>Directions:</u> Keep a log of your emotions for a full week. Below you will find a format for you to complete each day. You may use this worksheet for one day; you will need to use the same format for each of the other six days.

<u>Date:</u>_____

<u>Time of Day</u>	<u>Event</u>	<u>Emotion</u>	<u>Reaction</u>

Ask Yourself . . .

1.   How do your emotions vary throughout the day? Why?

2.   How do your emotions vary from day-to-day? Why?

3.   Who influences the emotions you feel?

4.   Do certain events seem to trigger the same emotions in you every day?

5.   Do you react to the same emotion in the same way every time you experience it? Why or why not?

6.   Write a paragraph that analyzes your emotional experiences over a seven-day period of time.

Name_____

Section_____

Instructor_____

Class Time_____

Personal Assesment

How Creative Are You

<u>Directions:</u> To determine whether or not your possess tendencies toward high creativity, circle the number that best reflects your relative position on each continuum. Use the scores below to interpret your results.

More interested in the meaning and implications of things and ideas than in details and the practical value of things and ideas	1 2 3 4 5	More interested in details and the practical value of things and ideas than in their meaning and their implications
A combination of relatively equal measures of both reasonableness and passion	1 2 3 4 5	More reasonable than passionate or more passionate than reasonable
A combination of relatively equal measures of both rationality and irrationality	1 2 3 4 5	More rational than irrational or more irrational than rational
A combination of relatively equal measures of scientific interests and artistic interest	1 2 3 4 5	More interested in science than in art or more interested in art than in science
A combination of relatively equal measures of masculinity and femininity	1 2 3 4 5	More masculine than feminine or more feminine than masculine
More likely to concentrate on the possibility of finding the deeper meaning and possibilities inherent in something	1 2 3 4 5	More likely to be interested in becoming aware of discovering something
More productive and contributive when working alone	1 2 3 4 5	More productive and contributive when engaged in group activities and brainstorming

Your Total Points: _____

<u>Interpretation</u>

26 - 35   Relatively low creativity
17 - 25   Average creativity
 7 - 16   Relatively high creativity

Personal Assesment

Quiet Time

<u>Directions:</u> Set aside a minimum of 20 minutes a day as "Quiet Time;" keep a log of your experiences. Do this for a minimum of 7 days. When the week is over, consider the questions posed after this assessment.

Day	Time	Locale	Activity	Thoughts and Feelings
#1				
#2				
#3				
#4				
#5				
#6				
#7				

Consider this . . .

1. What did you find the most difficult part of this assignment? What was the least difficult?

2. Will you continue to schedule quiet time? Why or why not?

3. Was it easy to make yourself take a scheduled quiet time? What might have made it easier?

4. Of what benefit was this to you, of any? What would need to be changed for it to be more beneficial?

5. Did your reactions to this vary from day to day? Why or why not?

Learning Objectives: Review of the Content

<u>Directions:</u> After reading Chapter 2 of the textbook, you should be able to complete the learning objectives below. The number(s) in parentheses at the end of each objective is (are) the page number(s) on which the information appears.

1.   Describe what is meant by a mentally healthy person. (23)

2.   Explain what distinguishes the difference between those who are mentally healthy and those who are not. (24)

3.   List the two major factors that influence personality. (25)

4.   Explain what is meant by the term "normal range of emotions." (25-26)

5.   Define depression and list its common symptoms. (26)

6.   Explain the distinction between "being alone" and "feeling lonely." (27)

7.   Explain why self-esteem may be the key to overall mental health. (28-29)

8.   Name and describe the five needs noted in Maslow's hierarchy of needs. (30-32)

9. Describe all of the characteristics of the transcenders noted by Maslow. (31-32)

10. List all of the traits that characterize creative people. (32-33)

11. Identify the two stages that college students may go through as they develop their own faith. (33-35)

12. List in order and briefly describe the four components of the cyclic process of emotional growth. (35-38)

Terms: Review of New Vocabulary

Directions: Match the appropriate term with its definition by writing the term next to the definition. So that you can check your answers, the page number on which the term appears in the textbook is presented in parentheses.

Affect	depression	self-actualization
authentic self	faith	self-esteem
cognition	individuative-reflective stage	synthetic-conventional stage
creativity	loneliness	transcenders
demythologization	performance	validity

Actualizer/Manipulator

1. Dictator—will stop at nothing in his attempt to control his victims' every thought and action; dominates orders, quotes authorities. Examples: mothers, fathers, rank pullers, bosses, teachers.

2. Leader—forceful but not dominating; leads by consent of group.

3. Weakling—dictators' victim; forgets, does not hear, passively silent.

4. Empathizer—not only talks but listens; is aware of his/her weaknesses.

5. Calculator—exaggerates his/her control. He/she deceives, lies, and constantly tries to outwit and control other people. Examples: high-pressure salesperson, seducer, poker player, con artist, blackmailer, intellectualizer.

6. Nice Guys—exaggerates his/her caring—love and kills the kindness; a pleaser, non-violent, non-offensive, never-ask-for-what-you want.

7. Carer—is genuine, affectionate, friendly, deeply loving.

8. Judge—exaggerates his/her criticalness. He/she distrusts everybody and is blameful, resentful, and slow to forgive; know-it-all, blamer, shamer, comparer, vindicator, convictor. She/he knows everything, and at any time she/he is wiling to tell you all about it. She/he blames others for her/his shortcomings and resents anyone who is successful.

9. Expressor—is not judgmental of others but is able to express his/her own convictions strongly.

10. Protector—exaggerates his/her support and is non-judgmental. Spoils others, is over sympathetic, refuses to allow those he/she protects to grow up, cares for others needs only. Try as he/she might, the protector can't do enough for you. In his/her great supporting role he/she manages to stifle every idea but his/her own. The thought of anyone else making a decision is completely appalling to him/her. Examples: mother/father hen, defender, embarrassed for others, fearful for others, martyr, helper, ;unselfish one.

11. Guide—does not protect or teach others but gently helps each person find his/her own way.

12. REspector—rather than using or exploiting, the actualizer respects himself and others as "thons."

13. Clinging Vine—she/he exaggerates her/his dependency. She/he is the person who wants to be led, fooled, taken care of. She/he lets others do the work for her/him. The crier, the perpetual child, the hypochondriac, attention demander, helpless one.

14. Appreciator—does not simply depend on others, but appreciates the different skills that others have to offer. Appreciates different points of view from her/his own and does not need to have other people think the same as she/he does.

15. Bully—exaggerates his/her aggression, cruelty, and unkindness. He/she controls by implied threats of some kind. He/she is the humiliator, tough guy, threatener, or nagger.

16. Assertor—enjoys a worthy joke but is direct and straightforward; he/she is not hostile or dominating.

Your Image: Fact or Fantasy

Do you see yourself as others see you? Particularly in intimate human relationships, it's especially interesti[ng] to see if your partner has an image of you that corresponds with your own. It's not unusual (and perhaps beneficia[l]) if your mate idealizes you, and you him or her; but if you see yourself as open, trustworthy, and unselfish, and your mate finds you secretive, untrustworthy, and selfish, you both would benefit by being aware of the discrepancies. The following exercise, granted, is very superficial—its purpose is to help you see if you are communicating to others the person you think you are.

On the form that is presented on the following page you will find a list of characteristics. Put an A, B, C, or D after each trait. Then in the "Partner" section mark the degree to which your boyfriend or girlfriend, husband or wife, possesses each quality. Then fold the form so that your mate cannot see your responses and ask him/her to complete the form. If you are brave, look over the evaluation and discuss your answers.

Image Worksheet

A = Not at all   B = Hardly at all   C = Fairly well   D = Very well

Characteristic	Self	Partner	Self	Partner
Tactful				
Careful				
Easygoing				
Overbearing				
Confident				
Hardworking				
Unselfish				
Frivolous				
Generous				
Overgenerous				
Lazy				
Cool and detached				
Shallow				
Overindulgent				
Smug				
Dull				
Self-controlled				
Indecisive				
Cruel				
Spiteful				
Understanding				
Emotional				
Irritable				
Neat				
Reliable				
Trusting				
Childish				
Self-centered				
Idealistic				
Tender				
Self-reliant				

Personal Assessment

How Does My Self-Concept Compare with My Self-Ideal?

Below you will find a list of 15 personal attributes, each portrayed on a 9-point continuum. Mark with an X where you think you rank on each attribute. Try to be candid and accurate; these marks will collectively describe a portion of your self-concept. When you are finished with the above task, go back and circle where you *wish* you could be on each dimension. These marks describe your self-ideal. Finally, in the spaces on the right, indicate the number of the discrepancy (between self-concept and self-ideal) for each attribute.

Decisive   **Indecisive**

9   8   7   6   5   4   3   2   1   _____

Anxious   **Relaxed**

9   8   7   6   5   4   3   2   1   _____

Easily influenced   **Independent thinker**

9   8   7   6   5   4   3   2   1   _____

Very intelligent   **Less intelligent**

9   8   7   6   5   4   3   2   1   _____

In good physical shape   **In poor physical shape**

9   8   7   6   5   4   3   2   1   _____

Undependable   **Dependable**

9   8   7   6   5   4   3   2   1   _____

Deceitful   **Honest**

9   8   7   6   5   4   3   2   1   _____

A leader   **A follower**

9   8   7   6   5   4   3   2   1   _____

Unambitious   **Ambitious**

9   8   7   6   5   4   3   2   1   _____

Self-confident   **Insecure**

9   8   7   6   5   4   3   2   1   _____

Conservative   **Adventurous**

9   8   7   6   5   4   3   2   1   _____

Extroverted   **Introverted**

9   8   7   6   5   4   3   2   1   _____

Physically attractive   **Physically unattractive**

9   ·8   7   6   5   4   3   2   1   _____

Lazy   **Hardworking**

9   8   7   6   5   4   3   2   1   _____

Funny   **Little sense of human**

9   8   7   6   5   4   3   2   1   _____

To carry this further . . .

1.   Overall, how would you describe the discrepancy between your self-concept and your self-denial (large, moderate, small, large on a few dimensions)?

2.   How do sizable gaps for any of your attributes affect your self-esteem?

3.   Do you think that any of the gaps exist because you have had others' ideals imposed on you or because you have thoughtlessly accepted others' ideals?

4.   Identify several attributes that you realistically believe can be changed to narrow the gap between your self-concept and your self-ideal.

Cancer

Self-Test and Instructional Objectives on Cancer

In written and/or oral form:

1. Explain the four basic groups of cancer causes. Give at least three examples for each group.

2. List three characteristics of cancer cells.

3. Present at least five possible sites of cancer in the body.

4. Describe the three major types of cancer.

5. Give seven danger signals of cancer.

6. Describe at least five techniques or instruments used for cancer diagnosis.

7. Describe four treatments of malignant tumors.

8. List three conditions that often lead to the deaths of cancer patients.

9. Give survival rates for at least three different types of cancer.

10. Define the following: cancer, malignant, benign, carcinogen, neoplasm, sarcoma, acute, chronic, biopsy, Pap smear.

11. Define the following: invasive ability, metastasis, proctoscopic, epithelial, leukemia, cervix, laser radiation, hormone, remission, anemia, debility.

12. Explain four guidelines for preventing and/or conquering cancer.

Cancer

Cancer is a general term for abnormal and uncontrollable growth of cells or tissue. A cancer cell can be distinguished from a normal cell by its nucleus. Often larger than normal, the nucleus of a cancer cell will often contain an increased number of chromosomes and/or abnormally shaped chromosomes.

Important Definitions

Benign tumor A tumor that is not malignant or cancerous.

Carcinogen Any substance that causes cancer.

Carcinomas Cancer that originates in epithelial tissue (skin, glands, and lining of internal organs).

Leukemia Malignant disease of the blood-forming system.

Lymphomas Tumor originating from lymphatic tissue (neck, groin, armpit).

Malignant tumor A tumor that is cancerous and capable of spreading.

Metastasis The spread of cancer cells from one part of the body to another.

Remission Condition in which there are no symptoms or other evidence of disease.

Sarcomas Cancers arising from bone, cartilage, or striated muscle.

Cancer Incidence

Cancer primarily strikes older age groups, but several types can affect individuals of any age. Cancers that can affect college-age students include leukemia, Hodgkin's disease, and cancers of the breast, uterus, and brain. Cancer can take many years to develop, so cancers that strike older groups often begin in the first 30 years of life.

Cancer often progresses slowly. It can affect an individual in different ways, depending on the type of cancer and how far it has progressed.

- Cancer cells grow and multiple out of control, stealing nutrients from normal cells.

- Cancers developing within specific organs can impair organ function and inflict permanent damage.

- Tumors (both benign and malignant) can grow large enough to interfere with bodily functions.

- Cancers of the blood damage the immune system, leaving the body unable to fight infection, and often cause anemia.

Personal Assessment

Are You at Risk for Skin, Breast, and Cervical Cancer?

Some people may have more than an average risk of developing particular cancers. These people will be identified by certain risk factors.

This simple self-testing method is designed by the American Cancer Society to help you assess your risk factors for three common types of cancer. These are the major risk factors and by no means represent the only ones that might be involved.

Check your response to each risk factor. Add the numbers in the parentheses to arrive at a total score for each cancer type. Find out what your score means by reading the information in the right column. You are advised to discuss the information with your physician if you are at a higher risk.

Skin cancer

1   Frequent work or play in the sun
    a   Yes (10)   b   No (1)

2   Work in mines, around coal tars, or around radioactivity
    a   Yes (1)   b   No (1)

3   Complexion—fair skin and/or light skin
    a   Yes (10)   b   No (1)

Explanation

1   Excessive ultraviolet light causes skin cancer. Protect yourself with a sun screen medication.

2   These materials can cause skin cancer.

3   Light complexions need more protection than others

Your total points _____

Interpretation

Numerical risks for skin cancer are difficult to state. For instance, a person with a dark complexion can work longer in the sun and be less likely to develop cancer than a light-complected person. Furthermore, a person wearing a long-sleeved shirt and a wide-brimmed hat may work in the sun and be less at risk than a person who wears a bathing suit for only a short period. The risk increases greatly with age.

The key here is if you answered "yes" to any question, you need to realize that you have above-average risk.

Breast cancer

1 Age-group
   - a 20-34 (10)
   - b 35-49 (40)
   - c 50 and over (90)

2 Race/nationality
   - a Oriental (5)
   - b Black (20)
   - c White (25)
   - d Mexican American (10)

3 Family history of breast cancer
   - a Mother, sister, or grandmother (30)
   - b None (10)

4 Your history
   - a No breast disease (10)
   - b Previous noncancerous lumps or cysts (2)
   - c Previous breast cancer (100)

5 Maternity
   - a First pregnancy before age 25 (10)
   - b First pregnancy after age 25 (15)
   - c No pregnancies (2)

Your total points _____

Interpretation

Under 100   Low-risk women should practice monthly breast self-examination (BSE) and have their breasts examined by a doctor as part of a cancer-related checkup.

100-199   Moderate-risk women should practice monthly BSE and have their breasts examined by a doctor as part of a cancer-related checkup. Periodic breast x-rays should be included as your doctor may advise.

200 or more   High-risk women should practice monthly BSE and have the examinations and mammograms listed above.

Cervical cancer*

1 Age-group
   - a Less than 25 (10)
   - b 25-39 (20)
   - c 40-54 (30)
   - d 55 and over (30)

2 Race/nationality
   - a Oriental (10)
   - b Puerto Rican (20)
   - c Black (20)
   - d White (10)
   - e Mexican American (20)

3 Number of pregnancies
   - a 0 (10)
   - b ·1 to 3 (20)
   - c 4 and over (30)

4 Viral infections
   - a Herpes and other viral infections or ulcer formations on the vagina (10)
   - b Never (1)

5 Age at first intercourse
   - a Before 15 (40)
   - b 15-19 (30)
   - c 20-24 (20)
   - d 25 and over (10)

Explanation

1 The highest occurrence is in the 40 and over age-group. The numbers represent the relative rates of cancer for different age-groups. A 45 year-old woman has a risk three times higher than a 20-year old.

2 Puerto Ricans, Blacks, and Mexican Americans have higher rates of cervical cancer.

3 Women who have delivered more children have a higher occurrence.

4 Viral infections of the cervix and vagina are associated with cervical cancer.

5 Women with earlier intercourse and with more sexual partners are at a higher risk

*Lower portion of uterus. These questions would not apply to a woman who has had a complete hysterectomy.

6   Bleeding between periods or after intercourse
    a   Yes (40)   b   No (1)

6   Irregular bleeding may be a sign of uterine cancer.

Your total points _____

Interpretation/To carry this further . . .

40-69   This is a low-risk group. As your doctor for a Pap test. You will be advised how often you should be tested after your first test.

70-99   In this moderate-risk group, more frequent Pap tests may be required.

100 or higher You are in a high-risk group and should have a Pap test (and pelvic exam) as advised by your doctor.

Personal Assessment

Assessing Your Cancer Risks

<u>Directions:</u> There are a number of risk factors which have been associated with the development of cancer. Below are listed a number of those risk factors. Beside each risk factor noted, rate yourself in terms of "often," "sometimes" or "never;" then, respond to the questions below.

		<u>Often</u>	<u>Sometimes</u>	<u>Never</u>
1.	I smoke cigarettes.	_____	_____	_____
2.	I spend a great deal of time outside and at the beach without any sunscreen.	_____	_____	_____
3.	I do not do monthly breast or testicular self-examination.	_____	_____	_____
4.	I tend to eat a high fat diet.	_____	_____	_____
5.	My job exposes me to many carcinogens.	_____	_____	_____
6.	I avoid foods high in fiber.	_____	_____	_____
7.	I am overweight.	_____	_____	_____
8.	I consume alcohol.	_____	_____	_____
9.	I pay little or no attention to changes in my body.	_____	_____	_____
10.	I avoid regular medical check-ups.	_____	_____	_____
11.	I an unaware of the warning signs of cancer.	_____	_____	_____
12.	I live with a cigarette smoker.	_____	_____	_____

Consider This . . .

1. Look at those "risk factors" for which you have checked "often." For which forms of cancer does this put you most at risk?

2. Which of those "risk factors" for which you have checked "often" or "sometimes" could you change?

3. Based on this, would you consider yourself at "high" or "low" risk for developing some form of cancer? If you are at "high" risk, what steps can you take to reduce that risk?

4. Would others in your family have rated themselves similarly to you for each of these risk factors? Why or why not?

Aging

Self-Test and Instructional Objectives on
Aging

In written and/or oral form:

1. State at least five characteristics of America's aged minority.

2. Describe at least five changes in physical characteristics that occur as we age. (Effects on hair, brain, heart, etc.)

3. Explain five effects of aging on the digestive system, the immune system, and the musculoskeletal system.

4. Describe three effects of aging on the cardiovascular system.

5. Explain five life-extending measures that have positive health effects.

6. State five reasons why the elderly should be concerned with the control of hypertension and diabetes.

7. Describe some of the changes of aging that younger people should recognize and understand.

8. List five known causes of aging.

9. Discuss five advantages of being elderly today in the United States.

10. Explain why we should change the public's perception about aging and the elderly.

Personal Assessment

Preparing for the Future

<u>Directions:</u> Answer each of the following 3 questions. Based on your responses, write a brief paragraph describing your preparation for healthy midlife years.

1.   What am I doing now that will enhance the quality of my health during my midlife and elderly years?

2.   What am I doing now that will decrease the quality of my health during my midlife and elderly years?

3.   What could I be doing, that I am not, to enhance the quality of my health during my midlife and elderly years?

Summary Paragraph

Personal Assessment

What Do You Know About Aging?

Erdman Palmore, author of the *The Facts on Aging Quiz: A Handbook*, developed the following quiz to stimulate discussions and identify misconceptions about aging. Test your knowledge about the elderly by answering yes or no to the following items:

		Yes	No
1	A person's height tends to decline in old age.	_____	_____
2	Older people have more acute (short-term) illnesses than people under 65.	_____	_____
3	The aged are more fearful of crime than are people under 65	_____	_____
4	More of the aged vote than any other age-group.	_____	_____
5	There are proportionately more older people in public office than in the total population	_____	_____
6	Most old people live alone.	_____	_____
7	All five senses tend to decline in old age.	_____	_____
8	When the last child leaves home, the majority of parents have serious problems adjusting to their "empty nest."	_____	_____
9	Aged people have fewer accidents per driver than drivers under 65.	_____	_____
10	One tenth of the aged live in long-stay institutions like nursing homes.	_____	_____
11	Most old people report they are seldom angry or irritated.	_____	_____
12	Most old people are socially isolated and lonely.	_____	_____
13	Most old people work or would like to have some kind of work (including housework or volunteer work).	_____	_____
14	Medicare pays more than half of the medical expenses for the aged.	_____	_____
15	Social Security benefits automatically increase with inflation.	_____	_____

Interpretation

Odd-numbered questions are "yes"; even-numbered questions are "no."

To carry this further . . .

What were the sources of the information on which you based your responses? How would you describe the quality of the relationships you have had thus far with older adults? What aspects of middle age do you find most and least attractive? Have you identified any misconceptions about older adults that you may have had?

Death and Dying

Self-Test and Instructional Objectives on Death and Dying

In written and/or oral form:

1. Explain how most scientists and legislators believe death is most reliably defined.

2. List five reactions to death and suicide.

3. Explain eight ways of learning to cope with death.

4. Explain five of the decisions and plans that must be made as death approaches.

5. State five reasons why making a will is so important.

6. Explain three important issues concerning euthanasia?

7. Define three aspects of the living will.

8. Explain five of the tasks a family must do after a family member dies.

The Living Will

The living will is a legally binding document in many states; it allows individuals to express their wishes concerning dying with dignity. When such a document has been drawn, families and physicians are better able to deal with the wishes of persons who are near death from conditions from which there is no reasonable expectation of recovery. Individuals can construct their own living wills or use forms supplied by concerned organizations.

ADVANCE DIRECTIVE
Living Will and Health Care Proxy

Death is a part of life. It is a reality like birth, growth and aging. I am using this advance directive to convey my wishes about medical care to my doctors and other people looking after me at the end of my life. It is called an advance directive because it gives instructions in advance about what I want to happen to me in the future. It expresses my wishes about medical treatment that might keep me alive. I want this to be legally binding.

If I cannot make or communicate decisions about my medical care, those around me should rely on this document for instructions about measures that could keep me alive.

I do not want medical treatment (including feeding and water by tube) that will keep me alive if:
- I am unconscious and there is no reasonable prospect that I will ever be conscious again (even if I am not going to die soon in my medical condition), <u>or</u>
- I am near death from an illness or injury with no reasonable prospect of recovery.

I do not want medicine and other care to make me more comfortable and to take care of pain and suffering. I want this even if the pain medicine makes me die sooner.

I want to give some extra instructions: [Here list any special instructions, e.g., some people fear being kept alive after a debilitating stroke. If you have wishes about this, or any other conditions, please write them here.]

The legal language in the box that follows is a health care proxy.
It gives another person the power to make medical decisions for me.

I name_____, who lives at _____
_____, phone number _____
to make medical decisions for me if I cannot make them myself. This person is called a health care "surrogate," "agent," "proxy," or "attorney in fact." This power of attorney shall become effective when I become incapable of making or communicating decisions about my medical care. This means that this document stays legal when and if I lose the power to speak for myself, for instance, if I am in a coma or have Alzheimer's disease.

My health care proxy has power to tell others what my advance directive means. This person also has power to make decisions for me, based either on what I would have wanted, or, if this is not known, on what he or she thinks is best for me.

If my first choice health care proxy cannot or decides not to act for me, I name _____
address, _____, phone number, _____,
as my second choice.
(continued)

I have discussed my wishes with my health care proxy, and with my second choice if I have chosen to appoint a second person. My proxy(ies) has(have) agreed to act for me.

I have thought about this advance directive carefully. I know what it means and want to sign it. I have chosen two witnesses, neither of whom is a member of my family, nor will inherit from me when I die. My witnesses are not the same people as those I named as my health care proxies. I understand that this form should be notarized if I use the box to name (a) health care proxy(ies).

Signature _____

Date _____

Address _____

Witness' signature _____

Witness' printed name _____

Address _____

Witness' signature _____

Witness' printed name _____

Address _____

Notary [to be used if proxy is appointed] _____

Drafted and distributed by Choice in Dying, Inc.--the national council for the right to die. Choice In Dying is a national not-for-profit organization which works for the rights of patients at the end of life. In addition to this generic advance directive. Choice In Dying distributes advance directives that conform to each state's specific legal requirements and maintains a national Living Will Registry for completed documents.

CHOICE IN DYING, INC.
the national council for the right to die
(formerly Concern for Dying/Society for the Right to Die)
200 Varick Street, New York, NY 10014 (212) 366-5540

Personal Assessment

Planning Your Funeral

In line with this chapter's positive theme of the value of personal death awareness, here is a funeral service assessment that we frequently give to our health classes. This inventory can help you assess your reactions and thoughts about the funeral arrangements you would prefer for yourself.

After answering each of the following questions, you might wish to discuss your responses with a friend or close relative.

1   Have you ever considered how you would like your body to be handled after your death?
_____ Yes   _____ No

2   Have you already made funeral prearrangements for yourself?
_____ Yes   _____ No

3   Have you considered a specific funeral home or mortuary to handle your arrangements?
_____ Yes   _____ No

4   If you were to die today, which of the following would you prefer?
_____ Embalming_____ Ground burial
_____ Cremation_____ Entombment
_____ Donation to medical science_____ Organ donation

5   If you prefer to be cremated, what would you want done with your ashes?
_____ Burial   _____ Entombment   _____ Scattered   _____ Other, please specify

6   If your funeral plans involve a casket, which of the following ones would you prefer?
_____ Plywood (cloth covered)
_____ Hardwood (oak, cherry, mahogany, maple, etc.)
_____ Steel (sealer or nonsealer type)
_____ Stainless steel
_____ Copper or bronze
_____ Other, please specify _____

7   How important would a funeral service be *for you?*
_____ Very important
_____ Somewhat important
_____ Somewhat unimportant
_____ Very unimportant
_____ No opinion

8   What kind of funeral service would you want *for yourself?*
_____ No service at all
_____ Visitation (calling hours) the day before the funeral service; funeral held at church or funeral home
_____ Graveside service only (no visitation)
_____ Memorial service (after body disposition)
_____ Other, please specify _____

9 How many people would you want to attend your funeral service or memorial service?
_____ 1-10 people
_____ 11-25 people
_____ 26-50 people
_____ Over 51 people
_____ I do not care how many people attend

10 What format would you prefer at your funeral service or memorial service? Select any of the following that you would like.

	Yes	No
Religious music		
Nonreligious music		
Clergy present		
Flower arrangements		
Family member eulogy		
Eulogy by friend(s)		
Open casket		
Religious format		
Other, please specific _____		

11 Using today's prices, how much would you expect to pay for your *total* funeral arrangements, including cemetery expenses (if applicable)?
_____ Less than $4000
_____ Between $4001 and $5000
_____ Between $5001 and $6000
_____ Between $6001 and $7000
_____ Above $7000

To carry this further . . .

Which items had you not thought about before? Were you surprised at the arrangements you selected? Will you share your responses with anyone else? If so, whom?

Personal Assessment

The Emotional Stages of Dying

Directions: Below you will find the psychological phases dying people often experience. Think back to a time in your life when you <u>lost</u> something or someone which was very important to you. Beside each of the phases listed below, describe something you did that would be illustrative of that phase.

Phase	**Illustration**
1 Denial	_____ _____
2 Anger	_____ _____
3 Bargaining	_____ _____
4 Depression	_____ _____
5 Acceptance	_____ _____

Points to Ponder

1. Was there any overlap between or among any of these phases?

2. Did the phases occur, for you, in this order? I not, how did they differ?

3. How long did it take you to go from denial to acceptance?

4. Do you think the time line would be the same if <u>you</u> were suffering from a terminal illness? Why or why not? If not, how might it different?

Personal Assessment

Writing Your Own Eulogy and Epitaph

<u>Directions:</u> Below you will find space provided for you to create the following: your own eulogy and your own epitaph. When you have completed these, answer the questions found at the end of this page.

<u>EULOGY</u>

<u>EPITAPH</u>

Questions:

1. How did you determine what should be included?

2. How do you think your perceptions may change over time?

3. Would your family and friends have chosen to include the same items about you if the had been asked to complete this exercise for you?

    a. What would have been the same?
    b. What would have been different?

Health Action Guide

Making an organ donation is one of the most compassionate, responsible acts a person can do. Only a few simple steps are required:

1. You must complete a uniform donor card. Obtain a card from a physician, a local hospital, or the nearest regional transplant or organ bank.

2. Print or type your name on the card.

3. Indicate which organs you wish to donate. You may also indicate your desire to donate all organs and tissues.

4. Sign your name in the presence of two witnesses, preferably your next of kin.

5. Fill in any additional information (for example, date of birth, city and state in which the card is completed, date the card is signed).

6. Tell others about your decision to donate. Some donor cards have detachable portions to give to your family.

7. Always carry your card with you.

8. If you have any questions, you can call the United Network for Organ Sharing (UNOS) at (800) 24-DONOR.

UNIFORM DONOR CARD

of _____

(print or type name of donor)

In the hope that I may help others, I hereby make this anatomical gift, if medically acceptable, to take effect upon my death. The words and marks below indicate my wishes.

I give: (a) _____ any needed organs or parts
(b) _____ only the following organs or parts

_____

specify the organ(s), tissue(s), or part(s)

for the purpose of transplantation, therapy, medical research or education;

(c) _____ my body for anatomical study if needed.

Limitations or special wishes, if any: _____

Signed by the donor and the following two witnesses in the presence of each other:

_____   _____
Signature of Donor   Date of Birth of
                              Donor

_____   _____
Date Signed   City and State

_____   _____
Witness   Witness

This is a legal document under the Anatomical Gift Act or similar laws.

____Yes, I have discussed my wishes with my family.
For further information consult your physician or

The National Kidney Foundation
30 East 33rd Street
New York, NY 10016

Aerobic Dance

Aerobic Dance

Completion of this chapter should enable the reader to:

- Recognize the benefits associated with regular participation in aerobic dance

- Organize and design a safe and effective aerobic dance program, including the sequencing   of activities

- Select appropriate music, movement patterns, and exercises for an aerobic dance program

HISTORY

Aerobic dance, defined as continuous and rhythmic movement to music, was introduced by Jackie Sorenson in 1969. The combination of vigorous dance steps and exercises performed to popular music in a group setting soon became one of the fastest growing leisure activities in the United States. Today more than 20 million exercise enthusiasts participate in this multimillion dollar industry. Virtually every community offers some form of aerobic dance class. Even home exercises can participate in this physically demanding activity by following popular aerobic dance leaders on television programs and videotapes.

Aerobic dance has evolved from rigidly choreographed dance routines intended for female participants to free-style routines that incorporate random combinations of dance, sport, and exercise movements designed to attract men and women. To further challenge enthusiasts, creative instructors have developed innovative aerobic dance programs that include water aerobics, bench stepping, sports conditioning, and interval and circuit training.

Professional aerobic dance associations are helping meet the demand for qualified instructors. Organizations such as the International Dance Exercise Association (IDEA) and the Aerobic and Fitness Association of America (AFAA) provide their members with services that include subscriptions to exercise journals, access to aerobic conventions and workshops, and opportunities to become certified as an aerobic dance instructor.

BENEFITS OF AEROBIC DANCE

Aerobic dance is an excellent activity for developing overall physical fitness. Balancing health-related components of fitness, aerobic dance can improve a participant's flexibility, strength, cardiovascular fitness, and body composition. The rhythmic movements performed to music also help develop coordi-

nation and balance. In addition, exercising in a group setting provides opportunities for social interactions not afforded by many other aerobic activities.

FACILITY

The ideal aerobic dance setting includes:
1. Good ventilation with a temperature of 60° to 70° F.
2. A floor that will absorb shock while controlling lateral motions of the foot and providing adequate traction. A hardwood sprung floor is an ideal aerobic dance surface.
3. Space for each participant to move comfortably. A good guide is enough space for each participant, with arms outspread, to take two large steps in any direction without touching anyone.
4. Acoustics that will allow the instructor's voice to be heard over the music.
5. For large groups, a raised platform for the instructor.
6. Mirrors to help participants observe and correct their posture and exercise positions.

EQUIPMENT

Equipment needs vary according to the type of facility and the size of the class. All programs require a sound system and a collection of audio tapes or records. A wireless microphone for the instructor may be necessary if teaching in a large space. In addition, mats and certain strength training equipment such as light hand weights and rubber bands are useful during the floor exercise segment of the class.

APPAREL AND SHOES

Participants should wear lightweight, well-ventilated clothing. Cotton fabrics are recommended because they absorb moisture while allowing air to circulate through the material. Many of the fabrics used for aerobic dance apparel are made of cotton blends. Knee-length tights or fitness shorts worn with a leotard or T-shirt provide the greatest comfort and mobility. Wearing cotton socks will help absorb perspiration and reduce the likelihood of blisters. Participants should be encouraged to layer their clothing in cool facilities and remove outer garments (such as a warm up suit) as the body temperature rises with increased levels of activity.

Shoes are perhaps the most important item worn by the aerobic dancer. Since certain aerobic dance steps can generate vertical forces on the feet of up to four times ones body weight, participants need to select a shoe designed to dissipate these impacts. A well-constructed aerobic dance shoe has an adequately cushioned sole, especially under the ball of the foot, to help absorb the shock of forefoot movements characteristic of most aerobic dance steps. Proper support and stability are particularly important for lateral movements. The traction provided by the shoe should match the surface on which activities are being performed. For example, less traction is needed on a carpeted surface while greater traction is necessary on a hardwood floor. Finally, a shoe should be selected for its durability, flexibility, and lightweight characteristics.

FUNDAMENTAL SKILLS AND TECHNIQUES
Components of an aerobic dance class
A well-designed aerobic dance class consists of:
1. Warm-up and prestretch (10 minutes)
2. Aerobic activity (20 to 30 minutes)
3. Cool-down (2 to 5 minutes)
4. Strength work (5 to 10 minutes)
5. Final stretch (5 to 10 minutes)

Warm-up and prestretch
The purpose of the warm-up is to increase blood flow to the muscles, increase the rate of oxygen exchange between blood and muscles, increase the speed and force of muscle contraction, increase muscle elasticity as well as the flexibility of tendons and ligaments, and reduce the risk of cardiac abnormalities. Using a moderate tempo, movements during the warm-up should include rhythmic, full range-of-motion exercises designed to prepare the body for movements used during the aerobic routines. The initial warm-up should concentrate on large movements for the shoulders, arms, and legs. A warm-up routine might consist of shoulder rolls, arm circles, marches, step-touches, and toe and heel raises. After the muscles have been warmed, static stretching exercises should be performed to increase joint range of motion. Stretching positions should be help for at least 10

seconds, paying special attention to muscles of the shoulders chest, hips, low back, thighs, calves and feet.

Aerobic activity
The purpose of the aerobic dance segment is to improve cardiovascular endurance. The physiological benefits of aerobic activity include increased heart and lung efficiency and decreased body fat. Aerobic benefits are achieved by using prolonged and continuous movement of the large muscles. Ideally, the aerobic segment of class will last 20 to 30 minutes performed at an intensity of 60% to 75% to the heart rate reserve.

To determine appropriate exercise intensity, participants need to determine their resting heart rates (RHR) and then calculate their target heart rate zones. Upon waking in the morning, the RHR can be determined by lightly placing the middle and index finger on either the carotid artery (at the neck) or the radial artery (on the thumb side of the wrist) and counting the number of beats occurring in 60 seconds. The target heart rate zone is then calculated by completing Karvonen's formula twice, once to establish the 60% value and again to establish the 75% value. The target heart rate zone lies between these two values. The formulas are:

220 - age - RHR x .6 (training percentage) + RHR 6 (to provide a 10 second heart rate) = 60% value

220 - age- RHR x .75 + RHR 6 = 75% value

For example, the target heart rate zone for a 40-year-old person with a resting heart rate of 72 beats per minute would be 23-26.

[(220 - 40 - 72) x .60 + 72] 6 = 22.8
[(220 - 40 - 72) x .75 + 72] 6 = 25.5

Exercise heart rate is taken for 10 seconds at the end of the aerobic segment (heart rate should be taken more frequently than this for beginners) and should be within the target zone. Participants above the target heart rate can reduce the intensity of exercise by keeping the feet closer to the floor, be decreasing the amount to arm movement or by minimizing the extent of traveling. Conversely, exercise intensity can be increased by lifting the feet higher off the floor, be increasing the amount of arm motion, or by adding directional movement.

The aerobic segment consists of movement patterns choreographed to music. Movement patterns can be extremely varied ranging from calisthenic exercises such as jumping jacks to dance movements such as leaps and lunges. Instructors can enhance their movement repertoire by using steps common to other dance forms including jazz, modern, folk, and ballet, or by borrowing movement patterns used in sports and games (such as basketball dribbling).

Common basic steps used in aerobic dance include jogs, marches, hops, jumps, knee lifts, kicks, twists, step touches, jumping jacks, and lunges. These steps can be varied by changing the rhythm (half time, double time), the direction of movement (forward, backward, sideways, diagonally, or in circles) and by adding arm positions to accompany the leg movements.

Steps can be combined into movement patterns in several ways. Routines can be rigidly choreographed repeating the same movements each time the routine is performed. Choreographed routines help participants become secure with a movement sequence, allowing them to concentrate on the intensity of exercise and correct exercise positions. However, choreographed routines require a great deal of preparation by the instructor and can take extra class time to teach. Many instructors prefer to use a freestyle approach to combine movement patterns with music. Rather than using routines, instructors using the freestyle technique select movements in a random fashion, building combinations of step patterns as the music progresses. When skillfully led, participants enjoy the movement variety associated with the freestyle method. If, however, the step patterns are too complex for the group, participants may be unable to maintain appropriate exercise intensity as they struggle with unexpected and unfamiliar movements.

Foot pattern: 8 knee lifts in place.

Foot pattern with arms: 4 knee lifts in place while pressing the arms overhead, 4 knee lifts in place while pressing the arms down to the feet.

Foot pattern with arms and traveling: 4 knee lifts moving forward while pressing the arms overhead, 4 knee lifts moving backwards while pressing the arms down to the feet.

The first aerobic dance routine following the warm-up should be performed at a moderate pace to give the cardiovascular system ample time to adjust to the increasing demands of exercise. As the class progresses through the aerobic segment, the intensity and music tempo should be increased. Participants should be instructed to adjust the intensity of their movements to correspond with their level of cardiovascular fitness.

Cool-down

The purpose of the cool-down is to lower the heart rate gradually toward normal, prevent excessive pooling of blood in the lower extremities, and promote removal of metabolic waste products from the muscles. Slow but continued rhythmic contraction of the leg muscles is important to help return the blood from the lower extremities to the heart. A cool-down of 2 to 5 minutes can consist of walking around the room while gently swinging the arms or a slow aerobic dance routine.

It is wise to take a recovery heart rate at the end of the cool-down. A decrease in recovery heart rate over time is a measure of improved cardiovascular fitness. For comparative purposes, the recovery heart rate must be taken the same number of minutes following the end of the aerobic segment. A record sheet for recording exercise and recovery heart rates is useful for observing the progress of participants.

Strength exercises

Muscular strength is important for preventing injuries by helping the participant maintain proper alignment and body mechanics. It is therefore important to strengthen the muscles that help maintain good posture and aid in the proper execution of aerobic dance routines and floor exercises. Weak upper back muscles (upper trapezius and rhomboids) contribute to rounded shoulders while weak abdominals can lead to a swayback posture. Aggravated by vigorous movements on the feet, these anatomical deviations can result in nick, shoulder, and low back pain. Therefore it is prudent to strengthen the upper back muscles and abdominals in each class session. Rowing exercises and prone shoulder raises can be used to strengthen the upper back while curl-ups, diagonal curls, reverse curls, and pelvic tilts will help strengthen the abdominals.

It is also important to strengthen muscles of the shins (tibialis anterior). The most common injury reported by aerobic dancers is shin splints. While there are many causes for shin pain, a typical problem results from a muscles imbalance between the strong calf muscles (gastrocnemius) that contract vigorously for a prolonged period of time during the aerobic dance segment and the weak shin muscles which are used less frequently during class. Various forms of toe tapping, walking on the heels, and ankle flexion with light weights or rubber bands can help to strengthen tibialis anterior muscles.

If time allows, instructors can include strength exercises for other parts of the body. These include side leg lifts for the hip abductors and adductors, leg curls and lifts for the hamstrings and gluteals, knee extensions for the quadriceps, arm curls for the biceps, elbow extensions for the triceps, lateral pull downs for latissimus dorsi, and lateral raises for the deltoids. Muscular strength is achieved by overloading the muscle with adequate resistance so that the student can complete 12 to 15 repetitions of an exercise. Surgical tubing, elastic bands, or light hand and ankle weights can provide appropriate resistance. In addition, holding a contraction for 5 seconds at different points in the movement pattern can provide added resistance to the muscles. To continue strength gains, the resistance for each exercise should be increased when participants can comfortably complete three sets of 12 to 15 repetitions.

To encourage controlled movements during the strength exercises, music tempos should be moderately paced and participants should be instructed to adjust the tempo (half time or double time) and on the number of repetitions required to meet their personal levels of strength. To encourage proper exercise technique, the instructor should move around the room providing appropriate exercise cues while observing and critiquing performance.

Final stretch

The purpose of the final stretch is to improve overall flexibility, which helps maintain good posture and proper body mechanics throughout the day. Stretching after a vigorous exercise session is often easier than stretching before since the joints are well lubricated and the temperature of the muscles is increased following the aerobic workout. It is best to perform these stretches on the floor allowing participants an opportunity to relax and concentrate on each stretch. The final stretch is most effective when performed to slow background music that does not have a strong beat. Flexibility exercises, held for 10 to 30 seconds, should include stretches for muscles of the arms, shoulders, chest, back, hips, thighs, and calves.

Low, moderate, and high impacts

In the past, most aerobic dance routines consisted of high impact movements including variations of jogs, hops, and jumps. High impact aerobics (HIA), characterized by movements that require both feet to leave the floor frequently, can produce vertical forces of up to four times the weight of the body. Researchers reporting on injuries suffered by aerobic dancers found a fairly high incidence of pain to the shins, feet, knees, and lower back. Although the injuries were seldom serious enough to require medical attention, concern that high impact movements were in part responsible for these aches and pains led to the development of a new form of aerobic dance

called Low Impact Aerobics (LIA). LIA, characterized by movements that use a wide base of support while keeping one foot one the floor at all times, have not been without their share of unique problems and injuries.

In an attempt to stay close to the floor during LIA, the use of a wide base of support and the extreme lowering and raising of the center of gravity produces a great deal of prolonged and often extreme knee flexion. This can result in a number of knee injuries for individuals already suffering from structural knee problems. In addition, the larger arm movements used to maintain exercise intensity during LIA have resulted in shoulder injuries among participants using uncontrolled arm flinging motions.

Generally, LIA is not recommended for anyone who complains of knee discomfort during prolonged knee flexion or for well-conditioned individuals who are unable to achieve appropriate intensity levels using low impact movements. On the other hand, HIA are generally not recommended for individuals who are conditioned, especially if they are obese, for women in the latter stages of pregnancy, for anyone who is susceptible to injuries related to impact shock such as shin splints, or for individuals who are uncomfortable with high impact steps, such as people suffering from incontinence. To accommodate individual differences in each class, many programs use a combination of high and low impact steps throughout the aerobic routines. This results in a decrease in the number of high impact steps being performed.

Aerobic dance instructors are also beginning to use a new technique which combines the best elements of HIA and LIA. It is called moderate impact aerobics (MIA). MIA movements require that one foot remain on the floor most of the time as in LIA, although the base of support is narrower and the center of gravity is lifted up and down as in HIA. MIA steps are therefore characterized by a springlike motion. All MIA movements should begin by lifting the body upward, rising onto the balls of the feet. Each step should be completed by gently pressing the heels against the floor. The advantages of MIA include less prolonged and extreme knee flexion often associated with LIA and smaller vertical impacts found in many HIA movements.

Aerobic training modes

Traditionally, the aerobic segment of an aerobic dance class consisted of continuous exercise. Today, interval and circuit training have become common.

Aerobic interval training involves high intensity work bouts (near maximal heart rate) followed by active rest or recovery periods of an equal length of time. Exercise and rest intervals vary from 3 to 5 minutes in length and are repeated four to six times during the aerobic segment of class. Since interval training requires high intensity exercise during the work bouts, high impact movements such as jumps and runs are commonly choreographed to fast-paced music. During the active rest, moderately paced movements such as walks and step touches are performed. Some programs incorporate light weights or rubber bands to develop upper body strength during the active rest. Due to the fast-paced, high-intensity nature of interval training, this activity is recommended only for the more advanced aerobic dancer. Interval training is associated with greater physical pain than experienced in continuous forms of training because more metabolic waste products are produced and accumulated in the muscles during the near maximal efforts of the activity.

Circuit training is another popular technique used in aerobic dance programs. A circuit consists of a specified number of exercise stations used to promote all-around physical fitness. The emphasis is on development of muscular strength and endurance, cardiovascular endurance, flexibility, and sometimes coordination and balance. Most circuits have between 10 to 20 stations. Each area is posted with a sign indicating the task to be completed. Participants are instructed to remain at a station for a given number of seconds, moving to the next station on command. The circuit moves in a clockwise or counter-clockwise direction and can be repeated two to three times. Time spent at each station can vary from 30 to 60 seconds. A typical aerobic dance circuit includes strength exercises with light wights or rubber bands, aerobic exercise such as knee lifts, jumping jacks, and lunges, and agility and coordination stations such as running drills and rope jumping. Instructors should encourage participants to work as hard as possible at each station.

TEACHING CONSIDERATIONS
Patterns of class organization
An aerobic dance class should be arranged so that everyone can hear the instructor's verbal cues and see the demonstrations. Above all, it is important that the instructor be able to observe all class participants. In a typical aerobic dance class, the instructor stands at the front of the room with the participants facing forward. The disadvantage of this system is that the advanced participants usually stand at the front of the room while the less skilled stay at the back. The instructor cannot clearly observe those who are in greatest need of feedback. To resolve this problem, the instructor can periodically move from the front of

the room to the back of the sides, asking participants to turn and face the instructor. A system of rotation is another effective way of observing class participants. At the end of each song the teacher instructs the participants to rotate. The front line moves to the back of the room while every other line moves forward one row. Other patterns of class organization include circle formations (where the instructor stands at the center) and movement patterns that travel from one end of the floor to the other.

Cuing
Cuing is a very important part of teaching aerobic dance. Participants depend on the instructor's verbal and nonverbal cues for every step they take. Each verbal cue should be brief and called on the preceding measure, giving ample time to move smoothly from one step to the next. Instructors can use a combination of types of cuing including footwork cuing (indicates whether to move the right or left foot), directional cuing (refers to the direction of movement such as forward, backward, left of right), rhythmic cuing (indicates the correct rhythm of the routine such as slow or quick), numerical cuing (refers to counting the rhythm such as "one, tow, three and four"), and step cuing (indicates the name of the step such as "step touch"). Initially, participants will be most dependent on footwork, directional, na numerical cuing. Once they become somewhat skilled and learn the names of each step or movement pattern, the participants will rely more on step cues and pay most attention to nonverbal cues such as hand signals indicating direction.

When leading aerobic dance routines, the instructor should face the class using mirroring techniques (the instructor moves to the left when the class moves to the right). To avoid potential collisions between students, instructors should begin lateral movements to the same side each time. Most instructors prefer moving first to the right followed by movements to the left.

Music
Music provides the timing and style for exercise movements. In addition, it adds fun, variety, and excitement to an aerobic dance class. The tempo, or rate of speed, at which music is played determines the progression and intensity of exercise. Aerobic dance instructors determine the tempo of the music by counting the beats per minute (bpm). Over the years, the following guidelines have been adopted by instructors for selecting appropriate music tempo for aerobic dance:

Warm-up, prestretch and cool-down: 100 to 120

bpm
Floor exercise: 110 to 130 bpm
Aerobic activity: 130 to 144 bpm (LIA)
144 to 160 bpm (HIA)
Final stretch: under 100 bpm

Instructors must be cautious when using fast music tempos (more than 160 bpm). To avoid uncontrolled movements, participants should be encouraged to use the arms through a small range of motion and take short steps. Since beginners are not proficient nought to perform fast movements under control, they should not be expected to dance to fast-paced music. When using music with fast tempos, instructors should be aware that participants with long arms and legs need more time than participants with short limbs to cover the same spatial area. For example, people with short arms can raise them above their heads more quickly than people with long arms. Tall participants should therefore be encouraged to bend their arms in order to keep in time with fast music. The most efficient way to use music in class is to record a 40 to 60 minute audiotape which includes music for the warm-up, prestretch, the aerobic segment, the cool-down, the floor exercises, and the final stretch. However, instructors reproducing and playing music in an aerobic dance class should be familiar with the copyright laws. The Copyright Act of 1976 states that a person wishing to play copyrighted music for a "public performance" must obtain permission from the copyright owner. Using music during an aerobic dance class consists of a public performance. Since it would be time consuming to obtain permission form the copyright owner of each piece of music used in a class, instructors can save valuable time by joining performing rights societies including ASCAP and BMI. These societies have been assigned the nondramatic rights of copyright owners and grant their members permission to play the music of numerous artists. Under the "fair use" doctrine, instructors teaching in the public schools or at institutions of higher education may be exempt from having to obtain copyright permission. It is wise, however, for instructors to consult with an attorney to determine if their use of music qualifies as "fair use."

Developing music tapes can be one of the most time consuming tasks for the aerobic dance instructor. To save valuable time and to stay current with popular music selections, instructors can subscribe to a number of music services that provide complete aerobic dance tapes classes.

SAFETY CONCERNS
To ensure the safety of class participants, instructors should comply with the following guidelines:

1. Screen participants for common anatomical problems such as kyphosis, lordosis, and excess pronation of the feet. Also evaluate them for tight and weak muscles. Early detection and correction of such problems can reduce the risk or aerobic dance injuries.

2. Encourage appropriate body alignment throughout the class period. Proper posture includes: head up, shoulders back, chest up, buttocks tucked under the hips, and knees relaxed.

3. Avoid or minimize the use of the following potentially harmful exercise positions: (1) sustained and unsupported forward flexion in a standing position, (2) unsupported forward flexion in a standing position with rotation, (3) trunk rotation against a fixed axis, (4) neck hyperextension, (5) fast head circles, (6) the yoga plough, (7) deep knee bends, (8) hurdler stretch, (9) hyperextension of the elbows and knees, (10) straight leg sit-ups, (11) double leg raises, and (12) side leg lifts supported on the knees and hands or elbows.

4. Avoid ballistic stretching. Static stretching is effective and tends to be safer than bobbing or bouncing techniques.

5. Insist that participants wear shoes during the aerobic segment of class.

6. Be aware of the placement of class members to avoid collisions during rapid movements across the floor.

7. Encourage participants to control the placement of their arms, avoiding any flinging motions. Shoulder injuries are becoming increasingly common in aerobic dance.

8. Avoid having the participants keep the arms at or above shoulder level for a prolonged period of time. This increases blood pressure, places stress on the tendons and muscles of the shoulder, and increases heart rate in a manner not related to increased cardiovascular conditioning.

9. Avoid prolonged and excessive deep knee flexion. Make sure the knees of participants remain over the first and second toes.

10. Be cautious of lateral movements on carpeted surfaces. The added friction associated with carpet can result in ankle inversion sprains.

11. Avoid dancing on concrete surfaces.

12. Reduce the risk of common musculoskeletal injuries during aerobic activity by progressing slowly and by not exceeding intensity levels of 75% heart rate reserve, exercise durations of 30 minutes and exercise frequencies of 4 days per week on alternate days.

13. Avoid too many consecutive movements on one foot such as dozens of hops.
14. Avoid rapid changes of direction.
15. Do not require participants to stay on the balls of the feet for extended periods of time. The lowering of the heels to the floor provides additional shock absorption for the feet.
16. Face the class as often as possible to effectively observe everyone's performance.
17. Do not allow the participants to hold their breath while performing strength exercises. Encourage them to exhale on exertion.
18. Control the movement of light hand and ankle weights at all times.
19. Be aware of exercise restrictions and modifications for special populations. for example, people with high blood pressure should not perform isometric contractions and should avoid keeping the arms above shoulder level for extended periods of time.

Jogging

Jogging

Completion of this chapter should enable the reader to:

- Know the guidelines for starting a jogging program

- Select and care for proper jogging equipment, particularly shoes

- Demonstrate correct running form

- Construct a proper training schedule according to one's goals

- Prevent and treat jogging injuries

- Teach fundamental jogging principles and skills

HISTORY

For many years jogging has been a major activity in the YMCA, the Boston Young Men's Christian Union, Boys Clubs, and many college physical education programs. However, the benefits of jogging were never completely realized until a scientific study was conducted by Dr. Kenneth H. Cooper, Major, USAF Medical Corps, in the early 1960s. His research made a significant contribution by correlating oxygen consumption and pulse rate with various types of exercise and the vigor and duration of each. He described a sort of pharmacopoeia of exercise that describes the training effect of each of several types of exercise and gives the value of each in building cardiorespiratory efficiency. He differentiated between "aerobic" and "anaerobic" exercise, based on the oxygen consumption each requires, and substantiated the effectiveness of aerobic types, such as jogging.

Jogging is popular as an exercise medium for an increasingly fitness-conscious American public. Increasing numbers of participants seem to be joining in this activity for a variety of reasons.

Most beginning runners view jogging as a means to health and fitness, including prevention of hear disease and weight loss. Others use exercise to relieve tension and frustration built during daily activities. "It feels good to run," say most. The run itself may not always be pleasant, but the effects usually are. The physical and mental glow after running is real and important to the runner.

GETTING STARTED

Jogging is usually defined as running slowly at a comfortable pace of about 9 to 12 minutes pr mile. Running is an individual activity, so some will be able to run farther and faster than others with seemingly the same effort. A good guideline for the beginning runner is to utilize the talk test: run just fast enough so that you are still able to carry on a conversation.

Running need not be a form of self-torture. To have a successful running experience, a sensible program should be initiated. The following guidelines ar applicable to almost everyone:

1. Consult your physician before initiating any type of exercise program. (This guideline increases in importance with an increase in age. After the age of 35 it is recommended that a novice jogger have an exercise stress test before embarking on a jogging program.)

2. Start slowly. If you overdo, your first day will probably be your last.

3. Be consistent. Set up a practical routine, and stick with it for at least 6 to 8 weeks.

4. Listen to your body. It will reveal your limits. Try not to become overly competitive and exceed those limits. If you become sore, back off for a day or two.

5. Take walking breaks frequently during the first few runs. Warm up and cool down by walking.

6. Get a pair of comfortable, properly fitting shoes (see next section). Clothing will be dictated by common sense and experience.

7. Do not always gear your schedule to how far you can run. Try using time as a guideline. Start with as little as 5 minutes of walking and easy running. Increase the time slowly, trying not to strain. By gearing your program to time, you allow the body to work to its own limits. Disappointment will not be part of your program when you fail to cover a set number of miles or kilometers.

Running can be enjoyable if it is done with a positive frame of mind.

SHOE SELECTION

Individual needs and requirements vary greatly from runner to runner, so that one brand of shoes cannot be recommended for everyone. Along with comfort and protection, various skill levels and competitive attitudes as well as differing body types and individual mechanical weaknesses must be considered.

The ideal shoe is designed to provide protection while leaving running motion unencumbered, so keep in mind that proper selection of a training shoe is essential for avoiding injuries while ensuring maximum performance and comfort.

The best place to start is with a good shoe specialist who offers a wide variety of brands and models. Try on several of the available choices and lace them up as if going for a run. Check the shoes for minor defects (which are common in this age of mass production), and then take them out for a short run. Take your time in making a selection.

Set your own requirements, keeping these questions in mind: Are you heavy on your feet, or do you run lightly with good form? What type of terrain will you run on (trails, roads, or grass)? As you strictly a fun runner, or training for a specific distance or time? Find the model shoe that fits your needs, then buy the pair that fits your feet best.

The sole should be durable yet soft enough to aid the body in absorbing the shock of each foot strike. You are seeking traction, flexibility, and good cushioning. The heel counter should be firm. Check the material used in the heel wedge and midsole. Is it soft and flexible yet not mushy? It too absorbs shock, but it should be firm enough to protect the foot from sharp objects and rocks. Check an older pair of shoes (if available) to see whether they have retained their softness.

The width of the heel is also important. Is the heel wide enough to provide good stability yet not change your normal running gait?

Check the ankle and Achilles tendon padding as well as the heel cup for the soft firm support that will help lock the heel in. They should be well-molded to prevent unnecessary side-to-side roll.

The side panel reinforcing should bring the arch support into proper position and fit snugly, yet not bind to the pint of causing blisters, and be made of durable material.

The forefoot or toe area should be high and well rounded to provide enough room for the toes to move around. You should be able to pinch the front end of the shoe and there should be enough space to fit the width of a finger between the front of the longest toe and the front of the shoe. It is not uncommon to require a running shoe to be a half size larger than street shoes.

The insole should provide some cushioning and also prevent the foot from slipping around when it perspires. If the insole is unsatisfactory it can be taken out and replaced with a popular commercial brand. The tongue should be well padded.

A soft yet firm arch support that fits well the first time is important. However, as with the insole, it can be replaced with a commercial product.

Width sizing has become popular with the expansion of the running shoe market in the past few years. Price is also a factor, but one should remember that expense does not ensure good fit or quality.

A good pari of shoes are a runner's most critical investment (outside of time), yet they are not a cure-all. The anatomy of your foot may call for something not offered by today's mass-produced shoes. If you cannot find a pair of shoes that fit comfortably, you may need to seek professional help from a qualified podiatrist or orthopedist.

Reserve your running shoes for running. Using them for casual wear causes different wear patterns, which will affect the life of the shoe.

Beginners should purchase a pair of training shoes. They offer more cushioning than a racing shoe. Always remember that it is important to wear high quality socks when jogging. Socks capable of "wicking" moisture away from the feet are a must.

RUNNING FORM

Many people believe long-distance running requires little or no skill. Simple observation of different runners shows that some seem to float along almost effortlessly, whereas others pound along, struggling with each step and exhibiting contorted expressions. The obvious difference is cardiovascular conditioning, but technique and efficiency of movement are also involved to a great extent and require skill and practice.

Distance running is a natural activity, so a runner should do what comes naturally as long as it is mechanically sound. The slower a runner travels, the easier it is to get away with poor form. Problems arise when the tempo is increased and mechanical inefficiencies become compounded by the increase in speed.

The keys to improving running technique are simple.

Foot placement

The slower you go, the flatter the landing. Try to land lightly and gently; do not pound. As you run faster you move higher on the foot, toward the toes. All runners land first on the outside edge of the foot, then roll inward. This absorbs shock. The precise point of contact varies with speed.

Stride

This is also a function of speed. The short stride is more economical and also slower. As the pace increases, so does the length of stride. Keep in mind that you should lead with the knee first. The foot should follow and extend to meet the ground. Do not overstride; keep your feet under you. The point of foot contact should be directly under the knee, with the knee slightly flexed.

Body carriage

Run tall and with a straight back. The head should remain level. Do not look at the sky or at your feet but out in front of you. This approach assures you of an erect, balanced running stance. The head should be in line with the trunk and the trunk in line with the legs.

The hips should be directly over the legs. Try not to "sit" or lean forward. A runner tends to "sit" when fatigue sets in, and this leads to shorter, mechanically inefficient stride.

The arms should play an active role in running. They are there for balance and driving and should not be ignored. Arms help the legs go faster as long as they remain rhythmic. Hold the hands loosely cupped and relaxed, palms turned inward. Bend the elbow and bring the arms parallel to each other, slightly inward but not across the midline of the chest.

The best time to practice technique is a short afternoon run. Stride six times over 50 to 60 yards (45 to 50 m) on a smooth, grassy surface, concentrating on any problem. Have someone watch you run several times before making suggestions. All runners

have innocent quirks in running styles that are their trademarks. If they do not affect mechanical efficiency they should be left alone.

TRAINING

A phenomenon that has occurred along with the large increase in the number of joggers in the country is the availability of races in which to participate. Almost every weekend a run is sponsored by some organization. Some are for serious runners, some for fun, some for raising money for charitable causes, some for recognizing local traditions and many are a combination of reasons. While it is possible to be a jogger and never enter a race, these events are motivational much like the recital that piano teachers use to motivate students to continue practicing. These races also can be fun social events. If you desire to enter a race, it shouldn't be done without advance preparation and training for the event's demands.

The word "training" like the word "jogging," can be ambiguous. The difference is sometimes artificial. Training indicates effort toward completing a specific distance or race; jogging is usually done on a more casual basis for fitness or health reasons.

There are several methods of starting training. Most are fairly simple. There are guiding principles, terminology, and systems of training for the beginning racer.

Fundamental principles of training

Stress. The body must adapt if it is to improve its general condition. Training stimulates the type of stress the body will encounter during a race. A fine line separates training from stress and strain during the run.

Overload. Overload means taking on a little more work than is comfortable. It should be done for brief periods at first, perhaps every other day. Stretch your limits gradually. If done too quickly it can result in injury or at least soreness.

Specificity of training. Training must resemble the type of race you are preparing for in both speed and distance.

Consistency. Body systems get into shape by regular training. Do not do a super workout one day and then be unable to walk the next. Be consistent.

Recovery. The body must be given adequate time to rejuvenate itself. Continuous hard training will bring you down eventually. Rest is just as important as stress.

Pacing. Take a long view toward running. Both in races and training, focus on gradual improvement. At first improvement comes quickly as mileage piles up. *Remember:* More does not always mean better.

Training schedules

Individualize your training schedule. Find a system that fits your life style and makes your running a part of you for the rest of your life. Keep yourself happy and eager. Undertrain rather than overtrain.

A program for a jogger who has been training for several months and is now interested in preparing for a 6- to 20-mile (9.7 to 32.2 km) run might look like this:

Sunday: Long easy run of 15 miles (24 km) or 1½ hours on relatively flat terrain.

Monday: MORNING--Easy 40-minute run. EVENING--Brisk 45-minute run followed by 8 to 10 strides on grass. Stretch and cool down. Do abdominal exercises.

Tuesday: EVENING--Medium to hard 1-hour run on fairly hilly terrain. Start easy, finishing with a long, hard sustained pace. Be sure to cool down.

Wednesday: MORNING--Easy 3 to 5 miles (4.8 to 8.0 km). EVENING--Forty-minute run according to the way you feel.

Thursday: MORNING--Forty-minute run. EVENING--Fartlek workout over hills, changing the pace often; 1 hour total time.

Friday: EVENING--Brisk 45-minute run.

Saturday: Try to find a race over 3 miles (4.8 km). Set predetermined goal. Experiment. Easy afternoon run or 4 to 5 minutes (6.4 to 8.0 km).

This sample workout is equal to about 70 miles a week, adequate even for a marathon of less than 3 hours. Using time as the basis for your program will allow you to individualize your training and respond to the way your body feels. If you feel good, cover more miles. If you need more time to recuperate, you will achieve fewer total miles. Get to know your own fatigue symptoms, because continuous overstress will result in a reverse training effect.

Types of training systems

LSD, or long slow distance. In this method of training a runner concentrates on running longer and farther, with little attention to speed. At least 95% of time you should be able to converse and feel comfortable while on a training run. Keep pulse rate and respiration well within your limits. Do all things in moderation.

Fartlek. "Fartlek" is a Swedish word meaning speed play. The basic principle is to change the pace endlessly by charging hills, stretching out going downhill, accelerating to a sprint, striding, jogging, and walking. Try to let changes in pace occur natu-

rally, such as when forced to stop at an intersection or pausing to admire the mountain scenery. Do it off the track on uneven and changing terrain. Fartlek is not a long distance run in the country with a 50-yard burst thrown in every mile!

Interval training. This method of training has five basic components: (1) distance of each fast run, (2) interval or recovery between the fast runs, (3) number of repetitions to be run, (4) duration of each run, and (5) activity done between each run (walking, jogging, or complete rest). When trying to build endurance, run longer training runs with shorter rest periods or jog for recovery. To sharpen and become faster, run as fast or faster than race pace, with almost complete rest for recovery. Interval training can bring quick results, but unless it is used in conjunction with a good endurance base, the results can be quickly wiped out by illness or injury.

Hard-easy-hard. This is more a philosophy toward running and training. The body must be given the opportunity to recuperate and rest after being placed under stress. There should be days when the activity is varied or when little or no training is done. Supplemental activities such as swimming, cycling, or weight training may be incorporated.

Hill running. Most runners believe that hills should be an integral of the training routine. Hill work is actually speed work in disguise, in that the hear rate is elevated and resistance work is done. Few runners enjoy hills, and may fear them when they are part of a race. However, by placing them on your training schedule you may gain not only strength but confidence. Because of the force producing braking action of the straining leg, pain in the lower back, hip or knee can result from downhill running. Downhill running should be done like sprinting or fast striding. Keep yourself balanced with the hips into the running action. Do not "sit"! Land on the ball of the foot. Keep the arms in rhythm.

INJURIES

Most running experts suggest that a stretching routine before and, perhaps more importantly, after jogging can reduce injuries. If you start your jog easily the initial stretching may not be as important, but a warm down routine is important. This is true not only for limbering up, but also to keep muscles constricting and pumping blood back to the heart. Even with adequate stretching, warming up and cooling down, injuries will occur to most runners. Most runners try to ease through their injuries by taking time off or running easier for a while.

Minor irritations are a way of life for most runners. As one disappears another arises, but they are usually not serious enough to make the runner five up the sport.

There are those who, through their own ignorance, are unwilling to heed the signs of trouble indicated by those minor irritations, Their excuse for avoiding medical attention is that the physician usually tells them to stop running for a while. However, the number of injuries to the lower limbs is on the rise and cannot be dismissed. Injuries present real problems, and the runner should seek a sensible solution based on fact rather than on hit-and-miss guesswork.

Problems with muscles or tendons are usually associated with fatigue or an aching pain. Burning or shooting pain may indicate nerve irritation. A consistent burning pain is probably caused by inflammation. Other injuries include blister, bone spurs, Morton's toe, muscle strain and tears, plantar fascia inflammation, and sciatic nerve problems.

It is necessary to isolate the location of an injury and determine the type of pain and its depth and point of maximum tenderness. Also important to not are: How did the pain start? Was it from new shoes or running a long way on roads or sharp downhills? Did you have a proper warm-up? Did you make unusual demands on the body?

Most injuries can be attributed to simple overuse or overstress. During training the foot can strike the ground 5000 times in 1 hour--a tremendous amount of stress for the leg to sustain.

Biomechanical deformities, structural susceptibilities, and postural malformations that may not be evident in everyday walking can show themselves as injury when the runner has been overstressed. Add to this poor running shoes, improper training methods, and poor running surfaces, and the runner is at risk of injuries.

The overuse syndrome usually is evidence by shin splints, Achilles tendinitis, chondromalacia of the knee, stress fractures, or bursitis, This syndrome can be treated by proper training, which includes a well-organized stretching program with a hard-easy approach to training. A well-planned conditioning period, proper shoes, and varied running surfaces all contribute to lessening the problems of overuse.

The knee is a common area of injury because it is a vulnerable hinge joint that takes most of the punishment inflicted by hard surfaces. The bottom edge of the knee-cap is often irritated, a condition medically termed chondromalacia. This condition indicates joint instability and usually affects the hyaline cartilage on the joint side of the kneecap. It can be a result of excessive rotation of the knee at foot strike. The best way to prevent this injury is by stabilizing the foot with heel or arch supports and by strengthening and quadriceps or thigh muscles through weight training.

The Achilles tendon connects the heel bone and the calf muscles. It is synonymous with vulnerability. Running tends to shorten this tendon and cause inflexibility and tightness. The best way know to prevent this is to stretch before and after a run. The inclined wall push-up is a good exercise to specifically work on the Achilles tendon. One method of reducing the stress placed on the affected tendon is to place a ¼-inch lift in the running shoes.

The term "shin splints" is a catchall for lower leg problems. Shin splints is a symptom, not a condition. It is primarily a swelling along the lower front of the legs and is usually a muscular problem. It results from (1) improper shoes, (2) insufficient shock absorption, (3) excessive training on hard surfaces, concrete, and all-weather tracks, (4) lack of flexibility, or (5) poor running form. Runners who suffer the least from shin splints are those who keep their feet and knees in line with their hips. Other potential causes include an imbalance between an overly strong calf muscle and weak anterior or front muscles. Soreness in the shins can be a common complaint of the beginning runner. The legs are not used to this type of muscular activity and should be give time to adjust.

Cryotherapy, or ice treatment, has been used for all of these problems with excellent results for many hears. The primary effect of cold--vasoconstriction (decrease in size of blood vessels)--takes place in the first few minutes of application. This is strictly a reflex action with an accompanying decrease in the capillary blood pressure and an increase in the arterial blood pressure. Ice is used for the first 24 to 48 house in acute muscular skeletal injuries. The secondary effect is vasodilation, an increase in the rate of blood flow to the injured area. A massive hyperemia is produced because of the increase in blood flow, with the peripheral blood vessels being constricted and the deeper blood vessels being dilated. (In contrast, with heat application there is dilation, with stagnation of blood in the area.) Cold also produces an anesthetic effect--a decrease in the spasticity of the muscles and an increase in the blood flow rate, rather an a gross increase in the circulation.

There are several methods of cold application. Crushed or shaved ice works best and produces a colder solution. A slush solution with a cold towel also works well. Massage with a frozen cup of ice is best for the knee and similar joint ares. The surface temperature when using ice treatments should be no higher than 55° F (31° C).

Remember: When ice therapy is first induced, the shock of the cold will cause an aching sensation. The skin will become numb in about 3 minutes and then redden. Therapy should be terminated at this point and repeated later.

These are some of the most common types of injuries and preventive measures as well as simple methods of treatment. If a problem persists, seek advice of a qualified podiatrist or orthopedic surgeon.

MISCELLANEOUS SUGGESTIONS

1. Do everything is moderation.
2. Start out by improving your cardiovascular efficiency. Work up gradually to at least a 30-minute jog three times per week.
3. Use the hard-easy=hard approach, allowing your body time to recuperate. Undertrain rather than overtrain.
4. Learn to calculate and measure your target heart rate (THR) and train at a pace to elicit this heart rate. THR is really a range and the object is to keep your heart rate in this range while jogging. THR can be calculated by subtracting your age from the value of 220. The resulting value is an estimate of your maximum heart rate. Multiply this value by .70 and by .85 to obtain the tow end points of the THR range, which is appropriate for young adults in good health. These percentages would be lower for older adults. For example, the estimated maximum heart rate for a 20-year-old is 200 (220 - 20). Multiplying this value by .70 and .85 results in a range THR of 140 to 170. Jogging at a pace to elicit a heart tare between these two values will produce a training effect over time.
5. Keep an accurate record of your mileage. Find out how much stress your body can handle comfortably. Take your pulse before getting out of bed and about 1 or 2 hours after your evening workout. Place the numbers on a graph. This will allow you to see the progress being made toward cardiovascular efficiency.
6. The recovery phase is also important to the jogger. It will take between 3 and 5 hours for the heart rate to return to preexercise levels. By taking your pulse 1 to 2 hours after evening workouts, you will begin to see what type of adaptations your body is making to running stress.
7. Eat sensibly. With an increase in calorie expenditure expect an increase in appetite. Eat a well-balanced diet. Be wary of fad diets.
8. Take fluids early if you are planning on running more than 1 hour, especially in warm weather. Water seems to work best for everyone. Be prepared and do not over-extend yourself, whatever the goal!
9. Vary the training program.
10. Run with someone. Making your jogging sessions enjoyable through social interaction will help ensure that you stick with them.

TEACHING CONSIDERATIONS

1. Instructional programs for groups must deal with two major factors:
   a. For clear training effects to be achieved students must exercise at least 3 days a week a minimum of 30 minutes for at least 5 to 6 weeks.
   b. Individuals will start at different levels of ability and will have different target goals.
2. If programs do not meet for the length of time required, additional work outside of the instructional period should be included.
3. Some type of preassessment should be used to determine beginning levels of students. Several tests using time (a 12-minute run-walk) or heart rate for a given work load are available. Programs should then be designed on this basis.
4. Heart rate is the best simple indictor of work-load. Teach students how to calculate their target heart rates as described earlier. Before set training programs are established, teach pacing for this rate. Begin increasing students' distance according to heart rate on a weekly basis. Have them keep records of progress. Give each student a target distance and time for the end of the program if possible.
5. Use the jogging experience to teach about the effects of exercise on the body and life-style of the student. Students are interested in this information. Jogging units can be combined with physical fitness experiences.
6. Provide a lot of encouragement, slow down overeager beginners, and be alert to adverse physical reactions. Become part of the class if possible.
7. Encourage students to be sensitive to their body to determine limits.

Archery

Archery

Completion of this chapter should enable the reader to:

- Recognize and select appropriate archery equipment

- Understand rules and scoring procedures

- Describe correct techniques for stringing the bow, drawing, anchoring, aiming, and shooting

- Identify and use proper safety procedures

- Instruct a group of students in the fundamentals of archery

- Recognize and use archery terms correctly

HISTORY

The bow and arrow is one of the oldest mechanical weapons and remains the weapon of many aboriginal races and tribes in certain parts of the world. The bow and arrow was first used by primitive peoples for hunting. It was the chief weapon of the American Indians, both for hunting and for war. It was used as a weapon of war by the Egyptians in overthrowing persia and in many other successful wars.

With the discovery of powder and the use of firearms in comparatively recent times, the bow and arrow has been retired to the realm of sport. In this capacity it has sporadically interested groups in various parts of the civilized world, particularly in England and the United States, but archery has not flourished to the same extent as many other sports.

The earliest contest in archer, "The Ancient Scorton Arrow," was held in England in 1673, created by the Ancient Scorton Arrow Society. This tournament is still in existence.

In the United States the first archery club, the United Bowmen of Philadelphia, was organized in 1828. The first tournament was held in Chicago in 1879, and tournaments sponsored by this club are still being held.

The formation of the Federation Internationale de Tir a L'Arc (FITA) in 1931 gave a great boost to target archery.

Archery, which had been a demonstration sport in the 1900 and 1904 Olympics, was give full status in 1908 but then dropped after the 1920 Games. Through the efforts of the FITA, archery was reinstated as a gold medal sport in the 1972 Olympic Games. Since this time the United States has done extremely well in this competition, with the men

winning the gold medal in every Olympics since 1972 except in 1980, when the United States boycotted the Moscow Games (gold won by Tomi Poikolainen). John Williams started the string by winning gold in 1972, Darrel Pace won in 1976 and in 1984, and Jay Barrs placed first in 1988. The United States women archers dominated the 1972 (gold to Doreen Wilbur) and 1976 (gold to Luann Ryon) Olympics but since the boycott of the 1980 Moscow Olympics (own by Keto Losaberidze of the USSR) the dominance has shifted to the South Korean women. They picked up the gold in 1984 (Hyang-Soon Seo) and in 1988 (Kim Soo Hyung).

In 1986 the FITA introduced a new scoring system to be used in the Olympics call the Grand FITA round in an attempt to make competition more exciting. The same total number of arrows (288) are shot as in the previously used Double FITA round. However, in the new system each archer shoots 72 arrows on the first and second day as before, but then an elimination process begins with previous cores being thrown out after every 36 arrows. On the third morning, the leading 24 archers shoot 36 arrows to determine the best 18 to shoot 36 arrows that afternoon. The final 12 archers shoot 36 arrows on the fourth morning to bring the field to six. These six, starting from scratch, shoot 36 arrows on the fourth afternoon to determine the Olympic champion.

In 1971 the College Division of the National Archery Association was founded. It serves to coordinate and promote collegiate archery throughout the United States.

Along with the revival of interest in all individual sports, archery is being enjoyed by an increasing number of men, women, and children.

Today, archery continues to hold interest for several reasons: (1) the evolution of a new method of shooting, which is easier to learn and more accurate that the old, (2) development of more efficient bows and arrows, and (3) the fascination many people find in the activities possible to the archer, ranging from target shooting, clout, roving, field shooting, and novelty shoots to the hunting of small and large game.

EQUIPMENT
The bow
The two types of bows most commonly used by the beginner are the recurved bow and the relatively recently developed compound bow. The compound bow's pulley system and its sophisticated weighting, balancing, and sighting devices have completely revolutionized the sport of archery. Of course, these advances increase the financial cost of the sport substantially, so the recurved bow is still popular, especially among beginners. A bow should be selected that can be pulled back full draw and held steady while aiming. This is determined by the weight of the bow--that is, the number of pounds of pull it takes to pull the arrow to its full length. Proper bow weight varies with age, sex, and strength of the archer. General recommendations for bow weights are: teen-age girls-20 to 25 lb; teen-age boys-20 to 30 lb; women-20 to 30 lb; men-25 to 40 lb.

The proper length of the bow is related to the length of the draw.

Draw length (in.)	Recommended bow length (in.)
24 or less	60 to 64
25 to 26	65 to 66
27 to 28	67 to 68
29 or more	69 to 70

The string consists of varied numbers of Dacron threads coated with beeswax, with loops at both ends. This type of bowstring is the most economical and requires least maintenance. New strings which increase the velocity of the arrow without increasing the bow weight are called fast strings and are made of Kevlar and other materials.

Points to look for in selecting a bow include:
1. The drawn bow bends evenly from the handle to the tips.
2. The upper and lower arms bend similarly.
3. When the bow is strung, the string divides it in half.
4. The cut of the bow follows the grain of the wood.
5. It feels comfortable in the hand.

6. It returns to its original shape after it is unstrung.
7. Pins and knots are plugged or there is extra wood around them.
8. Its weight and strength are suitable for the intended purpose.

The arrow
In the selection of arrows the beginning archer should make sure that the arrow is straight and that its length is appropriate for the length of his or her arm. To determine the proper arrow length measure the arm span and then refer to the following chart.

Arm span	Arrow length
57 to 59	22 to 23
60 to 62	23 to 24
63 to 65	24 to 25
66 to 68	25 to 26
69 to 71	26 to 27
72 to 74	27 to 28
75 to 77	28 to 29
Over 77	30 to 32

Another method for approximating correct length is to place one end of an arrow against the sternum and, while keeping the shoulders back, reach straight forward with both arms and use an arrow of such length that it extends 2 to 3 inches past the fingertips.

The proper arrow length is very important. If the shaft is too short, it is possible to overdraw the arrow beyond the arrow rest on the bow, possibly resulting in injury to the archer or to someone else.

Port Oxford cedar is the best wood for arrows and should be purchased unless the cost is prohibitive. If so, birchwood is cheap and sufficiently durable. Aluminum and fiberglass have proved to be quite satisfactory for more advanced shooting.

The quiver is used to hold arrows.

Protective devices
Finger protection is necessary for all archers. Without it the archer's shots will be inaccurate and painfully executed. There are two types of finger protection: (1) the finger tab, a leather pattern cut to cover index, middle, and ring fingers, and (2) the shooting glove, similar to an ordinary glove without the thumb and little finger.

The armguard protects the forearm of the bow arm from string contact.

The target
Homemade targets and stands are usually considered best and are least expensive.

The tripod stand should consist of three pine boards, 3 inches x 1 inch x 6 feet long. It should incline backward about 10 to 15 degrees from the vertical.

The target butt is approximately 48 inches (1.2 m) in diameter and 4 to 5 inches (11 to 12 cm) thick. It is constructed from rye straw or marsh hay would tightly in a coil and held firmly together with tarred cord.

The target face is made of heavy reinforced paper. On the face are painted five colored circles. The center is painted gold and is 9.6 inches (24 cm) in diameter. The other circles are 4.8 inches (12 cm) wide and are painted, from the center out, red, blue, black, and white. The target should be hung so that the exact center of the gold circle is 4 feet (1.22 m) from the ground.

RULES (USA)

The three major organizations governing the sport of archery are the National Archery Association (NAA), the National Field Archery Association (NFAA), and the Professional Archers Association (PAA).

NAA tournaments are conducted under International Rules (FITA), which place limitations on the equipment used; for example, compound bows, sight magnification, and release aids are not allowed. The NFAA tournament structure also includes many classifications and categories (such as limited and unlimited) that govern the equipment each archer may add to the bow. The PAA, a separate and complete association was formed when archery was officially inducted into the Olympics.

Crossbow archers compete in competitions organized by the National Crossbow Association; they do not compete officially against recurve or field shooters.

SCORING

Six arrows (an "end") are usually shot at one time. An arrow hitting the wrong target counts as a shot, but its score is forfeited. A loosened arrow may be retrieved if it can be reached by the archer with the aid of the bow without moving the feet. However, it is counted as a shot if it falls beyond the archer's reach.

An arrow that cuts two colors is always given the higher value of the two, even if the greater part of the arrow is in the ring of lower value. In tournament shooting all arrow holes are marked when arrows are drawn from the target. If an arrow rebounds or passes through the target mat, the hole is not marked and the score is recorded as the value of the unmarked hole. Local clubs or schools may elect

to count rebounds and pass-throughs as 7 points, providing they are witnessed. When ar arrow hits the petticoat, it counts for neither score nor hit. Scores are always listed with the highest score first, awarding 9, 7, 5, 3, or 1 point for the gold, the red, the blue, the black, and the white, respectively. Arrows must remain in the target until all are scored.

To call back to the archer the location of the arrow, the scorer reads the target like the face of a clock, for example, "6 o'clock red" if the arrow is in that location of the target.

SAFETY PRECAUTION WHILE SHOOTING IN GROUPS

Each archer shoots the end or flight of arrows and waits until the last arrow is shot. Following two blasts of a whistle, all archers retrieve their arrows, and no more shooting is permitted until all arrows are retrieved and all archers have returned to the shooting line. When this condition exists, the range supervisor permits shooting with one blast of the whistle. Three or more blasts of the whistle mean that a dangerous situation exists. The archers should stop shooting and remove all arrows from the bows.

TOURNAMENT SHOOTING

In NAA rounds the 5-color, 10-ring face is used, and score is counted from the center out: 10, 9, 8, 7, 6, 5, 4, 3, 2, 1. Shooting is in one direction only, beginning from the farthest range and finishing from the closest range.

Arrows are scored in groups of 6. A perfect score for 144 arrows is 1440.

Competition in a tournament usually consists of double rounds. Scores are tabulated after each end of six arrows is shot.

Archers are classified as follows:

Men	18 years old or older
Women	18 years old or older
Intermediate boys	15 to 18 years old
Intermediate girls	15 to 18 years old
Junior boys	12 to 15 years old
Junior girls	12 to 15 years old
Cadet boys	Less than 12 years old
Cadet girls	Less than 12 years old

Field shooting

Because of the vast increase of bow hunting in this country, the National Field Archers' Association of Redlands, Calif., sponsors a type of tournament and practice range called field shooting. Fourteen or 28 targets of different sizes are placed at random over a course with both hills and valleys.

Groups of four archers shoot a "field round"

and advance from target to target. Targets are black and white and have a bull's-eye that counts 5 points and an outer ring that has a 3-point value. Four arrows are shot at each target. The archer with the highest score is the winner.

FUNDAMENTAL SKILLS AND TECHNIQUES
Stringing the bow (bracing)
Push-pull method
Grasp the handle of the bow in the dominant hand with the back of the bow uppermost. Place the lower end against the inside of the arch of the foot on the same side, making sure that the tip does not touch the ground. Place the heel of the opposite hand on the back of the bow so that the loop of the string may be held between the thumb and first finger. By pulling on the handle with the dominant hand and pressing with the heel of the opposite hand, the bow may be bent and the string pushed up with the thumb and forefinger until it drops in to the nock. A bow stringer can also be used.

Step-through method
Grasp the bow with the dominant had (bow hand) and the string with the other hand (string hand). Put the back of the lower limb of the bow across the ankle of the foot on the string hand side. Step through the bow with the leg on the bow hand side. Put the bow handle high on the thigh of the leg on the bow hand side. Push the upper limb of the bow forward and with the bow hand and guide the string into the nock with the string hand.

Checking the bow after stringing
Make sure that the loop is slipped completely into the nock and that the bowstring is centered. The distance from the string to the deepest part of the handle should measure about 6 inches, which may be measured roughly by making a fist and letting the thumb extend perpendicularly from it. This is called the fistmele or brace height.

Unstringing the bow (unbracing)
The process is exactly the same as stringing, except that the string is pulled out of the nock and the loop is slid down over the upper limb.

PREPARATION FOR THE DRAW
Stance
The archer stands astride the shooting line with the target directly out from the bow arm side. The archer's feet should be spread enough to give a firm and comfortable footing. The body and the head should be in a normally erect, comfortable position; the posture should allow complete absence of tension at any point.

Possible errors in stance
1. Both feet on the same side of the line
2. Feet too close or too far apart
3. Too much weight on one foot

Position of the bow hand
As you raise the bow to position, allow the hand to tip up so that the pressure of the bow is against the part of the palm just inside the base of the thumb. Allow the thumb and fingers to encircle the bow only very lightly--just enough to keep it from falling. Never grip it.

Position of the string hand
Reach under the string and hook the first, second, and third fingers of the right hand onto the string, allowing the whole first joint to hook over the string. The index finger should be above the arrow, the other two fingers below it.

NOCKING
Be sure that the index feather (different colored) is up and the arrow is at a right angle to the string. Make a nocking (reference) point on the string by wrapping masking tape around the string about three times. Always nock the arrow below the tape each time. Hold the bow down and inside while nocking, with the index feather facing away form the bow.

THE DRAW AND ANCHOR
With simultaneous movement of the arms, slight pushing with the bow arm, and pulling with the string arm, the bow is brought to the desired position. As the draw is made, the outward pressure with the bow arm and the pull with the string arm should be equalized.

At the full draw, the bow arm is raised to shoulder height, with the elbow slightly bent and rotated downward to a 9 o'clock position.

The string hand is brought back to the face. In sight shooting (free style), the index finger is placed under the chin and lies in contact with the jawbone (low anchor). The string bisects both the nose and the chin for additional reference points. This point is known as the anchor point, and it is of prime importance that the string hand placement be exactly the same each time an arrow is drawn. At full draw the elbow of the string hand should be in line with the arrow.

In point-of-aim shooting, the string hand is brought back to the face; the string passes the nose to the side, and the index finger is locked in place under the cheekbone (high anchor).

Possible errors in the draw
Bow arm:
1. Elbow straight or hyperextended
2. Elbow bent too much
3. Left shoulder hunched

String arm:
1. Anchor point too far forward, too high, or below the chin
2. Some part of the hand other than the end segment of the forefinger or the string touches the anchor point
3. Elbow too high or too low

Aim, release, and follow through
Point of aim
Point of aim is a satisfactory method of aiming for the beginner, although sights may be used. With any bow and arrow there is only one distance at which a person may shoot and hit the center of the target by aiming directly at it while using point of aim. This will vary with the weight of the bow and with the length and weight of the arrow. In order that the arrows may be grouped on the target at distances farther or closer than this pint-blank range, the archer must use some auxiliary object in the background or foreground. This auxiliary object is known as the point of aim. At the completion of the draw, the point of the arrow should appear to be somewhere near the point of aim. The left hand is then moved slowly and steadily until the point of aim appears to be resting exactly on top of the point of the arrow.

At the instant the aim os adjusted to your satisfaction, release the string by allowing the fingers to quit holding. But allow only the fingers to relax; the muscles of the string shoulder and back must keep pulling, and the muscles of the bow arm and shoulder must remain steady until the arrow has hit the target.

Note the location of the group formed by the arrows that were properly shot. If they are high on the target, the point of aim must be lowered or brought toward the archer. If they are low on the target, the point of aim must be raised or moved toward the target. If the point of aim is in proper line and they group to the right or left or scatter over the target, check for faults other than in point of aim.

Possible errors in aiming and releasing
1. Shift in position
2. Both arms and shoulders relaxed at the moment of release

3. Point of aim not reached before releasing string
4. Point of aim to the right or left of a line directly between the archer and the center of the target
5. Aiming with the left eye
6. Sighting with both eyes
7. "Wrong arrow" used

Range finder
A device used for recording the established point of aim is called a range finder. It might be a piece of wood about 6 inches long. To record the point of aim, hold the finder at arm's length from the body toward the target, with the bull's-eye appearing just over the top of it. With the finder in this position, move the thumb up the stick until it is in line with the point of aim already established. At this point place a mark on the stick. In future shooting at this same distance, the point of aim can be reestablished by sighting through the mark recorded on the finder.

Bow sight (free style)
A device that is used for sighting and is attached to the back of the bow is termed a "bow sight." It has vertical and horizontal adjustments and is good for all ranges. In use, the line of vision is through the sight to the center of the target. For a right-handed archer (one who draws the string back with the right hand), the left eye should be closed, and the sight should be placed by the target's center. For a left-handed archer, the left eye is used.

Pin sight
One of the most economical types of bow sights today is the pin sight, in which the shooter uses masking tape or weather stripping with one or two large pins for sighting. Other shooters may use a tongue depressor held to the bow by adhesive tape and an pin or match stick for sighting.

When adjusting the sight:
1. Always start about 10 yards (9.14 m) from the target.
2. Set the pin about 4 inches (0.1 m) above the arrow rest. Sight through the pin to the yellow of the target.
3. Shoot a group of three arrows. If the arrows land high on the target, set the pin higher; if low, set the pin lower.
4. After resetting the pin, try again. Aim at the gold (yellow) and shoot.
5. When changing distances, adjust the pin sight. As the archer moves away from the

target, the pin sight should be moved closer to the grip of the bow.

Drawing arrows from the target

The back of one hand is placed against the target in such a way that the arrow is between the first and second fingers. Grasp the arrow close to the target with the other hand and pull the arrow from the target. Care must be taken to draw the arrow straight out so that it will not be bent or kinked. After being drawn out, drop the arrow on the ground, leaving the hands free for removing the remaining arrows. If an arrow penetrates to where the feathers have entered the target, it must be drawn on through the back of the target to prevent roughing or stripping off the feathers. If the arrow has penetrated one of the wooden legs of the wooden support of the target, it should be loosened with a pari of pliers before removal. At times, arrows that miss the target slither along the ground and into the grass. These must be pulled from the point end, much in the same manner as removing an arrow that has penetrated the target past the feathers. In looking for arrows that have missed target, keep the eyes on the ground as it is easy to step on an arrow and break it.

SAFETY PRECAUTIONS

Archery contains certain elements of danger if participants become negligent or careless. Proper conduct and behavior while shooting or taking care of equipment off range are exceedingly important. Safety rules are as follows:

1. Do not go to the target while others are shooting. All participants go at the same time to retrieve arrows.
2. When finished shooting, step back three paces and wait.
3. Draw an arrow only when directed at the target.
4. Shoot at targets only form the shooting line.
5. Remember that bows and arrows are not toys.
6. Faithfully obey the starting and stopping signals.
7. On the field range, shout "Timber" before the arrow is released so that persons nearby receive adequate warning.
8. While shooting, be certain that there is an adequate backstop behind the target or, if there is no backstop, that the area is clear behind target.
9. Never leave bows and arrows unguarded where children or careless persons might handle them.
10. Never shoot straight up into the air under any circumstances.
11. Never shoot with a faulty bow or arrow permit others to do so.
12. Never take changes or be in the least careless or negligent.
13. Do not pinch the arrow between the thumb and finger to shoot. Always use three fingers for drawing the arrow. This way you cannot accidentally release the arrow.

TEACHING CONSIDERATIONS

1. Teach safety procedures with no flexibility and strong consequences for any rule infractions. Establish and use consistent signals.
2. When teaching school populations, have the bows strung before the first class so that time is not wasted on this procedure and students get an opportunity to shoot during the first class period.
3. Assign bows and arrows to students the first day that they will use the entire unit unless adjustments need to be made.
4. Teach stringing and unstringing of bows on the second day.
5. Give students the whole idea of the skill before breaking it down into parts. This can be done through demonstration or the sue of audiovisual aids with a description of cures during the demonstration.
6. Practice stance, draw, and aim without an arrow, establishing clearly that the string is not to be released. Practice until each of these aspects is done correctly and with proper form. Do not go on until students have mastered the basics of each of these principles. Walk through each step if need be one at a time until mastered. In large classes use partners for feedback on:
   a. Straddling the line
   b. Raising the bow with the bow weight on the palm of the hand
   c. String hand position using first three fingers and whole first joint
   d. Level, straight pathway of elbow as it draws string back (9 o'clock position)
   e. Slightly flexed elbow on bow arm
   f. Correct anchor position
7. When students have mastered these steps, add nocking arrow, draw, anchor, aim, and release. Walk students through each step using cues before going to self-paced practice. Reemphasize rules for stepping in front of the

shooting line before students release any arrows.

8. Teach students how to retrieve arrows and how to score at one target before directing them to retrieve and score their own arrows.

9. Reemphasize point of aim and form after students have had an opportunity to shoot an end.

10. Help students analyze their errors in form based on clustering of arrows after enough practice results in consistent errors.

11. In longer units develop skills for shooting rounds and add novelty shooting (balloons, golf archery, etc.).

Golf

Golf

Completion of this chapter should enable the reader to:

- Recognize the values and benefits of participation in golf

- Be knowledgeable in the selection of golf equipment and in the uses for each club

- Practice proper technique in executing the basic golf swing and the several specialized shots.

- Know the rules of golf and be familiar with the etiquette that is so much a part of the game

- Teach a group of beginning students the fundamentals of golf

- Properly use the many and colorful terms associated with golf

Golf is one the most challenging and fascinating of modern sports. The thrill of striking a ball well over 200 yards and the satisfaction of successfully executing the soft touch needed for a 4-foot putt are of lasting pleasure. Whether one learns to play golf for relaxation and fun or aspires to achieve a high competitive level is the privilege of the individual. Few sports offer playing fields with such great variety and beauty as golf courses.

HISTORY

The game of golf is one of the most ancient of the modern sports. Historians do not agree on its origin, but it appears certain that golf was played in Scotland more than 500 years ago. As early as 1457 the Scottish Parliament ordained that golf should not be played by the people because it was distracting from the practice of archery, which was deemed necessary for defensive purposes. Old paintings and drawings show that similar games were also played about that time in Holland, Belgium, and France. The Dutch term "kolf," meaning a club, is considered by some to have give rise to the name of the present-day game. Regardless of how much Scotland invented on its own and how much it borrowed from others, it appears certain that that country was the source from which the game as it is known today spread to all parts of the world. St. Andrews in Fife, Scotland is believed to be the oldest existing golf course.

Courses or links of the early days differed greatly from those of the present. Golf was then distinctly a seaside game. It was played over stretches of land that linked the waterline of the seashore with tillable lands farther inland. It was this condition which led to calling the scene of play "links," which in fact means a seaside golf course.

Location of holes followed no definite plan. The landscape was partially covered by bushes, trees, and the like. Open areas were chosen as finishing points or putting greens. No official number of holes was adopted as standard for a round of play until 1858, when 18 holes were designated as a round.

Historical documents tell of the organization of golf clubs in the United States in the closing years of the eighteenth century. However, the game as we know it today had its start in the United States approximately 80 years ago. A few clubs were started in the eastern United States, and the rapid increase in popularity since then has greatly increased the number of private and municipal courses. Today, class instruction in golf is found in most secondary schools and colleges. Colleges and universities often own and operate golf courses; high schools use private and municipal courses. In recent years television coverage of major golf events has done much to stimulate interest in the game. In fact, in may urban areas of the country the number of golf courses has become insufficient to accommodate the demand. In 1980 the National Golf Foundation indicated that if a new golf course was built every day until 2000, there would still be a shortage. In 1989 they revised this statement to suggest that if five new courses were built every day until 2000, there would still be a shortage. It has been estimated that more than 16.5 million Americans play golf sometime during a year.

There are at least 16,000 golf driving ranges in America. Many people become enthusiasts and start playing golf as a result of experience on a driving range.

Golf today is not longer a game for those with a high income. It is played by individuals from a variety of economic backgrounds and includes the young and the old, duffers as well as masters.

Truly, golf is a sport that offers a life-long source of pleasure. One or two well-timed and well-directed shots often serve as the catalyst that causes the player to return for another round.

The social values and aspects of golf include the following: it encourages excellent compatibility of mixed groups; it clears and freshens the mind by diversion of interest; it brings urban dwellers into sunshine and nature; it provides restful activity for the working individual; the golfer is pitted against self as well as against opponents; each hole is a separate contest and challenge; and the game is played by people of all ages, sizes, and builds. As recreation, golf is one of the most desirable of all sports.

GENERAL DESCRIPTION

Eighteen holes make up the typical golf course. The first, ninth, tenth, and eighteenth holes are generally near the clubhouse. Any multiple of nine holes can be played, and each hole varies in length and general layout. Hazards are generally placed to penalize a poor shot. The object is to score as few strokes as possible for each hole. Play starts at the tee behind two markers, continues along the fairway, which is generally bounded by rough, and finishes at the green, which is often surrounded by bunkers. The ball is rolled into the hole marked by the pin or flagstick.

EQUIPMENT

The United States has contributed in large share to improvements in golf equipment, including, for example, the type of ball in use today; the steel-, graphite-, and titanium-shafted clubs and the peg tee.

Clothing

Dress should be comfortable and in accord with local custom on the course played.

Spiked golf shoes are an important part of a player's golfing equipment. However, if they ar not available, a pair of tennis shoes will suffice.

Clubs

It is not necessary to have the best set of golf clubs on the market to enjoy playing golf and to play it satisfactorily. On the other hand, one should not handicap his or her game by playing with inferior equipment. Purchasing clubs that are suitable to your characteristics and that are made by a dependable manufacturer is a sound policy for assurance of satisfaction and long wear.

Golf clubs come in a variety of lengths, weights, shaft flexibility, and other features. Club length is usually determined by a person's height, and club weight is often selected on a personal preference in relation to fee. Usually, the faster the swing, the less whip you should have in your club shafts. Ask your golf teacher or club professional for advice on the type of clubs to purchase.

The maximum number of clubs allowed to be carried by a golfer is 14.

Starter set

The beginning golfer should not invest in an expensive and complete set of clubs. Options include purchasing a set of used clubs or a start set. The advantages of purchasing a set of used clubs rather than a starter set are usually in the quality and number of clubs obtained for a comparable cost. On the other hand, with a starter set it is possible to purchase a brand that can be added to later as needed. In either case the minimum clubs to start with include a 3 wood; a putter; and the 3, 5, 7, and 9 irons.

Woods

The four common woods are the driver, or no. 1 wood; the no. 3 wood; the no. 4 wood; and the no. 5 wood. They have longer shafts and weigh more than the iron clubs and consequently can give more distance than an iron club having a similar loft or tilt to the club face. The driver is the longest hitting club and is usually used at the tee.

Driver. The driver hits 220 to 300 yards (201 to 275 m) (women, 150 to 220 yards [137 to 183 m]) and is used only on the tee.

No. 3 wood. This club hits 200 to 240 yards (183 to 220 m) (women, 150 to 170 yards [137 to 155 m]) and is used from a good lie for long shots.

No. 4 wood. This club hits 200 to 230 yards (183 to 210 m) (women, 145 to 160 yards [133 to 146 m]) and is used from a good lie where distance and height are needed.

No. 5 wood. The no. 5 wood hits 190 to 220 yards (174 to 201 m) (women, 120 to 150 yards [109 to 137 m]) and is used from a poor lie or in place of a long iron.

Irons

Irons are used from the fairway or from the tee on short holes. The player selects the proper iron according to the distance required.

Putter. This club is used for putting on the green

or from just off the green. Putters are manufactured in a great variety of styles and are chosen on the basis of individual preference.

Pitching or sand wedge. These clubs are used for short approaches from the rough and fairways, less than 125 yards (115 m), and as a trouble club from tall rough or sand traps. They are very versatile when properly used.

Golf balls

Golf balls are made by many manufacturers. Their construction varies from a solid one-piece ball to a ball developed from a small hard core wound with rubber bands and sealed with a durable cover.

Ball preference is left up to individual feel and style of play. The better players usually prefer a wound ball of higher compression, where beginners would use a one- or two-piece ball with a durable cover that does not cut easily. One should have at least three balls in the golf bag when going out to play.

Plastic balls may be used for the gymnasium, small field, or backyard practice.

THE COURSE

A golf course is usually built and constructed to best conform to the locale of the land. A complete golf course consists of 18 holes, which requires not less than 100 acres. In many communities 9-hole or 18-hole courses are constructed on less acreage with shorter holes that require less time to play. Par-3 courses, on which 18 holes can be played in 3 hours or less, are becoming increasingly popular.

A well-constructed golf course is architecturally planned so that each hole differs from the rest, yet certain elements are common to all.

Each hole is composed of a tee and tee markers, fairway, rough, trees, boundary, sand bunkers and sometimes water hazards, are left to the creativity of the golf course architect.

Par for the course is usually determined by the distance of the holes from the middle of the tee down the middle of the fairway to the middle of the green. Holes up to 250 yards (229 m) are usually designated as par 3, holes from 251 to 470 yards (230 to 430 m) as par 4, and holes from 471 to 600 yards (431 to 549 m) as par 5. Par 3 is a score usually obtained by reaching the green one shot and rolling the ball into the cup with two putts. On a par 4, the golfer should reach the green in two; and on a par 5, reach it in three. A championship course usually has a par of 72, or an average of four strokes per hole. A typical course has four par-e holes, 10 par-4 holes, and four par-5 holes.

Par for women differs somewhat from that for men, depending on the difficulty of each hole as to distance, hazards, and the like.

FACILITIES FOR PRACTICE

1. Outdoor driving range and putting green.
2. Any large room, preferably a gymnasium.
3. Two or three large pieces of canvas hun in front of a wall with fish netting along sides to form a cage-type setup.
4. Mats from which to hit
5. Clubs and balls (plastic balls may be used if nets are not available)
6. A large rung with short nap for putting
7. Putting cups for individual putting (water glasses an be used)

FUNDAMENTAL SKILLS AND TECHNIQUES

Because certain types of shots fall into natural groupings, the following material has been arranged to take advantage of these categories. For the left-handed player, it will be necessary to reverse the techniques as presented here because consideration has been given only to the right-handed player.

The golf grip

1. Ten-finger grip; sometimes used by players with small, weak hands or extremely short fingers
2. Interlocking grip; preferred by some players who like a solid feel
3. Overlapping or Vardon grip; the most popular grip, used by most professional players (described below)

One opens the left hand, and with the thumb and fingers together, places the club diagonally across the hand from the middle joint of the index finger across the heel of the hand. The hand closes over the club so that it is held by the fingers. The V formed by the thumb and index finger should point approximately to the right shoulder. When the club is held in the position of address, you should see the first three knuckles of the fingers. The thumb is above, one quarter turn over the club with the pad of the thumb on the grip of the club formed by the first and second fingers of the left hand. The correct rotation of the left hand allows cocking of the wrist at the peak of the backswing. It also allows the left arm to deal a backhand blow to the ball. At this point the player should try swinging the club head with only the left arm, watching that the arm remains comfortably straight and that the wrist cocks at the top of the backswing.

To place the right hand in position, the club handle should first contact the middle joint of the right forefinger. When the hand is closed, this forefinger knuckle must be on the right side of the shaft, never under it. Then one closes the hand, placing the thumb to the left, diagonally across the shaft so that it helps the forefinger to grip. The feel of the club head is controlled mainly by the fingers, giving more power and control. The left thumb should fit snugly into the palm of the right hand. The little finger of the right hand should be wrapped around the crevice formed by the first two fingers of the left hand (overlapping grip).

It should be emphasized that , regardless of the grip used, the back of the left hand and the palm of the right should face squarely toward the target.

The Stance

Square stance. The feet, knees, hips, and shoulders are parallel to the line of flight. This stance is used for almost all long shots of both woods and irons because it allows free movement of either side of the body. The knees are slightly bent, the toes turn slightly outward, and the weight is evenly distributed. The arms hand downward from the shoulders and away from the body but not forward. The body curves naturally, but not sharply, forward. The eyes re on the ball.

Open stance. The left foot is withdrawn slightly from the line of flight, but the knees, hips, and shoulders remain square. This stance is used rarely for wood shots but more often for the shorter iron shots. It tends to restrict the turning and pivoting of the left side but allows a better follow-through. This stance encourages the fade or slice but can result in increased distance.

Closed stance. The right foot is withdrawn slightly from the line of flight, but the knees, hips, and shoulders remain square. This stance is often used for wood shots and encourages a draw or hook.

The golf swing

Tempo

Maintaining an even tempo is one of the most important aspects of developing a proper golf swing. A player who is able to maintain good rhythm and smoothness throughout the swing will be able to develop an efficient and consistent golf swing. Most beginners attempt to hit the ball too hard, which results in an improper tempo or an uneven rhythm and causes many faults. In fact, as a variable, strength is much less important than proper tempo and clubhead speed in the successful golf swing. Beginning golfers should strive to achieve a consistent tempo or rhythm in all shots attempted. Often a simple key such as saying "Back," "Wait," and "Through" or "One, two, three" on the backswing and "One, two, three" on the downswing and follow-through will help to develop the rhythm necessary for success. Once the idea of tempo is understood and accomplished, the beginner will have the necessary basis for the development of a sound golf swing. Without proper rhythm it is difficult to hit the ball correctly, and much power is wasted. In general, the golf swing is developed by gradually

increasing the speed. The golfer should begin slowly, then accelerate on the downswing, keeping a continuous rhythm throughout. It takes approximately the same time to take the club from the address to the top of the backswing as it does to complete the downswing and the follow-through.

Addressing the ball

When addressing the ball, the player takes the proper grip and places the head of the club on the ground, with the sole of the club parallel to the turf. The feet should be placed approximately shoulder width apart or in a relative position for the club used, for example, wider for the longer clubs. The arms should fall naturally from the shoulders and not so far away from the body that the individual is stretching. For the woods, the ball is generally placed in line with the inside portion of the left heel. As the length of the club and the required distance decrease, the ball is addressed farther to the right of the left foot but seldom farther back than in the center of the stance.

The waggle

The waggle is a preliminary movement that takes a variety of forms, depending on individual preference. It is designed to help the golfer relax, adjust the grip, check alignment, and get ready to begin the swing. Usually, it involves slight body movement and the lifting of the club head several inches to check balance and position. When the golfer feels ready, there is a slight hesitation before the beginning of the full swing. This preliminary move tends to ease tension in preparation for the shot.

The backswing

Before beginning the swing, the golfer must fix his or her eye on the ball. The swing is started with a rotation of the shoulder and hips, which starts the club head moving to the back. The left arm should be kept straight and the club head low to the ground. The wrists begin to cock approximately halfway back on the swing. The right elbow is kept close to the body, and the weight is shifted from a balanced position to the right foot. The left knee is turned inward, and the left foot rolls to the right, keeping the left heel low to the ground. At the top of the backswing the left shoulder is pointing at the ball and the club is parallel to the ground and pointing toward the target.

The downswing

To make a smooth change of direction, the downswing is started with the left leg. The left foot comes down flat to the ground, and the knees and hips are moved forward toward the target. The knees are bent slightly to allow freedom of movement as

197

the weight is shifted from the right side to the left. There should be a feeling of pulling from the left side. The wrists should remain cocked until the arms are parallel with the ground. The left leg straightens and the left side becomes firm to provide a strong hitting position. At impact, there should be a straight line from the ball or club head through the hands to the left shoulder. The head must remain stationary and the eyes remain focused on the ball after contact is made.

Follow-through

After impact, the right arm becomes just as straight as the left arm was on the backswing. The head rises naturally but does not move forward as the right shoulder comes under. Both arms should be stretched out as far as possible toward the target. The wrists will begin to turn over after the arms have reached their limit, finishing with the hands high above the head.

The swing plane

When the golfer takes the club back from the ball, the club should come slightly inside the line of flight, maintaining a plane that will run back approximately between the shoulders and neck. One of the keys in a successful golf swing is to maintain this same plane on the downswing. To accomplish this, the golfer must maintain the proper sequence of body movements. The swing is started with the legs and hips, then the arms come into play, then the wrists begin cocking. This same order must be maintained on the downswing if the place is not to be broken. The downswing starts with the legs and hips then the arms come into play and next the wrists unlock so that they are straight at the point of contact. This sequence will enable the golfer to swing from slightly inside the line of flight out through the ball, maintaining proper control of the shot. Any deviations from this sequence will allow the club head to break the plane and will cause inconsistency or initiate numerous faults or problems with the flight of the ball. This sequence and having the clubhead square to the intended line of flight at impact are the two most important factors in a successful golf swing.

Common errors

The following are errors often made by beginners when learning the golf swing:

1. Swaying or moving the head to the right instead of pivoting the body over the ball
2. Backswing that is too fast, eliminating good tempo and throwing the golfer off balance
3. Bending the left arm
4. Raising the left shoulder
5. Backswing with a too flat or too horizontal plane
6. Raising the head from its original position
7. Pausing too long or not long enough at the top of the swing
8. Rushing the downswing
9. Uncocking the wrists too soon, which throws off the proper sequence and usually casts the club outside the correct plane
10. Hitting too hard with the right hand, which drops the right shoulder, causing contact behind the ball
11. Relaxing the wrists at the moment of impact or slowing the downswing, impeding proper rhythm or tempo
12. Failing to complete the follow-through with the hands held high

The short swing

One of the consistent factors in golf is that it is not necessary to learn a different swing for each club. The place varies slightly with the length of the club; however, there is no difference in what has to be learned to attempt the swing. When a shot reburies less distance than produced by the shortest club in the bag, a shorter swing must be executed. The short swing is a breakdown of the full swing, and the distance of the shot is commensurate with the length of the backswing. If a half swing is required for a particular shot, then the golfer uses less body turn and less wrist action than in the full swing, where the wrist break is not completed until the club is brought to the top of the swing. The shorter the swing, the less wrist action and body movement occur. The follow-through is the same as in the backswing. A one-quarter backswing requires a one-quarter follow-through; a one-half backswing requires a one-half follow-through; and so on. The rest of the fundamentals are exactly the same as described for the full swing. The golfer should practice short swings of various lengths to determine how far the ball will travel and to obtain the correct feel for the distance required.

The pitch shot

The pitch shot is usually executed with a no. 9 iron, pitching wedge, or sand wedge. This shot will fly high and is used to hit the ball over a bunker or hazard of some type and will stop on the green with very little roll. The stance should be square or slightly open, with the length of the backswing determined by the distance needed as described for the short swing. Some golfers prefer to choke down on the club for greater control, particularly for the shorter shots. Inasmuch as the swing is shorter, body movement is kept to a minimum, there is little wrist cock, and the left arm is straight throughout the swing. It is important that the follow-through be carried the same distance as the backswing, with care taken not to make any special effort to meet or hit the ball hard. Tempo is just as important in the short swing or pitch shot as it is in the full swing. Regardless of the distance of the shot, it is important that one hit down through the ball and not try to scoop the ball into the air. The club is designed to give the proper lift to the ball.

The chip shot

The chip shot is usually executed with a no. 7 iron and is effective when the golfer has an open shot to the pin and does not have to hit over any type of hazard. The stance is similar to that for the pitch shot, with slightly more weight forward at the address. The less-lofted club face will allow the ball to travel low and run much farther than the pitch shot. Again, the distance of the shot is determined by the length of the backswing, and the follow-through should be commensurate with the backswing. One should practice taking the club back various distances to determine the proper length of the backswing for the distance required. Club selection for this shot is usually determined by selecting the club that will allow the ball to hit as close to the edge of the green as possible and roll the remainder of the way to the cup. A short chip shot can be executed in a manner similar to a putting stroke. Again, the key to the chip shot is proper tempo and rhythm, with care not to chop at the ball with an uneven tempo.

Putting

Putting is individual in nature, although there are certain aspects of the stroke that must be maintained regardless of the golfer's style or the type of putter used. The stance may be wide, narrow, open, or closed, depending on the individual preference. However, there must be no body or head movement and the putter blade should be taken straight back in line with the direction required for a straight-through motion toward the hole. The following description of putting can be used as a guide; however, technique can be varied according to personal preference. The distance of the putt is determined by the length of the backswing. A shorter putt requires a shorter backswing and a longer putt a longer backswing, but the tempo must be consistent through-out.

Stance

1. The stance is fairly upright, with the neck and shoulders bent slightly.
2. The feet are 8 to 12 inches apart.
3. The stance is square.
4. The weight is balanced.
5. The left arm is kept close to the torso.

6. The right forearm is close to their right thigh.
7. The ball is at the left instep.

Grip

1. The back of the left hand and the palm of the right hand are square to the line.
2. Both thumbs are directly on top of the grip.

Swing

1. The swing is short and low to the ground.
2. It is in line with the intended roll of the ball.
3. It is completely relaxed, show, and steady.
4. There is no body or head movement.
5. The club head follows through.
6. The ball should be struck firmly enough to reach the hole.

Reading the green

1. The player checks the grass to determine whether the putt will be with or against the grain.
2. The player sights the hole from behind the ball to determine the angle of roll.

Sand bunkers

Executing the bunker shot properly can save the golfer many strokes. To control this hot, the player must hit the sand about 2 inches behind the ball and let the sand throw the ball out of the trap. The distance the ball travels is relative to the distance hit behind the ball. The object is not to bury the club but to continue to swing smoothly through the sand and under the ball, with a strong follow-through and finish.

General principles

1. Because sand traps vary from deep, soft sand to shallow, hard clay and sand, each shot is different.
2. The trap is entered from the lowest point so as not to destroy the bank or unduly disturb the surface.
3. The player positions his or her feet and then moves them back and forth in order to sink into the sand and have a firm stance.
4. In addressing the ball, one should not touch the sand with the club head until the ball is hit.
5. On leaving the trap, all irregularities made in the sand should be covered by smoothing them out with the club head or rake.

The explosion shot

1. The grip, stance, and swing are about the same as for the short, high approach.
2. The stance is open, with the feet fairly close together and well-set in the sand.
3. The grip must be firm but not tense.

4. The swing must be fairly long, upright, and U-shaped.
5. The club head must not stop in the sand because sand pushed ahead of the club will cause the ball to rise. The follow-through should be definite and powerful.
6. The amount of sand taken, or the distance back of the ball that the club head enters the sand, determines the distance the ball will travel. Thus the closer one is to the green, the more sand one must take.

Sidehill lies

When playing from sidehill lies, the golfer must adjust the stance and ball replacement to conform to the contour of the ground. The golfer should avoid trying to overswing and should first take one or two practice swings to become familiar with the changes in swing feel.

General principles
1. Do not overswing.
2. Play for accuracy.
3. Allow the club head to follow the contour of the ground.

Uphill
1. There is a tendency to pull or hook, so aim to the right.
2. Stand close to the ball with the feet almost together.
3. Put more weight on the right foot.
4. Play the ball forward of the normal position in stance.

Downhill
1. There is a tendency to slice, so aim to the left.
2. On a steep slope avoid wood clubs because it is difficult to achieve a rise.
3. Play the ball back of the normal position in stance.
4. Weight is naturally more on the left foot, which will restrict the action of the pivot to the left. "Shift the weight to the right foot.

Ball below feet
1. There is a strong tendency to slice, so play to the left.
2. The weight is on the toes, so open the stance somewhat.
3. Avoid topping by moving the grip closer to the top end of the club and concentrating on staying down until after the ball is contacted.
4. Do not pivot as much as on level ground; more of a U-shaped swing is natural.

Ball above feet
1. The tendency is to pull or hook, so play to the right.
2. Hold the club short.
3. Swing slowly; a fast swing will throw you back, causing you to top the ball.
4. There is a tendency to toe the ball with the club, so play it close.

Playing from the rough

When playing from the rough, set yourself firmly with a slightly open stance. The club should be brought back in a more upright motion. Hit down through the ball and finish the swing strongly.

General principles
1. Do not press in trying for too much distance.
2. Use the U-shaped swing.
3. Play the shot safely rather than gamble on a "lucky one."
4. Open the face of the club to cut the grass better and to give a quicker rise in long grass.
5. Each rough position will differ from the last, so judge each one as the occasion arises.

RULES
1. The ball must be played as it lies except as outlined by the rules. Local rules may permit preferred lies, or "winter rules," in which case the ball may be moved with the club head provided that it is not moved nearer the hole.
2. The ball must be fairly struck with the head of the club.
3. The player whose ball is farthest from the hole plays first.
4. If a ball goes out of bounds, the player must play the next stroke at the spot from which the ball was last struck. If the stroke was played from the tee, the ball may be teed; in all other cases it must be dropped. The penalty is loss of stroke and distance. (Add 2 strokes to score for the hole.) If any part of the ball lies in bounds, the ball remains in play.
5. In match play, if a player's ball knocks the opponent's ball into the hole, the opponent shall be considered to gave holed out on the last shot. A ball that has been moved by an opponent's ball may be left at the point or returned replaced in its original spot. In stroke play, the ball moved must be replaced as near as possible to its original spot. The golfer playing the putt has the right to ask the opponent to mark the ball.

   The player has the option of having the flagstick attended or removed. If the putted ball strikes an attended flagstick of a person attending the flagstick in stroke play, there is a 2-stroke penalty. In match play, if the flagstick

200

is held by an opponent or an opponent's caddy, the opponent loses the hole. If it is held by the player's caddy, the player loses the hole.

Note: If a ball is believed to be out of bounds, a provisional ball may be played before the golfer leaves the point from which the first ball was played.

6. Irregularities of surface that might in any way affect the player's stroke may not be removed or pressed down by the player, any partner, or caddies. However, ball marks on a green may be repaired before putting.

7. Any player may not move, bend, or break anything fixed or growing before striking at a ball in play. This applies to holding branches out of the way and to trampling weeds to improve the lie of the ball.

8. A ball lying or touching an obstruction, such as clothing, lumber, vehicles, ground under repair, and the like, may be lifted and dropped over the shoulder away from such an object without penalty but may not be moved closer to the hole.

9. If a player's stroke is interfered with by any object such as just mentioned, the ball may be moved two club lengths, no nearer the hole, without penalty.

10. When a ball lies in a hazard, nothing shall be done that can in any way improve its lie; the club may not touch the ground in addressing the ball or during the backswing; nor may anything be touched or moved by the player before the ball is struck.

11. If a ball lies or is lost in a recognized water hazard (whether the ball lies in water or not, or in casual water in a hazard) the player may drop a ball, under penalty of 1 stroke, either behind the hazard, keeping the spot at which the ball crossed the margin of the hazard between himself or herself and the hole, or in hazard, keeping the spot at which the ball entered the water between himself or herself and the hole. If the ball was played from the teeing ground, a ball may be teed under the penalty of stroke, as near as possible to the spot from which the original ball was played.

If a ball lies or is lost in casual water (unintentional hazard), the player may drop a ball without penalty on dry ground as near as possible to the spot where the ball lay but not nearer to the hole.

12. A golfer may have no more than 14 clubs when playing.

13. A ball is considered lost if not found within 5 minutes.

ETIQUETTE

Students should study golf etiquette carefully and govern their conduct accordingly. Golf developed as a mannerly game, and it still remains so. One should play the game by the rules without exception.

1. There should be nor more than four persons in one party, and each person should have a set of clubs.

2. No one should move or talk or stand close to or directly behind the ball or the hole when a player is making a stroke.

3. On the putting green, the player whose ball lies nearest the hole should hold the pin while other players putt.

4. No player should play until golfers playing ahead are out of range.

5. Players looking for a lost ball should allow other players coming up to pass them. They should signal to the players following them to pass, and having given such a signal, should not continue their play until these players have passed ahead and are out of range.

6. A player should see that any turf cut or displaced (a divot) by him or her is at once replaced and *pressed down*.

7. No practice shots should be attempted on any part of course when other golfers are following.

8. Slow players should allow a faster group to play through.

9. Local course rules should be observed.

10. All shots should be played according to the rules of the game.

11. The player farthest away from the hole shoots or putts first.

12. A player should avoid walking ahead of partners or opponents.

13. The tee shot should be played from behind the markers.

14. If any player or person on the course is in danger of being hit by your shot, "fore" should be called as a warning.

15. The golf bag should always be laid down off the green.

16. Footprints in a sand trap should be smoothed out after a shot.

17. When holding the flag on the green, a player should stand so that a shadow does not fall across the cup.

18. When all players have holed out, the party leaves the putting green immediately for oncoming players.

19. When one member of a twosome, threesome, or foursome has a lost ball, all members of the group should help look for it.

20. Above all, players should be courteous.

Golf teaches the highest principles of etiquette and consideration for others.

The game is no longer enjoyable when rules are broken at random. Golf etiquette is easily understood and, when correctly observed, affords pleasure and enjoyment of the game.

TEACHING CONSIDERATIONS

1. The basic swing is usually introduced with a no. 5 iron as a full swing. It is advisable to practice without the ball until basic form is established. Golf whiffle balls are useful once the ball is introduced. This enables students to get a great deal of practice with limited equipment. Repetition is critical. Nets to hit into avoid time wasted chasing balls.

2. As soon as possible give students a distance goal to swing toward so that maximum force can be attained and the importance of form can be established.

3. Introduce the woods and other irons as only slight variations of the basic swing. Emphasize the basic elements as well as critical differences between use of the woods and other irons. One wood and a no. 9 or wedge are all that are necessary for basic instruction before learners are introduced to playing a hole (or toward a distance target area).

4. Teach principles of putting but permit variations in style.

5. After learners have had experience with a wood, several irons, and putting, introduce concepts regarding the short swing, pitch and chip shots, and strategies for different lies. Each of these situations should be practiced separately and not just alluded to in instruction.

6. If possible, have learners go to a golf course before the end of the unit and not just as a culminating event. Prepare them for a particular course and review golf etiquette and rules. Learners will return to instruction highly motivated and willing to share their experiences and problems when they have had an opportunity to actually play golf.

Tennis

Tennis

Completion of this chapter should enable the reader to:

- Have a basic knowledge of the historical development of tennis
- Be informed about the proper selection of equipment
- Know the rules and scoring of tennis, and understand the etiquette of play
- Perform and demonstrate the fundamental skills for effective playing technique
- Know the principles of strategy for competitive play
- Teach others by using sound instructional and practice techniques

HISTORY

There is evidence that a form of tennis was played in the ancient Greek and Roman Empires, and that a game in which a ball was batted back and forth with a type of racquet may have been played in the Orient more than 2000 years ago. Still other indications are that tennis may have begun in Egypt and Persia 500 years before the Christian era.

Despite these obscure ancient origins, there is no doubt that a tennislike gamed was played in thirteenth-century France. Called *jeu de paume* (literally, game of the hand), it was first a barehanded game of hitting a stuffed cloth bag over a rope. When paddles, and later racquets, were a added, the game grew steadily in popularity. By the close of the fourteenth century it was also well established in England.

It is believed the game received its present name when English visitors heard French officials called *tenez*, which meant to resume play, an expression similar to "play ball" used by baseball umpires. The English thought tenez was the correct name for le paume. In time the English word tennis was substituted.

At he beginning of the fifteen century there were 1400 professional players in France, and yet the first standardized written rules of tennis did not appear until 1599. The game reached a peak of popularity in England and France during the sixteenth and seventeenth centuries; Paris alone having built 1800 courts. But the French Revolution virtually obliterated the sport (Paris was left with only court), and a civil war did much the same in England.

What remnant of the game was left in England seems next to appear at a particular garden party given in 1873 by British Army Major Walter C. Wingfield. His guests were introduced to a game called "spharistike," later to become more descriptively referred to as "lawn tennis." In attendance at the party was an army officer who took the game with him to Bermuda as a diversion for the British garrison stationed there. Miss Mary Outerbridge, who was vacationing on the island during the winter of 1873-74, became intrigued with the game and brought equipment with her upon returning to her New York home.

As a member of the Staten Island Cricket and Baseball Club, Miss Outerbridge received permission to lay out a court in an unused corner of the grounds. Within a few years tennis was included as an activity at nearly every major cricket club in the east, and soon it became a sport of the masses. But the rules were diverse, so in 1880 a brother of Miss Outerbridge called a meeting in New York to establish a standard code. An outcome of that meeting was the establishment of the United States Tennis Association (USTA), still the ruling body of American tennis today.

Later that same year the first tournament for the National Championship of the United States was held at Newport, Rhode Island. The site was moved in 1915 to Long Island, and in 1978 it was relocated to its present site at the National Tennis Center in Queens, New York City.

This tournament, now called the U.S. Open, is considered one of the four most prestigious in the world. It joins with the Australian Open, the French Open, and (the most venerable of all) the Wimbledon, named for the London suburb where it is played. A winner of all four tournaments in the same year will have accomplished the "grand slam" of tennis, the rarest feat in the game.

In 1988 tennis returned to the Olympics as an official sport for the first time since 1924, and it was open to professional players. The women's singles was won by Steffi Graf of Germany (who also had won the grand slam that year and had won in the Olympic competition in 1984 when tennis was a demonstration sport). The men's singles was won by Miloslav Mecir and the United States went home with both gold medals in doubles with Ken Flach and Robert Seguso winning the men's competition and Pam Shriver and Zina Garrison triumphing in the women's contest.

VALUES

Tennis is, without a doubt, one of the most popular of universally accepted games. There are many reasons:

1. It can be played by everyone.
2. It is a coeducational recreational game and is well suited for mixed competition.
3. It requires only two or four people to play.
4. It can be played indoors or outdoors.
5. Only a short time is needed to play either an easy game or a strenuous game that taxes the players' ability, endurance, speed, and agility.
6. It is an excellent game of eye-hand coordination.
7. It is a noncontact sport.
8. It can be adapted as a team sport in addition to being suitable for individual competition.

REASON FOR POPULARITY

The main factors to which tennis owes it popularity are:

1. Availability of court.
2. Availability of teachers.
3. Relatively low cost of equipment.
4. Stimulus of tennis associations and tournaments.
5. Trend toward individual sports.
6. Suitability of the game to both sexes and to a wide range of ages.
7. Onset of indoor tennis so that the sport is no longer seasonal.
8. Commercialization and publicity.
9. Growing demand in high schools and colleges for athletic programs for women.
10. Suitability as a sport for intramural as well as interschool competition.

For these and many other reasons, it is one of the best basic skill sports for carryover. All children should learn to play sometime within their school experiences, for its social values have a far-reaching influence on achievement of a full, rich life.

EQUIPMENT
Clothing

Tennis attire has evolved into multicolored clothing that is flexible in all the right places and has enough aesthetic appeal to be worn at a lawn party after a match. Orthopedic shoes have eliminated the plight of skidding around the court in discount sneakers, inviting self-inflicted hot-foot. Be sure, however, to buy only tennis (or "al -court") shoes, which are designed to support the constant changes of direction that tennis demands.

The ball

Tennis balls are made of two rubber cups molded together, covered with synthetic and wool felt, and inflated with compressed air. To maintain internal pressure, they are packed in pressurized containers and should be opened just before play. Once the can is opened, the ball will slowly lose its pressure. All tennis balls that have "Approved by the USTA" indicated on their packaging have met standards of constructions and playability.

The racquet

Racquet heads vary in size and shape for the purpose of affecting the sweetspot (the area on the strings that will produce the most reliable shot). Midsize racquets have around 85 square inches of strung surface, and oversize racquets have 100 or more. There is no "bigger is better" relationship. Overall, the midsize racquets offer the best combination of power and control.

Better racquets are composites—a crossbreed of several materials. The most satisfactory material is fiberglass, generally regarded as the best companion material for other fibers, such as graphite, boron, Kevlar, and even wood.

In general, a stiff racquet will produce more power and control than a flexible one. However, some are so still they will vibrate considerably on impact with the ball and could be tough on sensitive elbows. Still a general rule is that the stronger your game becomes, the more likely it is that you will appreciate a stiff racquet.

The "weight" of a racquet is misleading, for what one manufacturer calls light another may call medium. Moreover, racquets can be head-heavy or head-light, or have the weight evenly distributed. The real test is how it feels in your hand.

Also, there is no absolute way to measure your hand for the right grip size. Grips range from 4 to 5 inches (10.1 to 12.7 cm) (the extremes being rare) in steps of 1/8 inches (0.31 cm). The main factor is what feels comfortable.

Most strings are 15- or 16-gauge diameters, with 16 gauge being thinner and livelier. Conveniently, manufacturers have established recommended tension ranges for each of their products, varying from 55 to 80 or more pounds of tension. If you are a power hitter, opt for the upper end of the range. Otherwise, stay more toward the middle. Racquets that are prestrung will be in the middle of the recommended range.

The net

The net should be 3 feet (0.915 m) high at the center and 3½ feet (1.07 m) at the posts, with the bottom touching the ground or held down at the center by a net band. The posts should be located 3 feet (0.915 m) outside the sidelines and be equipped with a winch to raise or lower the net to desired height.

Cotton nets are best for indoor courts. The tarred hemp-type nets are best for outdoor because they are waterproof.

Courts

The surface of the court should be smooth, firm and level. It may vary from grass to cement. Hard-surfaced courts afford play soon after rain. Most clay courts in the United States are composition or Rubico and not the red clay of European courts. Clay is particularly suited for match play (from the spectator's point of view) because the ball tends to hit and bounce rather than skid as on a hard-surfaced court, thus producing longer and more involved points. Although hard-surfaced courts cost more to build, they cost less in upkeep.

Dimensions

1. Singles court: 78 x 27 feet (23.8 x 8.24 m)
2. Doubles court: 78 x 36 feet (23.8 x 10.98 m) (4½ foot [1.37 m] alley added to each side)
3. Height of net at center: 3 feet (0.915 m), commonly measured by taking the length of the racquet plus the width of the racquet head (using a normal-size racquet).
4. Height of the net at the posts: 3½ feet (1.07 m)
5. Height of the posts: 3½ feet (1.07)
6. Distance of the posts away from the sidelines: 3 feet (0.915 m)
7. Distance between the baseline and the service line: 18 feet (5.49 m)
8. Distance between the service line and the net: 21 feet (6.41 m).

The endlines are called baselines, and the sidelines are called sidelines. The forecourt is near the net, and the backcourt is near the baselines.

RULES AND SCORING
The singles game

1. One player remains the server for all points of the first game of a match, after which the receiver becomes the server for all points of the second game, and so on alternately for subsequent games of the match.

2. To start a match, the player who wins a "toss" may choose (a) to serve or to receive for the first game, whereupon the other player shall choose the end of the court on which to start, or (b) the end, whereupon the other player shall choose to serve or to receive. The "toss" is typically a spin of a racquet where one player guesses if an identifying mark will land up or down.

3. The server must take up a position behind the base line without touching that line, and between an imaginary extension of the center mark and the singles side line. From that position the server must project the ball into the air by hand and strike it in any fashion (underhand serve is *legal*) before the ball hits the ground.

4. For each point the server is given two opportunities to make one good service into the proper court. To start a game, the server stands to the right of the center mark and attempts to deliver the ball diagonally across the net into the receiver's right service court. When the first point has been completed, the server then stands to the left of the center mark and serves diagonally. Thus, when the total number of completed points is an even number, service attempts are made from the right of the center mark, and from the left when the completed points are an odd number. If a player inadvertently serves from the wrong side of the center mark, play resulting from that service is to be counted, but the improper position of the server must be corrected as soon as it is discovered.

5. A fault is an invalid serve, and is counted as a service attempt. The *foot fault* occurs when the server steps on the base line or into the court before the racquet contacts the ball, or when the server is in contact with the imaginary extension of the center mark or singles die line. However, the serve may legally be made while the server is completely in the air. Another service fault occurs when the server swings with the intent of hitting the ball but misses (although the ball may be tossed and then caught without penalty, so long as no serve is attempted). Finally, the service is a fault if the delivered ball does not land in the proper service court or on a line bounding that court. If the ball touches the net and then lands within the proper service court (including its lines) it is not a fault but a *let*.

6. Any service that is a let does not count as an attempt, and is retaken. In addition, a let may be called by a receiver who was not ready to receive the serve, unless the receiver makes an attempt to return the ball. Any other interruption in normal play from an outside source is

also a let, and the point is replayed. For example, if a ball from a neighboring court interrupts a rally or either of the services, the entire point is replayed, including the two service opportunities for the server.

7. There are no rules that govern the position of the receiver; a station may be taken anywhere, including within the service court. However, the receiver may not strike the served ball until after it has bounced.

8. With the occurrence of a legally served ball, play is continuous as long as the players succeed in making legal returns, even though a returned ball may strike another ball lying within the boundaries of the court. As is true with the service, a ball which lands on a line is considered to have landed in the court bounded by that line. After the service, it is not necessary for either player to allow the ball to bounce before making an attempted return.

9. After the service, a player has made a good return and play continues:
   a. When the ball lands from flight within the proper court.
   b. If the ball strikes and passes over the net and then lands within the proper court.
   c. When a player strikes a ball on his or her side of the net, even though the follow-through carries the racquet over the net without touching it. Note, however, that if a ball has bounced on a player's side of the net, and the spin of the ball causes it to rebound or it is blown back over the net again, that player may then reach over the net to strike the ball, provided the player does not touch the net or the opposing court.

10. The server wins a point when a legal service is not returned, or when a service hits the ground. The receiver wins a point when the server commits two consecutive faults (double fault) or otherwise delivers the ball in an illegal manner. After the service, a player loses a point:
    a. When the ball bounces twice before the player strikes it.
    b. When a returned ball lands outside the opposing court.
    c. When a ball lands within a player's court then strikes a permanent fixture before its second bounce.
    d. Any time a player strikes a ball before it has bounced and fails to make a good return, no matter where the player was standing when the ball was struck.
    e. If the player or the player's clothing or racquet touches the net or net post while the ball is in play.
    f. If the player hits a ball from flight before it has passed to that player's side of the net.
    g. If the ball in play touches a player or anything the player wears or carries except the racquet. A return may legally be made off any part of the racquet.
    h. If the player throws the racquet at and hits the ball.
    i. If the player intentionally interferes with an opponent.

11. Players change sides of the court at the end of the first, third, and every subsequent odd game of each set, and at the end of each set unless the total number of games in a completed set is an even number, in which case the change is not made until the end of the first game of the next set.

Scoring

A player must win at least four *points* to win a game, then at least six games to win a set, and usually at least two sets to win a match. When a player has no points in a game the score is called *love*; the first point is called 15; the second point 30, the third point 40; and on wining the fourth point, that player has won the game, provided that the player is ahead by at least 2 points at that time.

When both players have won 1 point, the score is called 15-all and when both players have won two points, the score is 30-all, but when both players have won three points, the score is called *deuce*. A score of deuce means that one player must win two consecutive points to win the game. The first point won by a player after a deuce score is called *advantage* for that player (often shortened to *ad*). If that point was won by the server it is called *ad in*, and if that point was won by the receiver it is called *ad out*. If the same player who won the advantage point also wins the next point, the game is won by that player. However, if the other player wins the next point, the score returns to deuce, and so on until one player wins two consecutive points after a deuce score.

When a player wins six games and has at that time a lead of at least two games, that player wins the set. If a player wins six games and the opponent has won at least five games, traditional scoring requires that the set by extended until one player has a two-game lead. However, this custom has been replaced by playing a tie-breaker game if the set becomes tied at six games each. In this game the first player to win 7 points with a 2-point advantage wins the set. To start the tie-breaker game, if it is player A's turn to serve the thirteenth game (with the set tied at six games each), that player serves for the first point. Then, player B serves for points 2 and 3. Note that player B serves from the left of the center mark for point 2, then from the right of the center mark for point 3. Next player A serves points 4 and 5, left then right of the center mark. Player B then serves point 6, then the players change sides, followed by player B serving for point 7. The game continues with players alternately serving for 2 points each until one player has won at least 7 points with the necessary 2-point advantage. Players continue to change sides whenever the total number of points played is any multiple of 6.

Points won in a tie-breaker game are called by their numerical value rather than the traditional scoring. After the tie-breaker game, player B becomes the server for the first game of the next set, and the players stay on their sides of the court for that game.

The doubles game

1. The server may stand anywhere between an extension of the center mark and the doubles side line, behind the base line. One player serves for the first game of the set, then a player on the opposing team serves for the second game. The partner of the player who served for the first game then serves for the third game, and the partner of the player who served the second game then serves for the fourth game, and so on for all subsequent games of the set, each player serving every fourth game. A team may elect to change its order of service for the next set.

2. Should a partner serve out of turn, a correction must be made as soon as the mistake is discovered, but play that has been completed before the discovery must be reckoned. If a game has been completed before the erroneous serving order is discovered, the order as altered must then remain for the continuation of the set.

3. One player of teach team must receive all serves in the right service court, and that player's partner must receive all serves in the left service court for the entire set. At the end of any set a team may change its order of receiving for the next set. The order of receiving is not determined by the order of serving.

4. Should a team receive out of turn, the altered receiving order must remain as it is until the end of the game in which the discovery is made, whereafter the partners must resume their original order for the next game they receive.

5. If a served ball strikes the server's partner (including that partner's racquet) it is a service fault, but if a served ball strikes the receiver's partner or racquet before it touches the ground, it is a point for the serving team.

6. If both partners strike the ball for any return, it is a point for their opponents.

7. To play a tie-break game, the player whose turn it was to serve for the thirteenth game of the set (with the score tired six games each) serves for the first point of the game. Thereafter each player serves for 2 points, holding to the same rotation as was used in the set, and following the same change of ends after every 6 points as is true for singles.

ETIQUETTE

There is an ethical code in tennis that obliges every player to maintain a certain spirit within the rules, including giving an opponent the benefit of doubt on line calls, avoiding foot faults during serving, never intentionally distracting an opponent, never stalling in an effort to upset an opponent, and always conducting oneself in a fashion that makes the game enjoyable for everyone. Specific situations are:

1. Any call of "out" on an opponent's ball must be made as soon as possible, before you have sent the ball back across the net.

2. You cannot ask for a replay of a point where you are unable to make a sure call. The rules do not allow it, so the doubt must be resolved in favor of your opponent.

3. You may, however, ask your opponent to make the call on a ball that lands on your side but which you did not clearly see.

4. If you hit a point-ending shot that you see as clearly out, but your opponent thinks is good, you should make the correct call. This applies also to your own serve.

5. However, if you hit a first serve that you saw as out and the receiver, nevertheless, returns the ball for a point-winning placement without making an out call, you must assume the receiver made the return in good faith; therefore, the point counts and you cannot make an out call (which would then allow for your second serve).

6. Whenever a player realizes he or she has committed a violation, that player should make the call immediately. This includes such things as hitting the ball after two bounces, touching the net, or hitting the ball before it has crossed over the net.

7. The server should announce the score of the game prior to serving each point, always calling the server's score first and the receiver's second.

8. If there is a disagreement as to the score and it cannot be resolved, the score should revert back to the last score on which there was agreement.

9. The server should never hit a serve until the receiver has had time to assume a ready position.

10. A serve that is clearly out should not be returned by the receiver.

11. After a point has been placed, return balls directly to the server; do not it them back carelessly.

12. If your ball goes into the adjoining court, wait until the players on that court finish their point before calling for the ball.

13. If a ball from an adjoining court comes into your court, return it to the owners as soon as possible. If it interferes with your point, play a let.

14. In doubles, call service faults for your partner when he or she is the receiver.

15. Try for every point. Tossing points and playing to the audience are insulting to your opponent.

16. In nontournament play, insist on furnishing the balls half of the time, and perhaps more often if you are much the inferior player.

17. Do not damage the court unnecessarily.

FUNDAMENTAL SKILLS AND TECHNIQUES

All strokes in tennis depend on a solid foundation of hitting techniques which give substance to ever shot. These are the basic skill performances that should become automatic for any court situation, as follows:

Stay Relaxed. Tense muscles produce rigid shots that are scattered and faulty. The first requisite for smooth coordinated hitting is to remain relaxed—not lethargic, but calm. Stay loose, yet alive and energetic.

Think rhythm and timing. Give each swing a fluid motion with an unhurried start, a solid middle, and an unrestrained finish.

Be ready to respond. Between shots, maintain a ready-to-reaction position with a low center of gravity, feet shoulder-width apart, knees bent, weight mostly on the toes, and buttocks down. Relax your shoulders, and ease your grip in the racquet.

Pivot the whole body. From the ready-to-respond position, as soon as you sight the oncoming ball, begin to rotate your entire body by turning shoulders, arms, and hips, all together in a neat, packaged backswing that coils the body ready for uncoiling into the foreswing. This is especially critical for hitting a backhand, in which the shoulders play an important power role.

Go forward at impact. At contact with the ball, your weight should be going forward—toward the direction of the intended shot. Bring everything (racquet, arm, shoulders, hips, and knees) forward with the stroke. Feel the energy of your body driving the ball where you want it to go.

Hit the ball early. Contact the ball in your groundstrokes diagonally in front rather than alongside or behind your body. Intercept the ball early in its flight during a volley. Reach up and forward for serves.

Hit through the ball. Make sure the racquet is not quitting its forward speed as it meets the ball. Keep your racquet alive, actively moving through the hitting zone for all shots, including a volley or a lob.

Bend your knees. Never lock your knees when hitting, waiting to hit, serving, or receiving the serve, or playing the net. Flexed knees will allow a smooth shift of weight and provide a uniform, rhythmical swing.

Keep your eyes on the ball. Focus on the ball as it leaves your opponent's racquet, then refocus again after the bounce. Notice how much the ball slows down from its bounce, giving you time to clearly set your sights and organize the coordination of your swing. And on the serve, keep your shin up to see the actual contact.

Coil and uncoil. Every swing is a continuous motion of wind and unwind—coiling into the backswing then uncoiling for the foreswing. No matter how strong the swing, every shot should be a flowing coil-uncoil of effortless energy in motion.

GRIPS

It is important to develop a "feel" for the racquet in your hand—a sensory awareness of the relationship of the racquet to the position of your hand. There is not exact way for every person to hold the racquet, although a grip called the "eastern" offers utility for most players. The "western" grip is seldom used.

Eastern

To achieve the eastern forehand grip, extend a racquet to you with the face perpendicular. Clutch the handle of the racquet as you would when shaking hands. Your palm should be in the same plane as the racquet face. Spread your fingers comfortably wide, and extend your index finger into a "trigger finger" position under the handle. Your thumb will wrap around the handle to contact or lie adjacent to the inside of your middle finger.

The eastern backhand grip has the palm on top of the handle, a quarter-turn from the forehand grip. There's less spread of the fingers, and the thumb runs at a 45-degree diagonal across the back of the handle.

Continental

The continental grip is halfway between the eastern forehand and backhand. There is some logic to employing this grip for the backhand, since it more properly aligns the wrist to provide for a stronger grasp than the eastern backhand.

Two-handed backhand

Players who hit a two-handed backhand can grasp the racquet with both hands effectively in an eastern forehand, or with the lead hand in a continental grip.

GROUNDSTROKES

Backhands and forehands are collectively called groundstrokes. They are the framework upon which all other aspects of the game are built. Effective groundstrokes have the following characteristics:

1. Keep the grip loose to start, firm to hit. Between shots, ease your grip. You'll automatically squeeze the racquet harder as you come into the ball.
2. Get a good shoulder turn for the coil into the backswing, especially for backhand shots, and emphatically if hitting a two-handed backhand.
3. When coiling for a backhand, look over the forward shoulder to sight the approaching ball. Pretend that an arrow extended through both shoulders would point at the ball. Bring the front shoulder down low for a low ball, high for a high ball.
4. Watch the ball all the way into the hitting zone. You do not need to see the ball actually hitting the strings,1 but keep a keen focus on the ball as it approaches the area of contact.
5. Take your weight off your front foot as you coil into the backswing so that you can step forward into the shot.
6. Point the handle of the racquet at the target (the area you want to hit the ball into) in your backswing.
7. Get all your weight into the shot. Accelerate the racquet into the contact point and have your weight going toward the target.
8. On two-handed backhands, keep the trailing arm directly behind the handle at contact, not lifted up with a hunched shoulder.
9. Extend your swing fully through the ball without hesitation, easing up only after contact.
10. Try to carry the ball on the strings as long as you can. Imagine that each ball has three other balls behind it. Try to thread the racquet through all four as you swing.

THE SERVE

Serving is a truly enthralling part of tennis. It's enlivening, arousing, and catalytic of the rest of one's game. However, the act is hardly more difficult than throwing a ball.

1. Serving is a dynamic, whole-body act. Start with an attitude of mental and physical freedom. If you hold back, you tighten your muscles and the swing has a cement-arm feeling. Instead, relax your whole self. Let your arm go limber.
2. To prepare for the serving motion, take up a throwing stance behind the base line. Stand as if you are going to toss a ball over the net.
3. Image the spot, in the air, where the racquet will meet the ball. Hold the ball in your tossing hand directly beneath that spot. Cradle the ball in the fingers, not in your palm, and point your thumb toward the imagined spot of contact.
4. Hold the ball and racquet in front of you, together, more-or-less pointed toward the target service court.
5. Start the serving motion with both arms, then continue into the windup without pause or hesitation. There is no hurry at the start, but no static halt at any point in the windup.
6. Lift the ball up unhurriedly, using your thumb as a guide to point toward the final destination of the toss.
7. Coil your body, similar to preparing for a forehand, and bring the racquet around behind you with the handle pointing toward the tossed ball.
8. Most or all of your weight should come to the back foot as you toss and wind up. Add some bend to your knees.
9. Start your foreswing into the ball from the ground up. That is, the knees rebound from their bend, the backbone uncoils, the hitting shoulder catapults toward the ball, and the arm thrashes up and over with the elbow unbending and the wrist adding a final vigorous snap that makes the racquet feel like a whip.
10. Build speed as you go. Feel like at the moment you hit the ball your swing is still gaining momentum. The whole swing is upward and forward in a clean arc that starts slows and finishes fast.

RETURN OF SERVE

There is no more neglected phase of tennis than the return of serve. Yet the techniques for success are surprisingly simple.

1. Stand in the middle of the widest possible area into which the server can hit, and as far in as you can and still feel confident in being able to hit under control.

2. Hold the racquet loosely, directly in front of you, with your body flexed and your weight on the front of your feet.

3. Go to meet a wide serve by moving diagonally forward, on a path 90 degrees to the flight of the ball. Move toward the ball, not away from it.

4. The harder the serve, the more the swing for the return must be compact, with less backswing, but no restriction on the follow-through.

5. Keep a solid, firm wrist as you come into the ball, especially on hard serves.

6. Have a "scrambling" attitude. Do anything to get the ball back.

PLAYING THE FORECOURT

The liveliest tennis occurs at the net. Go up to the net often, not only for the tactical advantage it presents, but also because it adds dimension to the game. However, approach the net only after your opponent hits a ball that lands shallow in your court or when you hit a ball that you believe will force your opponent to reply with a weak return. Once at the net, your two offensive weapons are the volley and the overhead.

The volley

1. A volley is a short stroke. It's a compact and firm black of the ball—a punch rather than a swing.

2. However, the weaker the opponent's return is, the more your volley stroke can resemble a regular groundstroke.

3. The ball should be contacted early, before it gets to the side of your body.

4. Generally, keep a vise-tight grip for the stroke and *drive* the racquet into the ball rather than just using the strings as a trampoline.

5. Reach for a wide ball by quickly turning your shoulders and pushing into a short step with your lead foot and, if necessary, following with a cross-over step with your trail foot.

6. Stay ready with your racquet head chin-high, in front of you.

7. Defend the net like an ice hockey goalie. Attach the ball! Hit every ball you can reach, aggressively when you can.

Overheads

1. You must get under and *in back* of the lofted ball. Skip-step into position. Keep your legs alive, with knees unlocked, for last-minute adjustments.

2. The overhead is like a serve, but the windup is more compact. Forget any fancy windup. Just get the racquet up and over your shoulder, like you were an archer reaching back to pull an arrow out of the quiver.

3. Turn sideways as you arrive at your hitting place and rivet your eyes on the ball.

4. Make contact with the ball more in front of you than for a serve.

5. Hit the ball with as much power as you can control. The overhead is not a push or a punch, so crack off a point winner.

THE LOB

Use a lob to loft the ball over an opposing net player, or when you need time to recover court position.

1. Let the racquet do the work. There is no need to lift your whole body into the shot.

2. Shorten the backswing. Get the racquet *under* the point of contact, then hit upward and forward in the same plane as the height you want to give to the ball.

3. Try to hold the ball on the strings as long as possible, and follow through into the path of the ball.

4. Keep a firm wrist for the stroke.

5. Whenever you can, hit the ball just over the reach of your opponent's racquet. Always provide enough clearance—hit too high rather than too low.

6. When under pressure, do anything to get the ball up and give it extra height.

HALF VOLLEY

This is a difficult shot and should be avoided by playing either at the net or in the backcourt. When this shot is necessary, use the following techniques.

1. Bend the knees to get down to the ball.

2. Watch the ball all the way to the racquet.

3. Use no preliminary swing but execute a full follow-through, hitting with a great deal of lift to make the ball drop into the court.

4. Stop and balance the weight forward at contact.

5. Use a firm rigid twist and get the proper angle to the racquet. This angle is somewhat over the ball.

6. After hitting the shot, move to the net rather than remaining in the middle of the court.

SPIN

A topspin (forward spin) causes the ball to drop rapidly and hence may be hit hard and fairly high above the net and still fall in court.

A cut or slice (backward spin) causes the ball to float or sail; it has a short, low, slow bounce. It may cause the net player to hit the ball into the net or out of bound.

On service, a right-hand slice bounces to the left and curves to the left. An "American" service curves to the left and down but bounces to the right and high.

GENERAL REMINDERS

At any level of play, there are on-court behaviors which are important parts of quality play.

1. Think positively about your game. Be in command of your physical responses.
2. Think of the racquet as part of you—an extension of your hitting arm.
3. Make every stroke a continuous, rhythmical, fluid action.
4. Hit the ball with your entire body, not just your arm.
5. Keep your style somewhat freelanced and not bound by a compulsion to have perfect, picture-book form.
6. Focus your attention on the ball in play, not your opponent, the net, the base line, or a previous errant shot.
7. Play dynamic, aggressive, spontaneous tennis.
8. Relish every chance to hit the ball. Enjoy the sheer physical pleasure of playing the game.

EFFECTIVE PRACTICE

Practice is the basis of improvement. It is the time to discipline your muscles so that in the next match your mind can focus on the enjoyment of the game instead of the mechanics of your swing.

Create muscle memory. If there is no structure to practice it becomes too easy to slip into lethargic habits such as not bending the knees or failing to transfer the weight properly. Keep your thoughts on the fundamentals of the game, looking first at your grip, then checking your pivot an backswing. Give special attention to accelerating the racquet into the ball. Try to train your muscles with free-flowing strokes.

Rehearse offense and defense. Offensive tennis is built around hitting the ball consistently deep into your opponent's court and hitting powerful serves. Practice these with flair, trying to land every ground stroke behind the opponent's service line, and hitting serves with extra flamboyance. But also rehearse the defensive shots you'll need in competition, such as a well-lofted lob and returns of strong serves.

Make practice like a game. Part of every practice should stimulate the game or segments of the game so that it's not merely hitting the ball back and forth without purpose. Creating gamelike circumstances makes practice more interesting and gives incentive to do well.

Practice specific shots. Have a partner feed you the type of shot you want to practice. For instance, if you want to rehearse overheads ask to have lobs hit to you. Often it's better if your partner hits a bucket of balls to you, without attempting to return your shots. After the bucket is exhausted, switch roles so that you can aid; your partner's practice.

Play specific points. Try to stage playing situations. Be inventive with these drills, but make them as close to reality as possible. For example, you can play a three-ball rally whereby your partner feeds a ball to you that you hit for a deep shot and then follow with a charge to the net. Your partner, hot bothering to flag down your shot, hits another ball to you that you can volley, and then lifts another ball for you to hit as na overhead. Or, while your partner is practicing serves, you could practice returns by attempting to return every serve, in or out, while your partner does not chase your returns but attends only to serving.

Include aerobic conditioning. Practice can be arranged to incorporate rehearsal of skills and aerobic conditioning for tennis play. A good drill is an all-court scramble where your partner has a bucket of balls and hits a variety of placements to any part of your court. You chase down and return every ball you can, and your partner continues to act as a feeder without retrieving shots.

Practice in logical sequence. Warm up properly, then hit easily for the first few minutes. Next, give your shots plenty of depth, then try for placements into a particular area of the court. Play some "rapid fire," when you and your practice partner stand across the net from each other, just inside the service line, and hit volley after volley to each other. Then hit serves and returns of serve. Play match situations. Then do drills that include aerobic conditioning and finish off the session with free hitting in which you focus solely on rhythm and form.

Make practice fun. Add variety to the session. Experiment with different techniques or add spin to the ball. Or, play some points when the only rule is that the ball must cross over the net. Let practice be therapeutic and spark renewed interest in the game. Remember that tennis is a game. Its purpose should be to add enjoyment to your life.

STRATEGY

The strategy for effective play in tennis is remarkably uncomplicated. Most situations in a game have automatic answers or, at least, sensible responses.

Singles

Keep the ball in play. The first rule of tennis strategy is to hit the ball over the net, land it in bound, and do this one more time than an opponent on each point. The worst mistake is to hit the ball into the net. It's a dead loss, never giving an opponent a chance to commit an error. Rather than trying constantly for point winners, loft the ball with enough room to clear the net by several feet. Give your opponent opportunities to misplay the ball.

Keep the ball deep. An associated tactic is to consistently place the ball deep. This will compel an opponent to stay back, hitting incessantly from behind the base line, with little chance to come up to the net to hit point winners. You'll also give yourself more time between points as the longer returns from your opponent allow you to move into a better hitting position on each ball and to collect yourself for a rhythmical, free-flowing swing.

Know when to use angles. When your opponent offers a shallow ball, take advantage of the expanded angles for placing your return. The further inside the court you can move to hit, the greater the potential is for hitting an angled shot toward either side line. If you are also pulled off to one side of your court for this shallow ball, the situation then becomes more favorable for hitting a cross-court return.

Use the forecourt often. Go up to the net as often as you can, even if you're still uncertain about your ability. Your presence alone may be enough to force a jittery opponent into committing errors. And once at the net, finish the point as quickly a possible. Try to hit every ball out of your opponent's reach.

Get the first serve in. Too often players assume they should bash away at the first serve and, upon failure, push the second. Instead, slow down the pace of the first serve and increase the pace of the second. This makes first serves successful more often, and keeps your opponent from stepping up to hit winners off your second serve.

Play percentage tennis. An overall guide is to ask (1) What do you do best? and (2) Where is your opponent weakest? Use your strengths. Note what an opponent cannot do well and play to that flaw often. That way you'll win instead of trying to avoid losing.

Doubles

Take the net. Doubles is a net game. The basic and overriding objective is to gain control of the net, from where most points are won. Both players should get into the forecourt at every opportunity to take command of the point.

Hit high percentage serves. Control the pace of your serve. If you can, hit it mostly to the receiver's backhand side where it will generate a softer return, giving your net-playing partner more time to reach the ball and volley a winner.

Hit away from a net player. When one opponent is at the net and the other back, hit the ball past the net player. It is especially important to return a serve back toward the server, deep if you can. Alternatively, lift a lob over the net player.

Exploit open space. Doubles teams are often overprotective of the alleys and thus play too far apart. Send the ball up the middle often, where the two of them may hesitate an instant due to uncertainty over who will take the ball. However, when given a chance to hit cross-court, take advantage of the wide doubles court. Use the angle opportunity, but provide a margin for error by aiming to land the ball on the singles side line.

Cover the empty space. Tie an imaginary rope between you and your partner. If your partner is forced off the side of the court, let the rope pull you over to cover the now-wider area of return space that is presented to your opponents. Always stay in the middle of the court space that's left over when your teammate is pushed out of position.

TEACHING CONSIDERATIONS

1. The techniques of skilled hitting have a common denominator of physics. Regardless of how contradictory different players' styles appear to be, at the critical microsecond when racquet and ball are in contact, everyone must impart the same force to achieve the same end. Learn the physics that apply to hitting a tennis ball, then help students to understand those laws and evaluate how well they are doing in relation to them.

2. Keep instructions simple. It's easy to become overloaded with instructional facts about each stroke. At some point a learner will no longer handle all the information while simultaneously trying to organize commands about what the muscles should do. The best method is often the simplest. Focus on only the most important aspects of hitting.

3. Attend mostly to the rhythmical patterns of the swing. Encourage learners to first develop

smooth, flowing motions for each swing, without necessarily judging their swings on the basis of where the ball goes. Emphasize the coiling and uncoiling and the position of the body relative to the ball. Have them think of the *art* of tennis. Make them "look good" as they hit. Focus their attention on the sensation of rhythm and timing for every swing.

4. Play lots of "mini-tennis" games to emphasize rhythm and proper position. Have one partner stand at the net and toss the ball on one bounce to the hitter; then switch roles. Or have partners stand on opposite sides of the net at the service lines and rally the ball trying to keep it within the boundaries of the service court. Provide students with games in which they can have instant success by making it possible to develop a "feel" for the game.

5. Become target oriented. Introduce rallying for specific targets. For example, to improve the depth of everyone's shots, stretch a piece of cord across the court several feet inside the base line to act as an aim point for deep groundstrokes. For the serve, stand a ball can inside each corner of the service court as targets. Or exchange groundstrokes using the alley as in the in-bounds area.

6. A common mistake is to turn the head prematurely, looking up to see where the ball is going before it's hit. Have players attend to all the dimensions of the ball as they follow it into the hitting zone. Focus on the spin, trying to actually see the seams of the ball. Or, note the color the ball and try to heighten its hues as it approaches. Create the habit of refocusing on the ball after its bounce. The play "bounce-and-hit" whereby both partners say "bounce" every time the ball bounces (including on the opposite side of the net), and "hit" every time a player strikes the ball. This will help players to refocus after the bounce and to concentrate on the ball rather than on mechanical parts of the swing.

7. The service toss is a major headache for many players. To often they throw it, or force it into the air with an exaggerated lift of the knees. Isolate the toss by practicing it alone, perhaps starting with the tossing hand resting against the inside of the forward thigh, then lifting and releasing the ball as if settling it on a shelf at hitting height. Place a racquet on the ground, the head in front and inside the forward foot. Toss the ball to proper height and allow it to drop to see if it will land on the racquet face.

8. Teach beginners to serve with a four-part but continuous sequence, as follows: (1) start with both hands held together, elbows bent, racquet pointed in the direction of the target court; (2) drop both hands down at the same time, toward the forward thigh; (3) bring both arms up together to release the ball and arc the racquet behind the hitting shoulder; then (4) deliver the racquet into the back of the ball with an accelerating forward swing. Have students say "down-together, up-together swing" as they practice the motion of the serve.

9. Arrange from variants of the game to encourage certain skills. For example, play a ground stroke game without the serve in which each point begins with one player hitting a ground stroke and the ball must cross the net three times before a point can be scored (this will encourage controlled rallies). Or practice second serves by playing games in which only one serve is allowed. Or, play games in which the server hits half-speed and only backhands are allowed thereafter.

10. Make practice fun. Add variety to the sessions, sometimes doing such things as hitting the ball with the racquet held in the nondominant hand. Play some points where the only rule is that the ball must cross over the net and land before the fence. Or, have a rule that after every shot players must run up and touch the net with their racquets. Try a game in which, on each side, a players hits a shot and then must hand the racquet off to another play for the next shot.

Badminton

Badminton

Completion of this chapter should enable the reader to:

- Appreciate the versatility of the game of badminton

- Be cognizant of the important considerations for selecting and caring for badminton equipment

- Understand the rules and scoring procedures of the game

- Describe the correct grip, wrist action, ready position, footwork, strokes, and shots

- Understand badminton strategy and etiquette

- Instruct a group of students in the fundamentals of badminton

- Emphasize skill, stamina, and athletic ability necessary for badminton competition

- Recognize and use badminton terms correctly

HISTORY

A game with some sort of racquet and a feathered object goes far back into history. A game similar to badminton (Shuttlecock kicking) was played in China as early as the fifth century AD, and there is mention of the game as long ago as the twelfth century in the Royal Court records of England.

Battledore shuttlecock was popular in King James I time, so it is not surprising that the game was played by early English settlers in America.

The portrait "Young Prince Sulkonsik" by Adam Mangoki, who lived about 1700, shows young members of the Royal Family of Poland holding a shuttlecock and racquet with a stance similar to that used by a modern expert preparing to serve. A portrait by Jean Simeon Chardin (1699-1779) hanging in the Uffizi Gallery in Florence depicts a girl with a racquet and shuttle.

"Portrait of Master Stephen Crossfield" hangs in the Metropolitan Museum of Art, New York, Painted by American William Williams (1727-1791), it depicts a young man holding a battledore (racquet) and shuttlecock.

It is generally accepted that the modern game of badminton, involving court boundaries and a winning objective, was named when a group of British army officers home on leave from India around 1873 played the game at Badminton, the country estate of the Duke of Beaufort in Gloucestershire, England. In 1878 the Badminton club of the city of New York was founded. Records in the New York City Museum of History substantiate that this is the oldest organized badminton club in the world. This club was the leading social rendezvous in New York for 25 years. Such names as Astor, Roosevelt, Rockerfeller, and Vanderbilt appeared on the membership list. Badminton was in its "heyday" in the United States in the 1930s when thousands of players, including famous athletes and Hollywood stars, enjoyed the game.

The American Badminton Association was founded in 1936. This association changed its name in 1977 to the United States Badminton Association.

The second organized badminton club was founded in Ireland in 1899. This organization was a founding member of the International Badminton Federation (IBF) in 1934. (The first badminton played internationally was a match between England and Ireland in Dublin in 1903.) The original IBF included nine national badminton organizations. By 1939 the tally had risen to 15; today there are more than 90. The Thomas Cup competition for men's teams was started in 1948; the Uber Cup competition for women's teams was started in 1956. Strangely, no European country has yet won either trophy. Malaysia, Indonesia, and China have shared the 15

216

competitions for the men's trophy. The women's trophy was won three times by the United States, three times by Japan, and then by Indonesia and China. Additional international competition is provided by the Asian games, the British Commonwealth games, the South East Asian games, and the Pan American matches. In 1977 the first official world championship was held in Malmo, Sweden; tournaments are now scheduled every two years.

Badminton was a demonstration sport in the 1972 Olympics and an exhibition sport at the 1988 Olympics. It will be a full medal sport for the first time at Barcelona, Spain in 1992. Badminton is now part of the U.S. Olympic Festival which is held every non-Olympic year.

CARRYOVER VALUES
Badminton offers fun and fitness for everyone. It is a sport that is easy to learn but difficult to master. A beginning player receives pleasure and exercise immediately, and an advanced player can get an extremely vigorous workout by playing just one game with an equally skilled opponent. Research studies of movement show that a badminton player uses more arm action in one match than the average baseball pitcher does in a nine-inning baseball game. Also, a top-flight badminton player runs more in one match than a running back or end does in a 60-minute football game.

Badminton is played by women, men, and children. Thus it is often called the family sport. Adaptability to small areas, indoors and outdoors, at a minimal cost provides an opportunity for everyone to participate. For advanced players who wish to compete, tournament play is available almost anywhere in the United States. Tournaments sponsored by local badminton clubs (there are over 250) sanctioned by the U.S. Badminton Association provide tournament competition for juniors, women's singles, men's singles, women's doubles, men's doubles, mixed doubles, senior men's singles, senior doubles (men's and women's), and senior mixed doubles. In addition most tournaments provide play for persons aged 40 years and older. The United States has junior (18 and under), adult (19 to 39), senior (40+), masters (50+), grand masters (60+) and golden master (70+) championships.

SELECTION AND CARE OF EQUIPMENT
In all sports, good equipment is a prerequisite to good play. Badminton is no exception. For the beginner, good used equipment is often preferable to cheap new equipment.

The racquet
1. Weight depends on the strength of the individual and the feeling of comfort with the racquet.
   a. Most good racquets are between 3 and 4 ounces (85-113 g).
   b. Smaller players should select light racquets for better maneuverability.
2. Racquets should be evenly balanced or slightly lighter in the head.
   a. Doubles players usually prefer lighter racquets because quicker shots are possible.
   b. Point of balance is normally 11 to 13½ inches (24-28 cm) from the bottom of the handle.
3. Handle (grip):
   a. Size depends on size of hand.
   b. Normal racquet grips vary between 3½ and 3 5/8 (8.9-9.2 cm) inches.
   c. The player should try several sizes and pick the ones that feels best.
4. Strings:
   a. Nylon is relatively immune to moisture, inexpensive, longer lasting than gut, and preferred for class use and beginners because of its serviceability and cost.
   b. Gut is expensive, less durable than nylon, not moisture proof, and requires special care, but it is preferred by more advanced and tournament players because of its resiliency and "playability."
   c. Gut and nylon are normally strung to tensions around 20 pounds.
5. Care of the racquet:
   a. Frayed strings should be replaced before they break to prevent loosening of string tension.
   b. Racquets should be kept away from extreme heat or extreme cold.
6. Other types of racquets:
   a. Metal racquets are very durable. Most are some combination of carbon, ceramic, graphite, or other material.
   b. Graphite racquets are popular among advanced players because they are light, give a whipping action, and provide a subtle sensitivity to the shuttlecock.

Shuttlecocks
Shuttles are made either of goose feathers or nylon. There are several kinds of feather shuttles, and the price varies depending on the quality of the feathers and construction of the shuttle. Feather shuttles are usually used for tournaments, but because of feather

breakage, these shuttles usually last only one or two games. Feathers can be pointed or rounded on the tip. The feather shuttle should be kept in a moist environment to prevent the feathers from drying out. This can be done by wrapping a moist towel around the tube 24 hours prior to use. Nylon shuttles are best for class use because they last several weeks and require no special environment.

The International Badminton Federation has defined the correct speed of a shuttlecock. Recorded in the IBF Statute Book, Law 4 states that "A shuttlecock shall be deemed to be of correct pace if, when a player of average strength strikes it with a full underhand stroke from a spot immediately above one back boundary line in a line parallel to the sidelines, and at an upward angle, it falls not less than 1 foot (30.5 cm) and not more than 2½ feet (76.2 cm) short of the other back boundary line." This statement needs to be further explained for those not accustomed to testing shuttles. The problem is to determine the shuttle speed at the particular time and place. The manufacturer has previously determined the speed by weighing the shuttle. The measure of weight is by grains (approximately 1/6 ounce). Shuttles weigh 73 to 85 grains.

In making the test, attention should be given to the point of contact of the shuttle and the racquet. It should be directly above the back boundary line, which means that the person testing the shuttle should have both feet behind the back boundary line, that is, outside of the court area.

The distance between the long service line for doubles and the back boundary line is 2½ feet. A shuttle of correct pace when tested properly will fall within 9 inches of either side of the doubles service line.

Students and teachers of badminton should know how to test a shuttle and should test those in use. When ordering shuttles, whether feathered or nylon, indicate a shuttle speed to suit the particular time (winter, summer), altitude, and area of the country (north, east, south, west) in which they are to be used. The speed of the shuttle determines the type of game that results. It requires an undue amount of effort and strain to clear a slow shuttle overhead from back line to back line; to clear a backhand the length of the court is almost impossible. The game becomes one of brute force, and the stronger person will prevail. The game should be one of speed, finesse, deception, control, and power.

The net and standards
The net is 5 feet 1 inch (1.56 m) in height from the surface of the court at the post. The posts should be sufficiently firm to keep the net stretched and are placed on the side boundary lines of the court. Where this is not practicable, some method must be used for indicating the position of the side boundary line where it passes under the net, such as by the use of a thin post or strip of material, not less than 1½ inches (3.8 cm) in width, fixed to the side boundary line and rising vertically to the net cord. Where this is in use on a court marked for doubles, it should be placed on the side boundary line of the doubles court irrespective of whether singles or doubles are being played.

The net is made of fine natural cord or artificial fiber of a dark color and an even thickness not exceeding 5/8 to 3¼ inch (1.5 to 2 cm) mesh. It should be firmly stretched from post to post and is 2 feet 6 inches (0.765 m) in depth. The top of the net is 5 feet (1.53 m) from the floor at the center and 5 feet 1 inch (1.56 m) at the posts, and it is edged with 3-inch (7.62 cm) white tape doubled and supported by a cord or cable run through the tape and strained over nd flush with the top of the posts.

HOW TO LAY OUT A COURT
If two or more courts are laid out side by side, a minimum of 6½ (2 m) feet should be allowed between them. In laying out a home court in the backyard, either tape of dry lime can be used for the boundary lines. For the gymnasium, the boundary lines are defined by white or yellow lines 1.5 inches (4 cm) wide. In laying ut a badminton court at home, the singles and doubles courts can be combined. The doubles playing court is the same length (13.4 m) as the singles playing court but is 0.92 m wider.

The ceiling height of a court used for international competitive play is a minimum of 39 feet (12 m) from the floor over the full court.

RULES
The object of the game is to hit the shuttlecock back and forth across the net with the racquet without permitting it to touch the ground, endeavoring to hit it into the opposing court so that it cannot be returned.

Scoring
The doubles and men's singles games consist of 15 points. When the score is 13 all, the side that first reached 13 has the option of "setting" the game to 5, and if the score becomes 14 all, the side that first reached 14 has the option of "setting" the game to 3. After a game has been "set," the score is called "love all," and the side that first scores 5 or 3 points (whichever set has been exercised) wins the game. In

either case the option to "set" the game must be made before the next service is delivered after the score has reached 13 all or 14 all.

The women's singles game consists of 11 points. When the score is 9 all the player who first reached 9 has the option of "setting" the game to 3, or when the score is 10 all the player who first reached 10 has the option of "setting" the game to 2.

The opposing sides contest the best of three games. The players change ends at the start of the second game and also at the start of the third game (if any). In the third game the players change ends when the leading score reaches 8 in a game of 15 points or 6 in a game of 11 points. When it has been agreed to play only one game the players change ends as provided for the third game.

If players forget to change ends, the ends are changed immediately as the mistake is discovered and the existing score stands.

Faults

A fault made by a player on the side that is "in" (has the serve) puts the server out; if made by a player whose side is "out," it counts as a point to the "in" side.

It is a fault:

1. If, in serving, the shuttle at the instant of being struck is higher than the server's waist, or if at the instant of the shuttle being struck, the shaft of the racquet is not pointing sufficiently downward that the whole head of the racquet is discernibly below the whole of the server's hand holding the racquet.

2. If, in serving, the shuttle falls into the wrong service court (into the one not diagonally opposite to the server) or falls short of the short service line, beyond the long service line, or outside the side boundary lines of the service court into which service is in order.

3. If the server's feet ar not in the service court from which service is at the time being in order, or if the feet of the player receiving the service ar not in the service court diagonally opposite until the service is delivered.

4. If before or during the delivery of the service any player makes preliminary feints or otherwise intentionally balks (tries to deceive) the opponent, or if any player deliberately delays serving the shuttle or getting ready to receive it, so as to obtain an unfair advantage.

5. If, either is service or play, the shuttle falls outside the boundaries of the court, or passes through or under the net, or fails to pass the net, or touches the roof or side walls, or touches the person or dress of a player. A shuttle falling on a line is deemed to have fallen in the court or service court of which such line is a boundary.

6. If the shuttle in play is struck before it crosses to the striker's side of the net. The striker may, however, follow the shuttle over the net with the racquet in the course of the stroke.

7. If, when the shuttle is in play, a player touches the net or its supports with racquet, person, or dress.

8. If the shuttle is held on the racquet (that is, caught or slung) during the execution of a stroke, or if the shuttle is hit twice in succession by the same player with two strokes, or if the shuttle is hit by a player and partner successively.

9. If a player obstructs an opponent.

General

The server may not serve until the opponent is ready, but the opponent is deemed to be ready if a return of the service is attempted.

The server and the player served to must stand within the limits of their respective service courts (as bounded by the short and long service, the center and side lines), and some part of both feet of these players must remain in contact with the surface of the court in a stationary position until the service is delivered. A foot on or touching a line in the case of either the server or the receiver is held to be outside the service court. The respective partners may take up any position, provided they do not unsight or otherwise obstruct an opponent.

If, in the course of service or rally, the shuttle touches and passes over the net, the stroke is not invalidated thereby. It is a good return if the shuttle, having passed outside either post, drops on or within the boundary lines of the opposite court. A "let" may be give by the umpire for any unforeseen or accidental hindrance.

If, in service or during a rally, a shuttle, after passing over the net, is caught in or on the net, it is a "let."

If the receiver is faulted for moving before the service is delivered or for not being within the correct service court, and at the same time the server is also faulted for service infringement, it is considered a "let."

When a "let" occurs, the play since the last service does not count, and the player who last served serves again.

If the server in serving misses the shuttle completely, it is a fault; but if the shuttle is touched by the racquet, a service is delivered.

If a player has the chance of striking the shuttle when quite near the net, the opponent must not extend the racquet near the net. A player may, however, hold up the racquet for protection to avoid being hit in the face if this action does not result in obstructing the opponent's stroke.

It is the duty of the umpire to call "fault" or "let" should either occur, without appeal being made by the players, and to give a decision on any appeal regarding a point in dispute, if made before the net service, and also to appoint linesmen and service judges at the umpire's discretion. The umpire's decision is final, but the decision of a linesman or service judge should be upheld. This does not preclude the umpire also from faulting the server or receiver.

Singles play

The players serve from and receive service in their respective right-hand service courts only when the server's score is 0 or an even number of points, the service being delivered from and received in their lift-hand service courts when the server's score is an odd number of points. "Setting" does not affect this sequence.

Both players change service courts after each point has been scored.

Doubles play

It having been decided which side is to have the first service, the player in the right-hand service court of that side commences the game by serving to the player in the service court diagonally opposite. If the latter player returns the shuttle before it touches the ground, it is to be returned by one of the "in" (serving) side and then returned by one of the "out" (receiving) side, and so on, until a fault is made or the shuttle ceases to be "in play." If a fault is made by the "in" side, its right to continue serving is lost, as only one player of the side beginning a game is entitled to do so, and the opponent in the right-hand service court then becomes the server; but if the service is not returned or the fault is made by the "out" side, the "in" side scores a point. The "in" side players then change from one service court to the other, the service now being from the left-hand service court to the player in the service court

diagonally opposite. So long as a side remains "in," service is delivered alternately from each service court into the one diagonally opposite, the change being made by the "in" side when, and only when, a point is added to its score.

The first service of a side in each inning is made from the right-hand service court. a "service" is delivered as soon as the shuttle is struck by the server's racquet. The shuttle is thereafter "in play" until it touches the floor or playing surface or until a gault or "let" occurs. After the service is delivered, the server and the player served to may take up any position they choose on their side of the net, irrespective of boundary lines.

Only the player served to may receive the service; however, should the shuttle touch or be struck by his or her partner, the "in" side scores a point. No player may receive tow consecutive services in the same game.

Only one player of the side beginning a game is entitled to serve in its first innings. In all subsequent innings, each partner has the right, and they serve consecutively. The side winning a game always serves first in the nest game, but either of the winners may serve and either of the losers may receive the service.

If a player serves out of turn or from the wrong service court and the serving side wins the rally, it is a "let," provided that such "let" is claimed and allowed or ordered by the umpire before the next succeeding service is delivered.

If a player of the "out" side standing in the wrong service court is prepared to receive the service when it is delivered, and the receiving side wins the rally, it is a "let," provided that such "let" is calmed and allowed or ordered by the umpire before the next succeeding service is deliver.

If in either of the previous cases the side at fault loses the rally, the mistake stands and the players' position is not corrected.

Should a player inadvertently change sides incorrectly and the mistake not be discovered until after the next succeeding service has been delivered, the mistake stands, and a "let" cannot be claimed or allowed, and the players' position is not corrected.

FUNDAMENTAL SKILLS AND TECHNIQUES
Grip of the racquet
1. Forehand grip: The handle of the racquet is held as if the player were shaking hands with the racquet.
2. Backhand grip: Similar to the forehand grip except the hand is rotated slightly to the left and the thumb is placed flat against the side bevel

for additional power. The changing of grips during play becomes somewhat automatic.

3. The racquet should be held at the extreme end of the handle with fingers well spread.
4. A standard grip may be secured by placing the racquet, as the player normally would, in front of the body, with the playing surface perpendicular to the floor and then grasping the racquet as one would grip the handle of a hatchet.
5. The standard grip can be used for both forehand and backhand strokes.
6. The hand, wrist, and arm should be entirely relaxed but the fingers should tighten on the handle just before the racquet contacts the shuttle.

Wrist action

1. Wrist action is used to disguise intentions. A simple flick of the wrist aids not only in directing the shuttle but also in sending the opponent in the wrong direction, since the flight is concealed until the last fraction of a second.
2. In starting all shots, the player should keep the racquet well back by cocking the wrist. The racquet's forward swing should not be checked; follow-through is important.

Ready position and footwork

To move properly on a badminton court, the player must start from a constantly maintained "ready" position. The ideal starting position on the court is approximately a step and a half from the short line and straddling the center line. The player who does not reach this ideal position on the court before the opponent hits the shuttle should stop and react to where the shuttle is hit. A player should never be moving as the opponent is hitting the shuttle.

The correct stance is similar to that of an infielder in baseball expecting a grounder. Weight should be on the balls of the feet, with the feet far enough apart to assure stable balance. The body should be ready to spring in any direction. The knees should be slightly bent. The racquet head should be held at about shoulder height comfortably away from the body.

In the ready position the feet are in the 12 o'clock position. To cover the court properly a speed line should be set up to get to the 1 o'clock, 3 o'clock, and 5 o'clock positions for a forehand stroke. Movement to the right, for a forehand stroke, at these positions on the court involves moving the body's center of gravity in the direction of the shuttle. For the backhand stroke the speed line should

be set up to 7 o'clock, 9 o'clock, and 11 o'clock positions.

STROKES
Service
High deep serve

The high deep serve is an underhand forehand serve hit high so that the shuttle will hand in deep court, near the back line.

1. Starting position: Feet in stride position with left foot in front for right-handed players. Shift weight to the rear on backswing, then forward as racquet comes forward. Both feet must remain in contact with the court; "stepping" is a fault.
2. A full backswing is made with the wrist cocked.
3. The wrist is uncocked just prior to contact.
4. Follow-through: Shuttle contact is made well in front of the body, not at the side, on the follow-through of the underhand stroke.

Low short serve

The low short serve should be made in such a manner that the shuttle barely clears the net, is on a downward trajectory the moment it passes over the net, and lands close to the short line in the opponent's court.

All basic techniques for the low short serve-- starting position, body rotation, shift in weight, and so on--are the same as for the deep high serve except:

1. This is a "push" type of serve, accomplished with the wrist remaining almost fully cocked throughout the serve, with little rotation of the forearm.
2. The server should attempt to contact the shuttle as close to the waist height as possible to achieve the desired flat trajectory.

Drive serve

The drive serve is comparable to hitting a line drive in baseball. This serve can be driven at the opponent preferably to hit just below shoulder level.

Basic techniques for the drive serve--starting position, body rotation, and so on--are the same as for the deep high serve except:

1. The racquet is partially uncocked at contact with the shuttle.
2. Inasmuch as the racquet does not go beyond half cock, there is not a complete follow-through in a full arc, as in the high

221

deep serve.

Forehand overhead shots
Forehand overhead shots begin with the player's weight from the right to the left foot. Body rotation occurs here.

Defensive clear shot
1. The racquet is angled slightly back from the perpendicular to attain a high trajectory.
2. Contact with the shuttle is high and slightly in front of the player.
3. The player should hit the shuttle high and deep and assume proper court position as a receiver.

Attacking clear shot
1. This is the same shot as the defensive clear, except the head of the racquet is almost perpendicular to the floor on contact with the shuttle, giving it a flattened trajectory.
2. This is a quick hit used primarily to place the shuttle deep and out of reach of the opponent.
3. The object of this shot is to get the shuttle past an out-of-position opponent.

Smash
1. Deception on this "put away" or kill shot is accomplished by making it appear that the return will be a "clear" or "drop."
2. The body should be facing the net on completion of the shot.
3. One should lead with the elbow as the body rotates. The arm should be straight on contact with the shuttle.
4. This shot is an extension of the overhead clear, except contact is made with the shuttle farther in front of the body and angle of the racquet is slightly forward.
5. Vigorous wrist action just prior to contact provides the velocity for the smash.

Drop
1. For a fast drop, the racquet is held at approximately the same angle as for the smash at contact. It should be hit like a smash, except with a softer touch.

Backhand overhead shots
The player's back is to the net. The forearm is bent toward the chest for the "ready" position. On striking the shuttle, the arm is extended and the forearm is simultaneously rotated in a clockwise direction. The angles at contact, the placement of the shuttle int eh opponent's court, and the use of backhand overhead

shots are the same as for forehand overhead shots.

Drive shots
The shuttle is hit quickly, forehand or backhand, on a flat trajectory. The forearm drive action is similar to that of throwing a baseball sidearm.
1. In both forehand and backhand, one should lead with the elbow and hit from a cocked position.
2. The arm should be straight on contact with the shuttle.

Underhand clear shot
The player swings up and through with the wrist in a cocked position, using the same mechanics as in a high deep serve.

Net shots
Net shots require a delicate stroke. The racquet, therefore, does not need to be held as firmly as it is in power shots.
1. Contact the shuttle as near the top of the net as possible.
2. Use arm movement instead of forearm rotation.
3. Stretch and reach for the shuttle.

Around-the-head shots
Such shots are within an arc around the head, above the shoulder, and ont eh left side of the body.
1. Body faces net, with weight on left foot at contact.
2. Right leg swings forward at completion of stroke.
3. Basic stroke is rotation motion.
4. The angle of the racquet at the time the shuttle is hit determines whether a clear, smash, or drop shot can be executed.

STRATEGY
Singles
1. Serve long unless opponent is playing back for just such a serve; in that case, serve short to take advantage of opponent's poor position.
2. Base use of long or short serve on opponent's strengths and weaknesses.
3. Return a high serve with a drop or clear shot.
4. Use a clear shot for a low serve, or if it can be reached before falling too far below the net, use a net shot.
5. Use down-the-line smashes or smash at opponent's right hip or shoulder.
6. Return a smash with a drop to the point on the court farthest from the point at which the smash

was made.

7. Drive down the sidelines.
8. Play your position; do not try to outguess your opponent.
9. Take advantage of your opponent's weaknesses, but not to the extent that such repeated effort improves the weakness.

Doubles

1. Play formulations:
   a. Side by side: Each person is responsible for half the court, form front to back. Disadvantages are that it is hard to run from the net to the back court and make a good smash or a good attacking stroke, and returns to the center cause confusion as to who will hit them.
   b. Front and back: One person plays the front court and one the back, with the front player taking all net shots and any other shot that can be returned with a better shot than the partner can deliver. Although this is a popular formation for doubles, a disadvantage is the resulting poor defense against smashes and drives down the sidelines.
   c. Combination: This formation combines the best features of the other two. The partners rotate in a counterclockwise circle, so that the backcourt player need never return for a backhand shot in the near court. When the team using this formation is on the attack, the players should be playing front and back; when on defense, they should be playing side by side.
2. Play shots that will give an opening for your partner on his or her return. Do not leave your partner open to a heated attack from the opponents.
3. Serves low and short, preferably to the corner formed by the center line and short service line.
4. Smash long services, but occasionally use a drop shot.
5. Rush short serves.
6. Do not play too close to the net. A position around the short service line is best for playing the net.
7. If servers are playing in front-and-back formation, the best return of a low serve is a half-court shot down the sidelines.
8. Make replacements to the least obvious spots.

BADMINTON COURTESY

Sportsmanship is the foremost courtesy. Be gracious never "needle" an opponent. If in doubt about a boundary decision, call it in favor of the opponent; the opponent, if a good sport, will disagree. If fouling occurs at the net, one should call it on one's self.

Hand a shuttle over to an adjoining court player at the end of a rally. Thank a player when your shuttle is returned.

Do not delay in calling a foul.

Do not play indifferently against an inferior opponent.

TEACHING CONSIDERATIONS

1. For school-age populations establish the grip and ready position as well as a basic underhand and overhead shot. It is not necessary to teach specialized shots until students can keep the shuttlecock going continuously with the basic shots.
2. Begin with singles, even if it means using half a court for practice.
3. Design experiences to have students change the placement, force levels, and trajectory of the shuttlecock from these basic shots.
4. Teach the short and high deep serve.
5. Introduce competitive play and stress placement of shuttlecock away from opponent. Introduce the clears and drop shot as students attempt to place the shuttlecock in front of the service line and near the back boundary. Practice the specialized skills and put them back into the game. Modify the games if need be by giving extra points for points won using one of these shots.
6. Begin doubles play with side-by-side strategies. Introduce combination up and back and side by side as soon as students are consistently returning to their home base position after being pulled out of position defensively.
7. Design warm-up activities that include combinations of skills using both forehand and backhand stokes.

Swimming

Swimming

Completion of this chapter should enable the reader to:

- Be familiar with the evolution of swimming and the various strokes
- Orient a group of student to being in water
- Instruct novice swimmers in basic swimming skills such as floating, gliding, and beginning propulsion
- Teach beginning and advanced swimming strokes
- Recognize the proper progressions for teaching beginning, intermediate, and advanced swimmers

HISTORY AND EVOLUTION

Early man probably learned swimming by observing animals that used a running motion to move about on or int eh water. Water is an unnatural medium for humans because it interferes with the breathing mechanism; animals are usually better equipped anatomically for swimming. Humans cannot easily keep the nose above water while horizontal.

Carvings showing people swimming have been found dating as early as 9000 B.C. In the Middle Ages, accounts in the Greek, Roman, Anglo-Saxon, and Scandinavian classics dealt often with great feats of swimming of the heroes of the day.

In 1538 Nicolaus Wynman, a German professor of languages, wrote the first book on swimming. In 1696 M. Thevonot, A frenchman, wrote a more scientific treatise.

The strokes listed here are still fundamental land sea-worthy for utility purposes but have been considerably refined for competitive swimming.

These strokes evolved in the following order:

1. The "doggy" or human paddling strokes.
2. The breaststroke (sailor stroke), the first scientific stroke taught.
3. The under arm sidestroke. This stroke was still too slow for speed because both arms recovered under the water as they did in the breaststroke. The kick was scissorslike.
4. The side overarm or English overarm stroke. This stroke was faster than either the breaststroke or the side under arm stroke because the uppermost arm recovered above the surface and thereby reduced undesirable resistance.
5. The trudgen stroke, discovered in South America in 1860 by an Englishman, John Trudgen. This stroke employed the method of recovering both arms above the water hand-over-hand and further reduced resistance to water and created greater speed. It was similar to the side overarm stroke except that the body turned over to the uppermost side to also permit the under arm to lift out of the water for recovery. In this stroke the scissors kick was used.
6. The Australian crawl, introduced to England by Richard Cavell of Australia in the 1902 championships. This was the first true hand-over-hand stroke with vertical thrash of the legs. Cavell explained the stroke as "crawling through the water." The scissors kick was eliminated for speed swimming because recovering the legs caused great resistance.
7. The American six-beat leg kick crawl. The Australian stroke was scientifically refined by American coaches. This style broke all existing freestyle records in speed swimming and became known as the fastest human stroke in water.
8. The inverted breaststroke. This is the breaststroke executed upside down wile swimming on the back.
9. The back crawl. About 1910 the crawl was turned upside down and was much faster in competition than the inverted breaststroke. Here again there was no recovery of arms or legs underwater as in the inverted breaststroke. It, too, minimized resistance and created faster speed on the back.
10. The butterfly breaststroke. This stroke was beginning to make its appearance in competition about 1934. The kick remained the same as in the breaststroke, but the arms recovered above the water simultaneously. They lifted out of the water at the hips and were swung laterally forward to the entry, resembling a butterfly in flight; thus the name.
11. The dolphin fishtail breaststroke. The newest of all the swimming strokes was created by Armbruster through the ability and skill of Jack Sieg. The purpose of this stroke is to obtain greater speed with the breaststroke by eliminating the recovery underwater of the legs in the kick. This is accomplished by beating the legs up and

down in unison. This kick actually creates greater speed when used without arms than does the alternating crawl flutter kick. It synchronized beautifully with the butterfly arm stroke and created greater speed.

Not only have all of these strokes been developed and refined, but they have been put to practical use by the average swimmer and are expressed in many different categories of water activities, usually called aquatics. Some of the categories of aquatics are:

1. Recreational
2. Lifesaving
3. Competition
4. Synchronized or ballet
5. Springboard diving
6. Water games—polo, basketball, baseball, and the like
7. Water safety
8. Survival
9. Skin and scuba diving

Most of these skill activities in water have as a basic background the fundamental skill strokes.

It is strongly recommended that the beginner be taught all of the basic strokes to gain an assurance of self-preservation, an at-home feeling, and the joy and relaxation in recreational swimming. To accomplish this, the beginner must know the fundamental skill strokes. This method of learning is the "Armbruster all-stroke method for beginners."

UNITED STATES OLYMPIC SWIMMING HISTORY
Men

In 1896 at Athens, there were only four swimming events, and competitors could use any stroke. The event took place outside in a lake. Over the years the competitions became increasingly organized in terms of distances, strokes, and facilities. By 1912 there were seven men's events and three women's events.

The first outstanding United States swimmer was Duke Kahanamoku of Hawaii who won the 100 meter freestyle in 1912 and again in 1920. His new style of kicking (the flutter kick) was later adopted by most freestyle swimmers. In 1924 Johnny Weissmuller, the next dominant U.S. swimmer, emerged. He was the first person to swim the 100 meter freestyle under a minute and won a total of five gold medals at two Olympiads.

In 1932 the Japanese men swimmers won five of six events and they won three of six events in 1936. Following these games the Australian men became the swimming power until 1964.

Don Schollander of the United States matched Johnny Weissmuller's feat of five gold medals by winning four in 1964 and one in 1968. Schollander's gold in 1968 was in the 4 x 200 meter relay, and Mark Spitz, a team member on that relay team, was destined in 1972 to win seven gold medals. At that time it was the most gold medals ever won at a single Olympic Games in any sport and each medal involved a world record (four were individual events and three were relays).

One of the most dominating team performances occurred at the 1976 Olympics when the U.S. men's team won 12 of 13 possible golds and 10 silvers in the 11 individual events. In 1980, when the United States boycotted the Olympics, the Soviet men's team dominated by winning seven of the 13 gold medals. In 1984, when the Soviets boycotted, the U.S. men returned to dominance by taking 9 of the 15 gold medals.

In 1988 a record 21 different nations earned medals in swimming (both men's and women's) but the men's events were once again dominated by a U.S. swimmer. Matt Biondi gathered five golds, one silver and a bronze for a performance eclipsed only by Mark Spitz.

Women

The first Olympic women's swimming events were held in 1912, and the next several Olympics were dominated by swimmers from Australia, Great Britain, and the United States.

In 1920 Ethelda Bleibtrey of the United States won the 100 meter freestyle, the 300 meter freestyle, and anchored the 4 x 100 meter freestyle relay to sweep all three events at the Antwerp Olympics. In 1932 the U.S. women's swim team, led by Helene Madison, won six of the seven swimming and diving events but won only three bronze medals in 1936.

As with the men's swimming events, the Australian women's teams, led by Dawn Fraser, dominated the Olympics after World War II. The U.S. women began to reemerge as a swimming power in 1968 when Debra Meyer won three gold medals. In 1972, when Mark Spitz was winning seven golds, the dominant women swimmer was Shane Gould of Australia with four golds, one silver, and one bronze. However, Melissa Belste of the United States also won three golds in two individual events and a relay.

In 1972, when the U.S. men had the great team performance, the U.S. and Australian dominance in the womens' events continued, but it came to an end in 1976 as the East German women won 11 of the 13 golds. Shirley Babashoff of the United States did manage a gold and three silvers, giving her eight Olympic medals in her career and establishing her as one of the United States' great female swimmers.

When the United States boycotted in 1980, the East German women repeated their feat of garnering 11 of the 13 gold medals. In 1984, when the East Germans boycotted, the U.S. women swimmers returned to power with 11 of the 14 golds.

In the 1988 Olympics, the stars of the women's swimming competition were Kristin Otto of East Germany and Janet Evans of the United States. Otto's six gold medals broke the record for most golds won by a woman in any sport at one Olympics. Seventeen-year-old Janet Evans won the 400 meter individual medley, the 800 meter freestyle and the 400 meter freestyle in a world record time of 4:03:85.

ARMBRUSTER ALL-STROKE METHOD FOR TEACHING BEGINNERS

The Armbruster all-stroke method begins by adjusting students to water; then several skilled and some low-skilled techniques are learned. When the student is comfortably adjusted to water and basically "stanced," the basic skill strokes can be learned quite rapidly.

Beginners can learn the strokes and make reasonable progress; however, not everyone can swim all strokes equally well. Therefore by teaching all of the students all of the strokes, everyone will naturally find the stroke most comfortable and suitable through a distance orientation program after the stroke skills are learned. People differ anatomically. If students are taught all strokes, in the distance orientation program, the stroke that takes the least effort will naturally be selected most often. Each student will find the stroke that gives the most self-satisfaction and pleasure, even though basically "grounded" in every stroke. The students are not first "grooved" in one or two strokes but are basically grounded for advanced swimming, lifesaving, or any other form of aquatic interest. The idea, too, is to do away with the intermediate level of swimming.

The secret of this method is really to work the legs by drilling them in the different kick skills. Ordinarily legs are clumsy and awkward, being composed of big muscles that in everyday living are trained only to walk, run, jump, and perhaps dance. To get legs to relax in water and become skilled, and to get the feel of the unnatural medium water, the swimmer must train and overlearn.

Correct breathing habits are the next essential skill to teach. One must breathe to swim. Water interferes with the breathing mechanism of the human

being. Even the quadruped holds its nose at the highest point of its body in relation to the surface level in order to swim. It, too, must breathe to swim. The human being has learned to exhale under the surface and inhale above the surface.

Instructors should emphasize skill learning by constant drill and action. Action creates interest and results in interested students who will work hard if they know they are learning. Swimming taught progressively and intensively accomplishes that. If students become fatigued (not exhausted) from constant exercise, they will naturally take it easy, and when they take it easy, the response is relaxation. Relaxation is learned through constant repetitions.

OBJECTIVES

1. To orient students to water, a medium that disturbs a person physically, physiologically, and mentally and brings about the following:
   a. Unstableness
   b. Apparent loss of body weight
   c. Loss of sense of balance
   d. Change in body position for locomotion
   e. Change in heat-regulatory mechanism
   f. Change in respiration
   g. Change in normal muscle tonus
2. To give confidence, using drills that have the following objectives:
   a. To eliminate mental hazards
   b. To teach the proper techniques of inhalation and exhalation
   c. To bring about relaxation in the water
   d. To encourage enjoyment of swimming
3. To teach self-reliance for self-preservation
4. To teach an appreciation of distance over water no matter how short or long
5. To teach respect for water generally while swimming
6. To impart confidence in skill and ability of accomplishment
7. To teach strokes in such a way as to motivate the student to persistent practice
8. To encourage swimming as a source of lifelong pleasure
9. To teach distribution of effort and conservation of strength
10. To teach how to delay fatigue
11. To teach how to dive into water

BASIC SKILLS AND TECHNIQUES
Adjustment to water

1. Examine the pool markings to know its depth at all locations before entering the water.
2. Wade waist deep into the pool and submerge repeatedly to chin level, rinsing up and down and washing the face.
3. Hold onto the splash gutter and allow water to lift the legs and body to the surface. Stay relaxed.

Breath control

Depending on the level and maturity of swimmers, the following activities can be performed while holding on to the pool gutter, holding on to a partner, or without support.

1. Standing in waist-deep water with the body inclined forward, practice breath holding; inhale through the mouth, close the mouth, shut the eyes, and submerge the face flat beneath the water. Hold for 3 seconds and recover. Repeat several times, lengthening the time of holding the breath underwater.
2. Inhale through the mouth, submerge the face with the eyes closed, exhale through the nose, and recover. Repeat several times.
3. Inhale through the mouth, submerge the face with the eyes closed, and exhale through the nose, mouth, or both, steadily but as slowly as possible. Recover and repeat several times.

Use of eyes underwater

Inhale, close the eyes, submerge, open the eyes, count the number of fingers visible on a partner's hand, and recover. Repeat.

Shipping water with mouth

Submerge, open the mouth, recover, and ship out water into splash gutter. Repeat several times.

Balance and control of the body

The following activities are designed to aid the student in developing confidence in the water. To ensure that confidence is generated and fear is not reinforced, it is important to discuss and practice (with partners) the procedures of returning to a stable position before assuming the various floating and gliding positions.

Jellyfish float. This float may be performed in either the pike or tuck position. Take a deep breath, submerge the face, raise the knees to the chest or extend the legs, and hold with the arms for 3 sec-

onds. Release the hold, allow the legs to extend to the bottom of the pool, let the arms float up a little, an then push them down and toward the hips while at the same time raising the head. The instructor should pay close attention to the swimmer in these initial float as individual differences, especially in amount of leanness and fatness, will result in large differences in ability to float. Repeat.

Prone floating position. The prone floating position is taken by lifting and extending the arms forward beyond the head beneath the surface, with the head held low in the water, and extending the legs (this is the only difference between the prone float and the jellyfish float). To recover to the standing position, pull the knees to the chest, round the back, then simultaneously press firmly downward with the extended arms, extend the legs to the bottom of the pool, and lift the face from the water. With the legs extended downward, the feet will settle on the pool floor. (Water must be at least waist deep.) Keep the eyes open. After recovery, exhale through the nose, open the mouth, inhale, and flutter the eyes open.

Prone glide and stand. For the prone glide, bend forward at the waist, with the arms extended forward. Lay the upper body and arms in the water, just under the surface. Take a deep breath at the side, bend the knees, and roll the face under the surface. Straighten the knees, push the feet off the bottom, and slide into a prone position and the glide. At the end of the glide, draw the knees into the chest and recover as in the prone float.

Back floating position. With a partner standing directly behind, assume a back floating position by submerging to the chin and, with the partner supporting the back of the neck with one hand and the small of the back with the other, lift the hips and extend the arms sideward. The ears will be under water. The partner gradually removes support, first from the small of the back and then from the neck. The body will not necessarily stay horizontal to the water. Some swimmer's legs have a tendency to sink. The important elements are to relax, keep the arms extended, and hold the neck back to keep the face above water. The partner should help you recover the first few times. To gain recovery from the back float, move the arms downward and forward in the water, round the back, bring the knees to the chin, and lift the head slowly forward. When the body moves to a vertical position, extend the legs to the bottom and stand.

Back slide and stand. For the back glide, sit back so the shoulders are submerged, push off with the feet, glide until forward motion stops, and then recover as in the back float. In the glide, keep the arms at the side and the legs straight and together.

Simple leg movements to keep body horizontal and to aid propulsion

Kick glide, prone position. For the kick glide, prone position, start in the same manner as in the prone glide, but as the body straightens out on the surface, move the legs in an alternate up-and-down maneuver, delivered with the knee fairly loose; continue to the limit of breathholding ability. (For additional practice, hold onto the splash gutter or a kickboard and kick the legs.)

Kick glide, back position. In the kick glide, back position, assume a back floating position but with the back flat and chin tucked well into the throat. Move the legs in a slightly bent-kneed flutter kick. Snap each knee into extension when finishing the kick. (For additional practice, hold onto the splash gutter and execute the flutter kick.)

Simple arm movements for support, propulsion, and balancing of body

Arm stroke on the front. For the arm stroke on the front (dog paddle or human stroke), assume the prone position in the water and extend the arms alternately forward and downward, following with a press backward under the body. Cup the hands slightly on the pull backward. In the recovery forward of each arm, straighten the hand, draw it up under the chin, and extend it to a forward position; cup the hand and repeat the stroke.

Arm stroke on the back. The arm stroke on the back (finning) is a paired movement of the hands and arms in a back position. The arms are first extended by the sides and then draw up about 1 foot, at which point they are thrust outward and then toward the feet in a sort of pushing movement, supplemented by a sort of fishtail flip of the hands and wrists.

Coordination of breathing with leg and arm movements

Combined stroke on the front. The combined stroke on the front is composed of up-and-down alternating beats of the legs and the dog paddle with the arms, with breathing done entirely above the surface or alternately inhaling above and exhaling below the water. Two or more beats of the legs should accompany each cycle of arm strokes.

Inhalation should be done with the head turned to the side. If the head is turned to the left to get air, inhale when the right arm is extended forward. Rotate the head into the water on this cycle, and when the left arm is extended, exhale under water through the mouth. To inhale to the right side, the left arm should be extended, and on this cycle, as the right arm is extended rotate the face into the water and exhale.

Combined stroke on the back. The combined stroke on the back consists of finning with the hands and flutter kicking with the legs. Assume the back floating position with the back flat and the chin tucked well into the throat. First, the leg beat is started using greater speed and more flexibility than is used in the front kick. The thrust of the hands (finning) is put into the stroke at regular intervals. Breathe naturally.

Turning, right and left. Begin the front stroke (human stroke), maintaining the body nearly horizontal, and execute a right turn and then a left turn. Try executing a complete turn. Extend the hands and pull in the opposite direction of the turn.

Change positions. In changing position or turning over from the front to the back, start swimming, keep the body nearly horizontal, and at the point of changing positions, roll the body either right or left to a back floating position. Keep the shoulders and head low in the water. The head, arms, hips, and legs will aid in rolling the body. In changing from a back float to the front, roll in a similar manner to a front position and resume the stroke.

SKILLED STROKE TECHNIQUES
Resting backstroke

The resting backstroke should be the first stroke taught to beginners. It requires little coordination and gives the student a sense of motivation. This is principally a resting stroke for an emergency or for easy swimming while resting, and it lays a sound foundation for the breaststroke and elementary backstroke as well as for treading water. The face is never underwater, and thus breathing is not a disturbing factor.

Whip kick (inverted breaststroke kick)

The recovery is executed by spreading the knees but holding the heels together. Press the heels down as they recover toward the buttocks so that the knees do not lift out of the water, and at the same time lift the hips to prevent the drop. Separate the heels and cock the feet outward toward the knees. Start the drive by sweeping the legs out and together, and engage the water with the soles of the feet, extending the feet as they kick. During this kick, when the knees are not quite straightened, squeeze the thighs together forcefully with the knees relaxed to give a whiplike motion to the foreleg and feet, resulting in increased propulsion. This stroke can also be introduced using a flutter kick first, as the whip kick can be difficult for some students to master.

Arm stroke

The arm recovery starts from the sides of the thighs by turning the palms downward and slightly at an angle in the direction of recovery, the little finger side of the hand leading and knifing through the water. The arms are held straight. The arms move outward away from the thighs to a point just above the shoulders.

The pull is executed by turning the palms to the rear and slightly downward and moving the straight arms forcefully to the sides of the thighs.

At no time during either the recovery or the pull of the hands or arms should they be above the surface.

Whole stroke

This stroke is easy to executive because the arms and legs work in unison. The arms and legs recover at the exact moment and kick and pull at the same moment. When the stroke is closed, stretch out straight and pause until momentum from the previous stroke is spent. Repeat.

Elementary backstroke

This stroke should be taught after the resting backstroke has been mastered.

This style affords a little more speed than does the resting backstroke and is still restful and easy to learn. However, more coordination is required to execute it because the arms are partly recovered before the legs recover.

Whip kick

The kick is executed exactly the same as in the resting backstroke kick.

Arm stroke

The arm recovery in the elementary backstroke differs from that in the resting backstroke. The arm recovery is executed by bending the elbows downward and sliding the hands from the sides of the thighs up along the sides of the body toward the shoulders. Then the hands, palms facing up, reach out diagonally from the armpit under the water until the arms are straight. Turn the palm facing backward and pull, straight-armed, to the sides of the thighs. Pause until the momentum from the pull subsides.

Whole stroke

In the recovery phase, hold the legs straight while the arms recover to about armpit level; then start the leg recovery at the same slow speed as the arms recover. When the arms have reached the pulling position, the legs have recovered to the kick position; that is, the knees and heels are apart, feet pointed outward. The kick and pull must start at the same instant. Stretch the body and legs straight, though relaxed, and pause for the momentum to spend itself. Breathe regularly.

Under arm sidestroke

The under arm sidestroke is easy to learn. It is the foundation stroke for lifesaving. Breathing is not difficult, because the nose and mouth are turned to the rear and the water passes by the side of the face. This is not one of the modern competitive strokes.

Scissors kick

The scissors kick is perhaps the most powerful of all kicks in the water, which is why it is used so much in lifesaving.

First the kick is learned on both sides by holding onto the sides of the pool. The body is held straight on its side, legs straight, feet extended, and one leg on top of the other. To start the recovery movement, flex at the knees and slowly draw the heels backward. Both legs are held together ad move simultaneously. This drawing of the heels backward gives just the proper amount of flexion at the hip joint. In this position, if an imaginary line were passed through the midpoint of the shoulder and hip joints, it would project out over the legs at a midpoint between the knees and ankles when the legs are in a full recovery position. The scissors is now opened by moving the underleg back and the top leg forward, still maintaining the fully flexed knees. The foot of the top leg cocks itself, or flexes toward the knee. The under foot remains extended. From this position the legs start the drive, sweeping outward and together by extension of the knees and the foot of the top leg. The under leg hooks the water and acts in the same manner as kicking a ball, whereas the top leg has a whip motion similar to a horse's pawing. The legs come together stretched straight and relaxed and pause long enough for momentum to be spent in the glide.

Arm stroke

While the body is on its left side, with the shoulder girdle in a true vertical plane, the under left arm is extended forward directly under the head, with the palm facing down and the hand just under the surface. The upper right arm is pulling back, hugging closely along the upper front part of the body with the palm of the hand resting on the front side of the upper leg—never on the top of the leg.

The learner should first get a clear mental picture of the arm stroke from the starting position, that is, both arms moving simultaneously along the longitudinal plane of the body. They meet just under the head, change direction, and simultaneously extend again to their starting position. The under arm moves forward; the upper arm moves backward. The student can "singsong," "Everything drawn in, everything thrust out." Actually, as the upper arm slides forward to recover to meet the under arm, the under arm should pull diagonally downward and backward to a line under the head. Here it changes direction and starts the recovery movement, with the hand and fingers pointing forward to its starting position. Even though the hands move in and out together, the under arm is always pulling on the "in" movement, while on the "out" movement the upper arm is pulling, or vice versa.

Whole stroke coordinated in four steps

It is recommended that each of the four steps be learned thoroughly before advancing to the next step.

Step 1—scissors kick only. Take a deep breath and lie on the left side floating position with the body straight and the left under arm extended in a line with the body. Turn the face into the water on to of the under arm and hold the breath. The upper right arm is in front of the upper thigh. Take at last four kicks in succession and pause between each stroke for the glide. The upper hand is in front of the upper thigh and remains on it during these kick exercises. This trains the upper arm to work in unison with the kick, as it must do in the whole stroke.

Step 2—the kick and upper arm. The body is still on its extended left side, with the face under water as in step 1. To execute step 2, the upper hand and arm recover at the same time as the legs. The hand planes forward beyond the face, with the elbow and hand submerged to a point beyond the face. The arm pull starts at the same time as the kick. Here again, as in the resting backstroke, the upper arm and legs recover at the same time, and the kick and pull occur at the same time.

Step 3—the kick, upper arm, and under arm. The body and face are still in the same position as in step 1. To execute step 3, press—do not pull—the under arm diagonally down and backward to a point under the face. At the same instant that the under arm starts its press, the legs and upper arm are recovered. The hands meet, cross over, and repass as the under arm hand recovers and thrusts forward to guide the glide. At the same time the under arm recovers, the upper arm and legs start the kick and pull. Pause and glide. Repeat the singsong, "Everything in, everything out," as in the under arm sidestroke. Glide. This makes the arms and legs simple to coordinate into the whole stroke. Repeat at least four strokes before stopping for air.

Step 4—breathing. Take one or two strokes in the step 3 position and then turn the face out of the water and face to the rear with the chin in line with the upper shoulder. Breathe in at the same time that the arms and legs come in; breathe out at the same time that the arms and legs go out. Remember, "Everything in, everything out." Once four or five strokes are correctly timed and coordinated, you have learned the skill of coordinating the whole stroke. Now repeat the same four-step procedure on the right side. The water level should remain constant at the face, leveling at the corner of the lower eye and lower corner of the mouth.

Note: These four-step procedures can also be performed with flotation devices such as kickboards.

Breaststroke

The breaststroke was the first competitive stroke and is still used in competitive events. However, it is also an excellent utility stroke and is used in many lifesaving skills.

Kick

There have been many modifications of the breaststroke kick in recent times. These modifications have resulted primarily from an interest in increasing the speed of the entire stroke. In general, the main characteristic of these modifications has been to reduce unwanted resistance by narrowing the knee spread and increasing the desired resistance by adding a slightly downward thrust in the propulsive phase of the kick. However, for the beginner the traditional kick is probably easiest to learn initially.

The breaststroke kick (whip) is almost the same as used in the inverted or the resting backstroke. The body is prone, arms extended, face under. The recovery beings with the heels close together and then drawn toward the buttocks just under the surface. This results in the knees being brought forward; however, the angle of the thighs to the upper body should be slightly greater than 90 degrees. In other words, the knees should not be drawn up quite so far as to be directly below the pelvis. When the heels are fully drawn up to the buttocks, the feet separate outward and the ankles are cocked, or the feet are flexed outward at the ankles and toward the knees. The legs are now in position to drive. The drive is made with an outward and together sweep, extending the ankles until the legs are again closed to the starting position, with the legs straight and the toes pointed. Pause with the legs fully extended until momentum from the kick is spent. During the propulsive phase of the kick, you should feel as though water is being pushed backward by the soles of the feet. Also attempt to get a whiplash to the legs during the kick phase. This is accomplished by driving the thighs in toward each other before the knees have fully extended. This movement gives the powerful whiplash kick.

Arm stroke

In the starting position, the arms are extended forward, hands close together, palms facing away from each other. The arms spread out and pull simultaneously in a lateral downward and backward movement, and the elbows bend as the hands reach shoulder width apart. The hands continue to a point under the chin. Pulling them farther removes the support from under the shoulders and head, causing them to drop and sink, which disturbs the body balance. At the completion of the arm pull, the face is lifted to breathe and the knees begin their flexion for the kick recovery. The recovery of the arms begins under the chin as the hands join each other and are thrust forward to the starting position. At this point, pause to allow for a glide. The entire arm stroke is a continuous, uninterrupted movement. Practice walking across the pool and coordinating the breathing with arm action technique.

Whole stroke

Push off from the side of the pool with the body prone on the surface, fully extended, the face underwater. The arms pull as just described to a point under the chin, at which time the breath is taken and the legs are recovered with the feet spread and cocked for the drive. By this time the arms are already thrusting forward. When the arms are almost fully extended, the legs start the drive. The arms pause for the glide when they have reached full extension. The legs also pause for the glide when they have closed at the end of the drive. The body is now fully extended. Exhale slowly during the glide. Repeat several strokes to time the movements smoothly and continuously from the start of the stroke to the end of the leg drive. The breaststroke can easily be executed with the face out of the water, as may be required in some lifesaving situations. To accomplish this the glide is shortened and the stroke requires more effort than normal.

Crawl stroke

The crawl stroke is the speed king of all strokes. Neither arms nor legs recover underwater, which accounts for its greater speed. The modern speed crawl is truly one of the most refined and specialized of all sports skills.

Flutter kick

The body is prone, with arms and legs fully extended, face under, and ankles stretched and close together. From this position the flutter kick is executed by alternately oscillating the legs vertically from the hips, forcefully and regularly. On each downward beat the foot turns inward (pigeon-toed). This occurs naturally if the ankles and feet are held loosely. This increases the surface area of the foot. In the upward beat the foot is extended, jot pigeon-toed. Beginners should first attempt this kick while learning to hold the legs straight yet not rigid. This originates the movements from the hips. When this is learned and the thighs move up and down, the knee action can be learned. For example, look at the action of one leg only. In some ways, it is similar to pedaling a bicycle. As the leg drives up, the sole of the foot pushes upward and remains there until the knee is almost straight on the downward beat. This movement results in a quick down-up whiplash of the foreleg and foot at the end of the downbeat, the same principle used in the breaststroke kick. This skill can be learned by daily drills with the aid of a kickboard.

Arm stroke (alternating)

This stroke is executed by alternately reaching hand-over-hand forward into the water and pulling the body forward over the surface. The arm stroke has seven components: (1) entry, (2) support, (3) catch, (4) pull, (5) push, (6) release, and (7) recovery.

For the entry, place the hand in the water at a natural arm's length, directly in front of the shoulder. The hand should enter the water before the elbow or shoulder. A comfortable reach should be made; never overreach.

In modern speed swimming, as well as in teaching the crawl stroke to beginners, an opposition rhythm type of stroke is prevalent. "Opposition-type stroke" means that the arms are nearly opposite each other at all times. However, if speed is desired, the fundamental mechanics of the stroke become quite complex and highly technical in obtaining the ease and balance necessary for good performance as well as speed. These technical essentials can be obtained once the fundamentals of the stroke have been mastered.

The beginner should not be concerned with speed in learning but should merely be able to execute the arm stroke with reasonably good opposition timing.

The catch and pull should start, first in the hand and then bending the elbow slightly for good lever-age. The pull shifts into a push as the arm passes under the chest toward the opposite hip. Then the push continues the drive to the release with the forearm and hand. At this point the shoulder begins to lift in preparation to recover the arm until the hand clears the surface at the hip.

The arm is then recovered to the entry by lifting the shoulder, bending at the elbow, and turning the hand so that the palm faces to the rear and gradually faces the water at entry. The arm recovery movement is up and outward, away from the hip, and forward to the water. The shoulder is held high while the hand and forearm enter the water. The desired high elbow position on the recovery, entry, and catch is made easier if the shoulders and hips are allowed to roll to both sides during a complete stroke. The rolling action should be symmetric, with the head held in a relatively stable position.

Whole stroke

While the arms execute a complete revolution, the legs complete some number of evenly measured beats. In walking, the arms and legs move in a 1 : 1 ratio, an opposite arm and leg counterbalancing movement. In swimming the crawl, preferred (though not mandatory) leg to arm ratio is 3 : 1; that is, the legs perform three beats to each arm stroke, or six beats to each complete cycle of both arms. This ratio gives the stroke a counterbalancing movement like that in walking or running.

Breathing

Breathing in the crawl stroke is executed as follows: just as the arm opposite the breathing side is put into the water for support, the head is turned to inhale and then immediately returned in line with the body. When turning the head for air, keep the chin in close to the throat and look to see if the mouth is inside the trough of the bow wave formed by the head. Take a quick breath as the mouth is opening; do not pause after opening the mouth. Curl the lips out away from the teeth when opening the mouth.

Back crawl stroke

The back crawl stroke is the crawl stroke inverted. However, it differs somewhat from the crawl in that the face is not under the water during the stroke, so that breathing is simplified.

Inverted flutter kick

Essentially the kick is the same as the flutter kick in the crawl stroke. The body is extended on its back, legs held closely together, ankles and toes pointed, chin low on the throat, water level at the lower earlobes and around, not over, the chest. The legs move alternately up and down with action originating from the hips. On the upward beat the toes turn in, and on the downward beat they are extended. AT the end of the upward beat the kneecap should not break through the surface and the foot should throw some water above the surface without projecting out of the water. To accomplish this skill, the thigh, as in other styles of kicks, forcefully drives down just before the knee has straightened. This action gives the foreleg and foot an effective propulsive up-down whip. The ratio of leg kicks to one complete stroke revolution is 6 : 1, the same as in the crawl stroke.

Arm stroke

The arms move in opposition to one another as if the swimmer has a broomstick across the back of the neck and shoulders with the arms extending out along the broomstick.

The moment the arm has finished its pull along the side of the thigh, the hand gives a final downward press as the shoulder is lifted out of the water and the hand is turned to face outward. The arm is bent slightly at the elbow at the beginning of the recovery phase, but it is straightened for the entry. The arm recovers to the entry with an upward swing and continues to the entry at a point not more than 6 inches outside the shoulder line. The hand and forearm should not be slowed as they near the point of entry but should accelerate so that they are in the water before the shoulder can sink under.

The power or pull phase of the stroke can be done with either a bent arm or a straight arm. The bent-arm stroke is used by high-level competitive swimmers but is more difficult to learn than the straight-arm pull, which is generally recommended when learning the backstroke. In the initial part of the straight-arm pull, the arm is shallow, about 2 to 6 inches underwater. As the arm reaches a point directly out from the shoulder the depth should be about 6 to 10 inches. From here, the arm continues until it reaches the leg and begins the recovery phase. The bent-arm pull is initiated slightly deeper than the straight-arm pull. As the pull progresses, the arm is drawn in toward the body by bending at the elbow. Just before the hand reaches a point directly out from the shoulder, the pull changes to a push. The arm and hand continue and finish near the leg, as in the straight-arm pull, to begin the recovery phase. In both types of pulls the arm stroke should be smooth and relaxed throughout. A slight hip and a more pronounced shoulder roll permit an easier recovery and catch, as well as more efficient action of the opposite arm.

Breathing

Breathing should be continuous and rhythmic. Hold the head with the chin always up on dead center, never moving from side to side. Try to keep the body stretched to prevent sagging at the hips.

Dolphin butterfly stroke

The dolphin butterfly stroke was created by Armbruster at the University of Iowa in 1935 with the aid of one of his swimmers, Jack Sieg. The legs in this stroke move in unison in an up-and-down wavelike action that resembles the tail of a dolphin in swimming. The arms also move in unison in both the propulsive and the recovery phases. The arms recover low above the surface, are held nearly straight, and resemble the wings of a butterfly in flight.

The stroke is definitely dominated by the kick. This dolphin wavelike kick by the legs only has become the fastest means of kicking through water. It is even faster than the alternating flutter kick used in the crawl and back crawl strokes, yet the basic characteristics of the dolphin kick are the same as those of the alternating flutter crawl kicks.

The dolphin butterfly stroke is very exhausting to the untrained individual. Except for use as a competitive swimming stroke, it has little, if any, value to humans. However, the stroke is included here because many students desire to learn it, for no other reasons than for its rugged, challenging action and for the satisfaction of being able to perform it.

Kick

It is essential that before learning the dolphin kick the beginner thoroughly master the crawl flutter kick, because the basic characteristics of the two are the same. When the flutter kick is learned and performed with ease, the student is well conditioned to attempt the dolphin kick. In daily training drills the practice of this kick works in well with the other stroke kicks in the all-stroke practice method.

As practice progresses, the student should lie face down on the surface of the water, kicking only, with the hands finning at the sides of the hips. As a final step of conditioning and training, and before the whole stroke is attempted, the student should submerge and practice the kick underwater during breath-holding intervals. The hands should be finning at the sides of the hips rather than extended in front of the head. By practicing the kick underwater, the student is able to determine that the progress is true forward and not down or up. If either occurs, adjustment should be made to equalize the up-and-down beat in relation to the forward plane of progress. It is also essential while performing underwater to stress relaxing the entire spine from the shoulders through all the joints to the end of the toes. To help beginners become familiar with this movement, it is often practiced with the aid of swim fins. When the true shortened up-and-down beat of the kick and the up-and-down action of the hips have been mastered, the student has been properly trained and conditioned for learning the arm action.

Arm stroke

The student should first practice the arm stroke by walking across the swimming pool, bent at the hips, chin at water level, stroking the arms. The stroke can also be practiced while stationary, in the same position.

The arms start the stroke from the point of entry, just outside the shoulders, pressing downward into a short lateral spread. The hands and forearms continue to pull backward with a quick inward action, elbows bending, until they reach a point just under and ahead of the shoulders. From this point the power drive is completed backward to the sides of the hips until the arms and hands have cleared the surface of the water. This final emphasis is delivered by straightening the elbows until shoulders, arms, and hands have cleared the surface of the water. From this action the arms also derive the impetus to swing laterally forward through the recovery phase to again reach the correct point of entry. During the recovery the arms are held nearly straight, palm facing the surface. The recovery should be executed without hesitation at the end of the power drive. The arms should enter the water with a soft plunge, the wrists slightly flexed toward the surface as they enter. Actually, the hands and forearms should enter the water slightly ahead of the upper arms and shoulders. At this point, without hesitation, the catch of the next stroke is started.

When walking or swimming across the pool practicing the arm stroke, the student should imagine the body moving toward the face of a large clock; the left arm should enter the water pointing to 11 o'clock and the right arm should pint to 1 o'clock.

There is no pause in the entire stroke turnover. This is what is known in swimming terms as a fast turnover stroke; that is, the moment the arms complete the power drive, they go into the recovery to start the next stroke. Not only must the arms recovery quickly, but the power drive of the arms must also be rapidly executed. It is this fast turnover cadence that makes the stroke so strenuous for the beginner, especially if the beginner is poorly conditioned. However, most students skilled in other strokes have an urge to learn the challenging, complex skills involved in performing this stroke.

Whole stroke

The stroke is started by moving the arms forward laterally to the point of entry. The hands enter the water just outside the shoulders simultaneously, pointing to the 11 and 1 o'clock positions, respectively. As the hands execute the catch, with a slight spread and downward press, the first downward beat of the kick takes place. This downbeat of the kick is a natural counteraction caused by the powerful downward catch and pull of the forearms, similar to the counterswing of the arms and legs in walking or running. While the hands and arms execute the inward drive or pull to a point just ahead of and under the shoulders, the first upbeat of the kick has taken place. From this point the arms continue to complete the final power drive as the second downbeat of the kick takes place. This action is again a natural counterbalancing movement of legs and arms. As the arms drive out of the water at the hips and move into the recovery phase, the legs execute the second upbeat. Note that during the entire arm recovery phase there is but one beat of the legs, which is up, and none supporting the body. For this reason it is essential that the swimmer moves the arms quickly from the end of the drive to the entry. This quickened movement will prevent the body from sinking below swimming level. The most troublesome part in learning the stroke is this latter phase. If the arms move too slowly or hesitate at any point between the final drive and the entry, rhythm and timing are lost.

In executing the entry, the arms plunge lightly into the water and immediately go into the catch to start the next stroke. The stroke should first be practicing without breathing until reasonably satisfactory timing is attained. Then too, in learning, beginners often make the mistake of starting the recovery of the arms prematurely before the arms and hands have cleared the surface of the water well back of the hips and straightened elbows.

Breathing

Correct breathing in the dolphin butterfly stroke is to too difficult, providing the beginner does not develop a tendency to climb too high to get a breath. In learning this kill, the student should again walk the arm stroke across the swimming pool with the face submerged while executing the breathing and correct timing action of the head in the arm stroke cadence. Taking a breath every stroke should be practiced. Correct breathing habits in this stroke are essential to obtain ease of performance of the entire stroke.

To inhale, the swimmer should lift the head just far enough for the mouth to clear the surface of the water. This action takes place just as the arms have passed backward from under the shoulders and are completing their drive. Air is actually taken just as the arms clear the water and move into the recovery phase. Note how the finishing "kick" of the arm stroke gives the head the necessary lift to inhale. Emphasis is placed on dropping the head quickly into the water (but not too deeply) after air has been taken and before the arm recovery has reached the point of entry. It should now be easy for the beginner to visualize why it is essential to quickly recover both the head and the arms to give support to the body during this phase of the stroke. Both the head and the arms are above the surface of the water during the second upward beat of the kick. If this phase of the stroke is. jot well timed and executed, the beginner will tend to sink too deep in the water and then have to climb too high to get air. With practice, proficiency is acquired and the tiring unnecessary movements are minimized.

LEARNING PROGRESSION FOR BEGINNERS

1. Review swimming pool landmarks regarding pool depths, any unique features of the natatorium, and personal safety rules.
2. Orientation and adjustment to water in order to overcome loss of body weight, loss of balance, and loss of body heat, all of which disturb the beginner psychologically, physiologically, and physically.
   a. Submerging the face, opening the eyes, and holding the breath
   b. Shipping water from the mouth
   c. Breathing with bobbing exercises
   d. Floating, tucked and body straight, on both the face and back
3. Adjustment of the hands and feet to paddling in shallow water
   a. Sculling with and without the feet
   b. Finning with and without the feet
   c. Treading water with and without the feet
4. Unskilled strokes on the face, sides, and back
5. Skilled strokes (basic strokes)
   a. Kicks
      (1) Flutter
      (2) Scissors (both sides)
      (3) Whip
   b. Arm strokes (basic strokes)
      (1) Alternating stroke with breathing
      (2) Sidestroke with breathing
      (3) Breaststroke
      (4) Resting inverted breaststroke
6. Synchronizing or timing of arms and legs in all strokes—part-whole method, that is, breaking down each stroke from the whole into its component parts and by progressive stages building it again into the whole stroke
7. Orientation in distance swimming

LEARNING PROGRESSION FOR INTERMEDIATE SWIMMERS

Instructions in intermediate swimming is given to those who have taken and passed the beginner's course; those who have never had instruction but can pass the beginner's test, although they have no knowledge of stroke technique; or those who can swim in deep water.

1. Study pool sanitation and personal health and hygiene.
2. Review strokes, and review techniques of proper breathing.
3. Practice and drill on the techniques and timing of the leg action in all the stroke kicks.
4. Coordinate and time the technique of the arm action and breathing action; review the diving techniques.
5. Start orientation to distance swimming, emphasizing relaxation and natural breathing.
6. Practice fundamental dives from the springboard.
7. Learn and practice safety factors for self and others, such as tired swimmer's stroke, a simple rescue, simple carries in towing, and resuscitation.
8. Swim distances, stressing ease in breathing, relaxation, and the distribution of effort over distance comfortably.

LEARNING PROGRESSION FOR ADVANCED SWIMMERS

Instruction in advanced swimming is given to those who have passed the intermediate course or have achieved the ability to swim ¼ mile (0.4 km) and have demonstrated all of the standard strokes.

1. Practice timing the strokes to develop ease of performance with added power and speed, thereby gaining confidence.
2. Swim each stroke 100 yards (90 m) with correct timing.
3. Swim 25 yards (22.5 m) on each side, holding the upper arm out of the water fully extended.
4. Swim 25 yards (22.5 m) on the back, holding both hands out of the water.
5. Swim ¼ (.04 km) mile in 8 minutes or less.
6. Learn a good racing start and good technique in turning at the end of the pool.
7. Be able to do at least three dives from the springboard in good form.
8. Learn safety factors in small craft.
9. Swim safely for 20 minutes.
10. Learn how to wade properly in water of unknown depth.
11. Learn how to swim out of a swift current.
12. Learn how to assist another person temporarily in distress in deep water.
13. Learn how to swim for two people.
14. Swim under water for a distance of 25 yards (22.5 m).
15. Learn how to conserve strength.
16. Learn how to rest while tired in deep water.
17. Learn boatmanship:
    a. Paddling and rowing.
    b. What to do when capsized.
    c. How to land safely when capsized.
18. Be able to teach others how to swim.
19. Learn how and when to make a safe rescue.
20. Be able to demonstrate proper resuscitation.

TEACHING CONSIDERATIONS

1. Skilled lifeguards should be on duty in the pool for all instructional sessions.
2. Beginning classes should contain fewer students than intermediate or advanced classes. All classes should be ability grouped as specified in the chapter.
3. Include review and practice in all sessions.
4. Basic stroke technique is easier to understand if demonstrations and initial practice take place out of the water.
5. Consider using a "buddy" system for safety and skill feedback.
6. Work first for technique and then using strokes for distance.
7. With intermediate and advanced swimmers, consider why students are taking the course. Competition, endurance, and recreational goals require different teaching orientations.

Volleyball

Volleyball

Completion of this chapter should enable the reader to:

- Appreciate the development of volleyball and describe the general rules and equipment used

- Practice the fundamental skills of passing, setting, spiking, serving, and blocking

- Explain aspects of team play and offensive and defensive strategies

- Teach the fundamentals of volleyball

HISTORY

Volleyball was invented in 1895 by William J. Morgan, who was physical education director of the YMCA in Holyoke, Massachusetts. He developed the game to provide an indoor game for the winter months in which relatively large groups of men could participate in a small gymnasium. The principal features of tennis were employed, but the net was raised and the players struck the bladder of a basketball with their hands instead of racquets.

The YMCA is chiefly credited with promoting this very fine game throughout the United States and in many foreign countries. In America volleyball is played regularly on playgrounds and in recreation centers, camps, and school and college classes and intramural programs. It recently has become one of the most popular sports in high school and college women's athletic programs. Also, it has become an excellent recreational game in the armed services and was used in both World War I and World War II.

The YMCA held its first National Volleyball Championships in 1922. The annual YMCA tournaments and the addition of the United States Volleyball Association (USVBA) Open Championships in 1928 further popularized the game, not only as a pleasurable sport but also as a competitive game.

Volleyball was adopted as an Olympic sport in 1964 at Tokyo. While at the time it was a sport played around the world, it was the Soviets and Japanese who took it most seriously. The Japanese women's teams introduced tenacious defense and increased the level of play by scraping and diving for every ball hit by an opponent. The Soviet's contribution to the game was the power offense. With the exception of 1976, when the Polish men's team defeated the Soviets for the gold medal, the Soviets of the Japanese won every men's and women's volleyball gold medal through 1980 (Soviet men three

gold, women three gold; Japanese men one gold, women two gold). In fact, in the women's competition from 1964 through 1980 the only time the gold or silver medal failed to go to the Soviets or Japanese was in 1980 when the Japanese boycotted the Olympics (silver to East Germany).

Until 1984 the highest finish by a U.S. men's team was seventh in 1968 and the highest placement by a U.S. men's team was seventh in 1968 nd the highest placement by a U.S. women's team was eighth, also in 1968. But in 1984 (when the Soviets boycotted) the U.S. men won the gold and the U.S. women won the silver (China won the gold). In 1988 the Soviet women's team regained the gold by beating Peru (with China capturing the bronze) but the U.S. men's team repeated its gold medal performance, this time by beating the Soviets 13-15, 15-10, 15-4 and 15-8.

Today the game of volleyball requires team strategies involving offensive and defensive plays and highly refined individual skills. Another modification that has become popular, especially on sand courts and beaches, is played with just two players on each side.

DESCRIPTION AND EQUIPMENT

Volleyball for men and women is played on a rectangular court divided by a tightly stretched net. The top of the net is 7 feet 11 5/8 inches (2.43 m) from the floor for men and 7 feet 4 1/8 inches (2.24 m) from the floor for women. A backcourt spiking line is drawn across the court 9 feet 10 inches (3 m) from and parallel to the centerline. Two lines, each 6 inches (15 cm) long, are drawn behind the endline to designate the serving area. One line is an extension of the right sideline. The other is 9 feet 10 inches (3 m) to the left of the first line. Six players constitute a team: three frontline players and three backline players.

An inflated leather ball 25 5/8 inches (65 to 67 cm) in circumference and weighing between 9 and 10 ounces (260 to 280 g) is used. It is somewhat smaller than a basketball and resembles a soccer ball of water polo ball in size.

The play begins with a serve by the right back player. The server stands with both feet in the service area, which must be at least 6 feet 6 inches (2 m) deep and is 9 feet 10 inches (3 m) wide to the right and in back of the endline. The right boundary line of this area is an extension of the right sideline of the court. The serve consists of hitting the ball with the hand (open or closed) or any part of the arm so that it goes clearly over the net and within the boundaries designated by vertical extensions of the sidelines called the net antennae. The receiving team must return the ball over the net before it reaches the floor. Each team may hit the ball a maximum of three times in returning it across the net (a block is not considered one of the three hits). The ball is returned back and forth until one team makes an error. Only the serving team may score points. If the receiving team commits a fault a point is scored. If the serving team makes the error or commits a fault, side-out is called and the other team serves following the rotation of players.

The ball must be cleanly hit in volleyball; it may not come to rest momentarily in the hands or on the arms. A player may not hit the ball twice in succession (*exception:* blocking rule). The server continues to serve until loss of serve or completion of the game. Following a sideout, the opposite team must rotate clockwise one position before serving. This rotational system is used so that every player rotates not only in serving but in position on the floor. Both teams must be in correct rotation order at the time the ball is served. However, after the serve players may exchange court positions.

ABRIDGED RULES AND REGULATIONS
USVBA rules and regulations are described here.

Playing area and court specifications
The height of the net is the only difference between court specifications for men and women.

Officials and their duties
1. The first referee is the superior official and decides whether the ball is in play or dead and when point or side-out is made and imposes penalties for rule infractions.

2. The second referee, stationed beneath and at the opposite end of the net from the first referee, assists the first referee wherever possible but is primarily responsible for net and centerline violations and for supervision of substitutions.
3. The scorer, seated on the side of the court opposite the referee, keeps the record on points scored, substitutions made, and time-outs called and supervises rotations of servers.
4. When two linesmen are used they are stationed diagonally opposite each other. They are responsible for decisions concerning boundary plays and serving errors.

Players and substitutes
1. If official matches each team must consist of only six players. Player positions along the net are designated right front, center front, and left front; those in the backcourt are called right back, center back, and left back.
2. When the ball is served, players must be in their positions. In the front line the center front must be between the right and left front. In the back line the center back must be between the right and left backs. Also, the back row players may not overlap with the front line players. As soon as the serve is contacted, players may move anywhere on their side of the court.
3. A substitute may replace any player when the ball is dead, provided the player has reported to the scorer and received permission of the referee. A player taken out of a gamy may reenter once but must return to the original position in the serving order.
4. A substitute who enters the game and is then removed cannot reenter until the next game.

Service and rotation of positions
1. Choice of playing area or service at the start of a match is determined by the toss of a coin. After each game the teams alternate who serves first. When teams are tied in the number of games won, the first serve in the deciding game is determined by a coin toss.
2. The player in the right back position makes the serve and continues as the server until side-out is called. After side-out is called, an opponent becomes the server.
3. Each member of a team, on receiving the ball for service, rotates clockwise one position and remains in this new position until side-out has been called on an opponent's serve.
4. When a game is completed, teams change courts, and alterations in rotation of players

must be made at that time. During the deciding game of a match when the score is tied, the teams change courts when one team reaches 8 points.

5. The server must stand entirely outside the court in the service area until the ball is struck. The server must bat the ball with one hand clearly over the net so that, if untouched, it will land within the opponent's court. A serve is good if it clears the net and is touched by an opponent, regardless of where it might have fallen.

Returning the ball

1. A return may be hit in any direction. A player may use any part of the body above and including the waist to hit the ball.
2. A return that passes over that part of the net between the net posts or their imaginary extensions is in play even if it touches the top of the net while in flight.
3. A return may be recovered from the net, provided the player avoids contact with the net.
4. After once contacting the ball, a player may not touch it again until it has been touched by some other player. (*Note:* After the ball has been blocked at the net, any of the blockers may make the next contact.)

Restrictions in the play of backline players

1. Backline players may not participate in the action of blocking.
2. Backline players may not spike from the attack area but may from behind the attack line.
3. Inasmuch as the attack line extends indefinitely, a backline player may not hit a ball into the opponents' court from above the height of the net while outside the court and within such limits of the attack area.

Infractions

If any member of the receiving team commits any of the infractions listed, 1 point is credited to the serving side; if the infraction is made by the serving team, side-out is called.

1. Serving illegally or serving out of turn.
2. Catching or holding the ball or failing to make a legal return.
3. Touching the ball twice in succession.
4. Contacting the net. A player is not considered to have contacted the net if a hard-driven ball causes it to touch him or her. (*Note:* Should two opponents contact the net simultaneously, neither player is penalized, and the serve is repeated.)

5. Touching the ball when it has already been played three times without passing over the net.
6. A player's foot completely touching the floor on the opposite side of the centerline. (*Note:* A player's foot or feet may contact the opponents' side, provided that some part of the foot or feet remains on or above the centerline.)
7. Reaching under the net and touching the ball or an opponent while the ball is in play.
8. Changing player positions before the serve has been made. Until the serve is made, players on each time must be in their relative playing positions.
9. Violating substitutions or time-out regulations.
10. Unnecessarily delaying the game.

Time-out

1. Time-out can be called only by the referee on request of a team captain or coach when the ball is dead.
2. Time-out for substitutions is not charged against a team, provided play is resumed immediately.
3. Time-out for rest is limited to twice each game, and play must be resumed in 45 seconds, except that if a player has been injured but is to remain in the game, the rest period may last 3 minutes.
4. Time-out between games is 2 minutes

Scoring

1. Failure of the receiving team to return the ball legally over the net into the opponent's court scores 1 point for the team serving.
2. A game is won when either team scores a 2-point lead with 15 or more points.
3. The score of a forfeited game is 15-0.
4. A match is won by the team that first scores two of three or three of five games. The three-of-five format is most common among college and international matches. Courts are changed in the middle of the third of fifth game.

FUNDAMENTAL SKILLS AND TECHNIQUES

Volleyball is a game that challenges the participant's skill in the use of the hands and agility in jumping, twisting, reaching, and hitting. Hitting motions that require the use of proper body control and muscular coordination are constantly demanded.

Passing

The most fundamental skill to be learned is the ability to pass the ball to a teammate, which is required on almost all plays.

Forearm pass

A forearm pass should be used to receive serves, low balls, and spikes. The forearm pass used to recover the opponents' attack is called a "dig." The official rules do not permit carrying the ball, which occurs during any open-handed hit below the chest. If the ball is hit underhanded, the player should clasp the hands together in any one of three methods: (1) clenched fist, (2) curled fingers, or (3) thumb over palm.

When possible the passer should move quickly to a position behind the ball, with knees bent, feet shoulder width apart, and trunk slightly forward. The hands and arms should be extended and together and parallel, with the elbows locked during contact. The hands should point toward the floor and the ball should be contacted on the forearm above the wrist. The arm movement should be an arc from the shoulders, with the legs actively involved.

One-arm pass

One-arm passes should not be used except at times when it is impossible to use both arms. In an emergency the player should hit the ball with a one-arm underhand fist, but when possible should be hit with the forearm.

Setting

The setter moves to a position so that the forehead is in line with the descending ball and faces the direction of the intended set. The setter's hands "form a window" 6 inches in front of the face with the upper arms nearly horizontal, wrists cocked, and fingers spread. The ball should be contacted with the inner surface of the thumb and fingers. A synchronized springing action of the fingers, wrists, and arms, as well as extension of the legs, pushes the ball forward.

Spiking

Spiking is the act of striking the ball with great force in a downward direction into the opponents' court. To accomplish this powerful offensive skill, the player must learn to coordinate the approach, takeoff, and arm movements. The spiker's preliminary position is near the sideline and attack line. Three of four steps are taken with the stronger leg.

The step-close takeoff is one method of transferring the momentum of the body into a vertical direction. During the last steps the heels of both feet contact the floor, and then the weight is shifted forward to the toes. Both arms swing backward to shoulder height when the heels contact the floor. The arms are swung forward and upward during the takeoff. The left arm extends directly upward above the shoulder, and the right arm bends into a throwing position. The left elbow leads the swing, followed by an extension of the spiking arm, contacting the ball with the heel of the open hand. The wrist should snap quickly over the ball to impart a topspin.

Tip

A tip is a soft shot contacted with the fingertips. The arm action is similar to the spike, but the attacker reduces the speed of the swing. The ball is contacted high above the net so that the tip is just over the opponent's attempted block.

Serving

Serves should never be missed at the beginning of a game, after a time-out or substitution, or near the end of a close game. Players should study the opposing team and serve to deep corners, weak players, areas between players (seams), and substitutes. Players should always concentrate on keeping the serve in bounds.

A player should learn to serve accurately and carefully, avoiding trick serves, because a team cannot score unless the serve is made good. The success of a serve therefore depends primarily on accuracy, control, and consistency. Regardless of the type of serve used, the server should attempt to place the ball in the opponents' backcourt, preferably in the corners or to the opponents' weakest receivers.

Types of service

The underhand serve is the easiest to learn and control. The use of the overhand serve will give greater speed to the served ball as well as a twisting line of flight deceptive to the opposing receivers. Sidearm serves can also be made.

Underhand serve. The underhand serve is the easiest and simplest for beginners to use to start the play.

In executing this serve, the player faces the net with the left foot in front (if right-handed) of the right, rests the ball in the left hand at about knee height, and hits it off the holding hand, which swings forward and upward during the hit. The hitting arm swings as in bowling a ball. The hand follows the ball straight through in the direction of the flight of the ball.

Overhand serve. There are two types of overhand serves--the floater and the top spin. the chief asset of the floater is its speed and its weaving line of flight, making it difficult for opponents to return. The top spin serve, while resulting in a more predictable path than the floater, tends to dive toward the floor after it crosses the net.

The overhand serve is executed by tossing the ball 2 or 3 feet in the air above and in front of the right shoulder. The left side of the body faces the net; with the feet in a stride position. As the ball falls to the desired hitting spot, the arm extends from a cocked position to contact the ball. The heel of the hand should be used. Contacting the ball momentarily at its midpoint and with little follow-through results in a floater, while contacting the ball on its lower midsection, snapping the wrist, and rolling the hand over the top of the ball imparts the top spin. The overhand serve is the one most used by players participating in power volleyball.

Sidearm serve. The sidearm serve is infrequently used. Its chief assets are its deceptive curves and the twist that the line of flight often has. Consistent use requires practice, but the serve can be used as a change of pace.

The ball is held at about hip level and is tossed about a foot into the air while the arm swings parallel to the floor. The left side of the body faces the net, left foot forward as in a forehand stance in tennis, and the swing of the arm is similar to the forearm swing.

Jump serve. A recent development is the jump serve. Hitting the serve while jumping allows the server to contact the ball at a higher point, thus permitting a steeper angle. The similarity of the body actions of this serve to the spike (except the angle of contact with the ball) makes this serve a natural and its use is increasing in high level competition.

Receiving the serve

The ball should be advanced from the backcourt to the front line in preparation for either spiking or placement in the opponents' court. The success of the receiving team depends on anticipating the flight of the serve and then on accurate passing.

Because the overhand serve is such a potent offensive weapon, formations for receiving the serve are necessary. An effective approach called the W formation is for the two front-line outside players to move back and toward their respective sidelines and the front-line center player stay near the net with the right shoulder turned slightly toward the net. The back-line center player becomes the primary serve returner by being positioned in the center of the court approximately 12 feet ahead of the back line. The back-line outside players move back to about 6 or 7 feet from the back line. In this formation the receiv-

ing team is best prepared to react to the rebound from the center back player, whose job is to nullify the effects of the opponents' serve.

Blocking

Blocking is a defensive play by an opponent or opponents against the spike or any other placement play near the net. Essentially, the block consists of a defensive player or players' jumping into the air directly in front of the spiker, with arms extended in an effort to block the ball and at the same time to rebound it off the arms back into the spiker's court. This results in the receiver's forming into a W arrangement. To block effectively, one should time the jump with that of the spiker. Multiple contacts by a player(s) participating in a block are legal provided they are during one attempt to intercept the ball.

Retrieving the ball from the net

To play the ball from the net, crouch low, legs spread and bent, with the body facing the sideline. As the ball rebounds from the net, use a forearm pass and an upward-backward striking motion so that a teammate may be able to play the ball. If the ball hits the net near the top, it will drop almost straight down. If it hits low in the net, it may rebound several feet, and the retriever must be stationed accordingly.

Team play

The idea of the game of volleyball is not merely to hit the ball back and forth over the net. Essentially, the game offers many opportunities for team play, both offensive and defensive. When these skills are smoothly developed and executed, a real sense of enjoyment is derived by all players.

Offense or attack

The basic offense consists of passing the ball from the back line to a setter at the net. The setter delivers the ball above and within 2 or 3 feet of the net to the spiker for the attack plays selected to take advantage of the opponents' weaknesses.

The attack is used to develop and establish a playing situation that will deliver to the opponents an unplayable ball. This requires team play. The spiker should aim the ball into an unguarded area of the opponents' court. Sometimes as a surprise play the spiker tips the ball just over the blockers' heads or directs it to either side of the blockers' hands.

The four-two is a simple, basic offense. Four players are designated as attackers and the tow best ball handlers as setters. In this system a setter always switches to the center of the front line. Success depends on the ability of the five remaining players to pass the ball to the designated setter. The service order should be arranged so that the two setters and two spikers are diagonally opposite each other.

Defense

Primarily, good defensive methods are formation plays to most effectively block or recover a hard-hit or well placed ball. A block is usually set up by grouping two (or occasionally three) front-line players. The back-line players are the secondary line of defense. The diggers must crouch low with hands held waist high, ready for a low, fast, spiked ball.

Return quickly to original position when drawn out on a play. The server should assume position immediately after a serve.

TEACHING CONSIDERATIONS

1. The overhead set is the basic skill upon which continuous play can be built. Therefore it should be the first skill taught. Teach the set using the following guidelines:
   a. Establish consistent good form in simple conditions from either a self-toss or a partner toss.
   b. Build the progression from:
      (1) Stationary setting to moving to receive the ball (stress getting into position before contacting the ball)
      (2) Returning the ball to the same direction, to returning the ball to a different direction
      (3) Simple tosses, to balls tossed across the net
2. Once the set is established one-on-one, two-on-two, and four-on-four, cooperative and competitive play can be introduced to teach positioning and basic offense and defense strategy. Offensive strategy includes:
   a. Playing the ball to an empty space on the opponents' court (back and to the sides).
   b. Changing the direction of the ball.
   c. Changing the dynamics of the hit (tip or spike).
      Defensive strategy for beginning players includes primarily returning to home base to cover space.
3. The serve can be introduced as court size increases. Introduction of the serve requires introduction of the forearm pass. Progression for the forearm pass is similar to that of the set.
4. combine practice of the forearm pass with the set and serve until students can receive a serve with the forearm pass from different directions and can set it to different directions.

5. Introduce the spike and dig only after consistency with the set and forearm pass is established.
6. Build new skills into the basic game gradually. Provide opportunities to play the game in modified form through the unit, increasing the number of players, size of the court, and skills used gradually as students develop consistency. Do not permit students to swing at the ball with one hand (make it illegal in game play if necessary). Modify rules to encourage good play (e.g., must be three hits on a side, or as many hits as needed).

245

Weight Training, Circuit Weight Training, and Weight Lifting

Weight Training, Circuit Weight Training, and Weight Lifting

Completion of this chapter should enable the reader to:

■ Describe the history of weight lifting and distinguish the differences among the activities in this chapter

■ Set up a personal weight training and circuit weight training program

■ Recognize the importance of safety in these activities

■ Identify appropriate exercises for various parts of the body

■ Explain the competitive and power lifting events

■ Teach basic weight lifting techniques to a group of beginning students

HISTORY

In its earliest form, weight lifting was a part of everyday life; however, the exact period in history when weight training became a practice or part of a training regimen is not known. There is, however, evidence that the first physical training programs were geared toward the development of only the strength component of fitness.

Ancient myth and folklore include accounts of strong men, such as Samson, Hercules, and the Greek warrior Milo. A legendary figure, Milo was said to have carried a calf up to a hayloft each night and then retrieved it each morning. As the calf gained weight Milo gained strength, until he was carrying a full-grown cow up and down a ladder daily.

In the days of the Greeks, Egyptians, and Romans, weight training played an important role in preparing soldiers for battle. During the Middle Ages, Romans trained their soldiers by marching them over long distances with heavier than normal loads. Throughout the seventeenth to nineteenth centuries, most of the empires and armies of Europe followed the Greek and Roman examples and trained with overloaded packs.

Weight lifting was introduced to the United States between 1859 and 1872, when Dr. G.B. Winship toured the United States and Canada giving lectures and exhibitions.

Weight lifting soon found its way into the carnivals, circuses, and vaudeville stages, where men and women performed unbelievable feats of strength that in fact were gimmicks and tricks, and which

probably are responsible for most of the myth and mystery that has surrounded weight training until recent times. Weight lifting survived this era and went on to find its way into YMCAs and athletic and health clubs. With these organizations promoting the activity, evidence of the value and worth of weight training began to grown.

Weight lifting has been included in the Olympic games since 1896. At first there were two events--a one-handed lift and a two-handed lift--and the lifter's body weight was not considered. In 1920 the press, snatch, and clean and jerk were introduced, and this system remained until 1972, when the press was eliminated. In the early Olympics weight lifting was dominated by European nations. In the United States an organized program for competition was not begun until the AAU held its first American National Championships in 1929. In 1932 the United States entered its first team in Olympic competition, and won the team championship for the first time in 1948 by winning four of the six weight categories. In the 1952 and 1956 Olympics, all the gold medals were won by United States or Soviet weightlifters. However, since the 1960 Olympics the Soviet and Eastern European countries (primarily Bulgaria, Hungary and Poland) have dominated the competition.

In recent years the sport of powerlifting has been the most popular form of competitive lifting in the United States. Since the AAU held its first American National Championships, the United States National team has won the Pan-Am and World Team titles with surprising regularity. In less than 10 years the sport has grown to the extent that more than 40 nations now compete in the International Powerlifting Federation World Championships. Although a comparatively new form of competition, the sport of powerlifting is now being considered as an additional event in Olympic competition.

Weight training is constantly increasing in popularity in colleges, health clubs, and YMCAs across the country. It is not uncommon to find a set of barbells in the recreation room of many American homes. In an age that has provided us with countless labor-saving devices, weight training has provided the much needed vigorous exercise that our push-button life-style has taken away.

Weight training
GENERAL CONSIDERATIONS

Frequency. Lifting should be done three times per week, with at least 1 day of rest between sessions. More advanced programs often follow different weekly schedules concentrating on specific areas on set days during the week. However, most basic programs start with working every body part equally, 3 days per week.

Logical order. Exercises should progress from multijointed muscle group exercises (bench press, squat) to single-jointed intrinsic muscle group exercises (arm curls, calf raises).

Beginning poundage. By trial and error one selects starting amounts of weight that can be lifted with proper form for 10 to 12 repetitions of an exercise.

Rest and recovery. During exercises one should allow 1½ to 2 minutes between each set to recover fully before proceeding to the next set. One exercise (all sets) should be completed before moving to the next exercise.

Sets and repetitions. A basic program usually consists of three sets of 10 to 12 repetitions, with proper recovery between sets.

Last set. The last set of each exercise should be difficult to complete using proper form. The weight should be such that a "momentary failure" is reached during the last set of each exercise.

Partners. It is important to lift with a partner and always consider safety first.

GENERAL TECHNIQUES FOR ALL LIFTS

Stretching. Basic overall stretching should precede any lifting, with particular attention to the muscle groups to be exercised. For example, before the bench press one should concentrate on stretching the chest, shoulders, and triceps. Many experts suggest that stretching activities should be used at the end of a workout as well.

Warm-up. Warm-up activities should be specific to the exercise; for example, a light bench press should be done in preparation for the bench press exercise. Usually a warm-up consists of 10 repetitions with a light, comfortable weight.

Breathing. One should inhale during the negative or lowering phase of all lifts, and exhale during the working or positive phase. One should never hold the breath during any part of a lift.

Full range. One should always complete the full range of motion during any lift, and never do any partial or half movements while learning the basic exercises.

Spotting. For any exercise culminating with the lifter in a fatigued state and still supporting the weights, a spotter should be used.

FUNDAMENTAL SKILLS AND TECHNIQUES
Exercises for the upper body
Free-weight bench press (for chest, shoulders, and upper arms)

Starting position. Lie on the bench with feet flat on the floor and arch the back slightly. The spotter lifts the weight from the rack and gives it to the weight lifter. The weight lifter should take the weight with the arms extended and the hands slightly wider apart than the shoulders.

Movement. Lower the bar to the middle of the chest. Then recover to the straight-arm starting position.

Technique and safety tip. Once the bar is pressed up approximately 12 to 14 inches from the chest, strive to angle the bar slightly back toward the head and shoulders. This places the bar at an advantageous angle for the shoulders and triceps to finish the lift.

Universal gym bench press

The technique for this exercise is the same as for the free-weight bench press but no spotter is required. The body should be positioned so that handles cross the middle of the chest.

Universal gym lat pull (for upper back, biceps, and posture muscles)

Starting position. Grasp the bar with a wide overhand grip. Kneel on one knee, with the head up and the back straight.

Movement. Pull the bar down behind the head until the bar reaches the base of the neck. Return the bar to the starting position.

Technique and safety tip. Return the bar slowly to avoid any loss of control or stabilization. No spotter is necessary.

Free-weight bent rowing (for posture muscles, biceps, and upper back)

Starting position. Stand with the feet shoulder width apart and the toes pointed out slightly. Bend over until the torso is parallel to the floor, and bend the knees slightly. Grasp the barbell with an overhand grip, with the hands at about shoulder width.

Movement. Pull the barbell up until it reaches the lower rib cage. Then return it to the starting position.

Technique and safety tip. Concentrate on raising the elbows as high as possible. No spotter is necessary. Always keep the knees bent to avoid lower back injury.

Free-weight overhead press (for shoulders and upper arms)

Starting position. Stand with the feet shoulder width apart and the toes pointed out slightly. Keeping the head erect, bend down and grasp the barbell with an overhand grip, with the hands also shoulder width apart. Return to the standing position and lift the barbell shoulder high.

Movement. Push the barbell straight up until the arms are fully extended. Return to the shoulder-high position. The knees should remain straight.

Technique and safety tips. Never bend or arch the back. Always look straight ahead or down during the lift to prevent lower back arching.

Free-weight arm curls (for biceps)

Starting position. Stand with the feet shoulder width apart and the toes pointed out slightly. Bend at the knees, grasp the bar with an underhand grip, then return to the standing position.

Movement. With the elbows tucked tightly against the rib cage, pull the bar up to the chest, and return to the starting position.

Technique and safety tip. To avoid arching the back, keep the head down and the eyes on the bar, or stand with the back against the wall.

Parallel bar dips (for lower chest, shoulders, and upper arms)

Starting position. Use an overhand grip on the parallel bar, and jump up to an arms-extended position. Cross the legs and arch the back slightly.

Movement. Bend or "dip" until the chest touches the crossbar or the elbow is bent 90 degrees. Push back up to the starting position.

Technique and safety tips. Keeping the back arched and the eyes forward help prevent swinging and rocking during the movement.

Three additional exercises for the upper body-- side lateral raises, bent lateral raises, and sit-ups--are described under Circuit Weight Training.

Exercises for the lower body
Free-weight parallel squats (for thighs, hips, lower back, and buttocks)

Starting position. Stand with feet shoulder width apart and the toes pointed out slightly. Grasp the bar with a comfortable, wide overhand grip. (The distance between the hands will vary with the individual.) Position the arms across the shoulders just below the base of the neck.

Movement. With the head up and the back slightly arched, squat until the tops of the thighs are parallel to the floor. Then extend the legs and return to the starting position.

Technique and safety tips. To avoid bending forward at the waist, keep the head up and the eyes focused ahead. The knees should be aligned directly over the toes while in the squat position. The rate of descent should be slow and controlled. Never try to bounce out of the squat position. Always use at least one spotter when doing this exercise. If it is difficult to keep the feet flat on the floor, use a heeled running shoe or stand with a 2- by 4-inch board the heels. Straddling a bench during the exercise is one way to avoid squatting too far down.

Universal gym leg press (for thighs and buttocks)

Starting position. Sit up straight at the station and place the feet on the lower pedals of the carriage. Grasp the handles on the sides of the chair.

Movement. Push until the legs are fully extended, and then return to the starting position.

Technique and safety tips. Position the seat so that the knees are flexed at least 90 degrees at the start of the exercise. Control the weight in the extended position. However, try to "pop" the weight up at the top of the stroke. Return slowly to the starting position.

Universal gym knee flexion (for hamstrings)

Starting position. Lie face down on the knee flexion table with the back of the ankles touching the carriage pads. The knees should be extended over the edge of the table.

Movement. Pull the carriage as far up toward the buttocks as possible. Then return to the starting position.

Technique and safety tips. The hips and buttocks have a normal tendency to rise during the movement, but this can be corrected by using a flexed table.

Free-weight heel raises (for calves)

Starting position. Grasp a dumbbell in each hand and position the balls of the feet over a board or stair step.

Movement. Stretch the calves by lowering the body until the heels are lower than the toes, then extend to a "tip-toe" position.

KEEPING A RECORD

When beginning a weight training or circuit training program, set down goals and chart the progress toward them. Fancy charts and printed graphs are not necessary. However, to keep track of current status and future plans, a diary or log is often helpful.

Most diaries start with the date and personal observations, such as body weight and current condition (for example, tired, energetic, strong, weak). This is followed by a renewal of goals (e.g., "Add two more repetitions to every exercise this week"). Next entered are the exercises to be done, and finally, the number of sets, numbers of repetitions, and amount of weight used for each exercise. Use one page for each workout session. When doing circuit weight training (describes in the next section), list the exercise to be done and the heart rate at the completion of each circuit.

Circuit weight training

Circuit weight training has become an increasingly popular form of weight training because it is believed to be one of the best forms of total body conditioning. Circuit weight training involves aerobic (using oxygen) as well as anaerobic (not using oxygen) as well as anaerobic (not using oxygen) work capacities. Normally, circuit weight training consists of 8 to 12 stations, with different weight training exercises at each. The participant moves form one station to another continuously. This provides the aerobic phase, with only enough time to get ready for the next exercise. Usually 10 to 15 repetitions are completed at each station. This provides the strength and local muscle endurance components. Rest time between stations is normally 10 to 15 seconds. The exercises should progress from the large, major muscle groups to the smaller groups and alternate between the upper and the lower body.

TYPICAL PROGRAM

1. Frequency: Program should be done 3 days per week on alternate days.
2. Intensity: 30 seconds at each station.
3. Repetitions: 10 at each station.
4. Rest time: 15 seconds between stations.
5. Order of exercises:
   a. Parallel squat
   b. Bench press
   c. Universal gym leg press
   d. Universal gym leg pull
   e. Back hyperextensions
   f. Overhead press
   g. Leg curls
   h. Arm curls
   i. Leg extensions
   j. Side lateral raises or alternate exercise
   k. Sit-ups

After the circuit is completed, the participant should fully recover before starting another cycle.

SETTING UP A PERSONAL CIRCUIT

Below are a few stations, listed by body part. When setting up a circuit, choose one or two exercises from each section. (Be sure to choose exercises that can be done with available equipment.) Nest, decide time intervals to be used; and finally, determine how many repetitions will be used at each station.

Another technique is to complete as many repetitions as possible in a chose time limit (e.g., 30 to 45 seconds). If this procedure is adopted, times 2, 3, and 4 above change to (2) Intensity: desired time limit; (3) Repetitions: maximum; and (4) Rest time: longer than 15 seconds to accommodate recovery. Also, only one cycle may be necessary when using this technique.

As an alternate exercise to side lateral raises, start with the arms at the sides with the elbows flexed at 90 degrees. Move the elbow backward until the weights are next to the hips and then return to the starting position. The arms remain flexed 90 degrees at the elbow throughout the exercise. This exercise is less stressful on the shoulders and elbows than side lateral raises.

Section 1--lower body (large-muscle group)

1. Free-weight parallel squat
2. Universal squat
3. Squat jump; remember, do not bounce or sag in squat position; jump as high as possible; alternate which foot is forward in the squat portion of the exercise.

Section 2--upper body (large-muscle group)

1. Bench press
2. Incline bench press
3. Resistance push-ups

Section 3--lower body (small-muscle groups)
1. Back hyperextensions
2. Universal leg press

Section 4--upper body (small-muscle groups)
1. Overhead press
2. Parallel bar dips
3. Bent rowing
4. Lat pull-down
5. Pull-ups (wide overhand grip)

Section 5--lower body (single muscle group)
1. Knee extensions
2. Calf raises
3. Leg curls

Section 6--upper body (single muscle group)
1. Arm curls
2. Sit-ups
   a. Unanchored
   b. Stand bent-knee sit-ups
3. Side lateral raises
4. Shoulder shrugs
5. Bent lateral raises

Weight lifting
COMPETITIVE LIFTING (OLYMPIC AND POWER)
Weight classification

Flyweight	114½ pounds (52 kg) and under
Bantamweight	123½ pounds (56 kg) and under
Featherweight	132¼ pounds (60 kg) and under
Lightweight	148 3/4 pounds (67.5 kg) and under
Middleweight	165¼ pounds (75 kg) and under
Light heavyweight	
	181 3/4 pounds (82.5 kg) and under
Middle heavyweight	
	198¼ pounds (90 kg) and under
	220½ pounds (100 kg) and under
Heavyweight	242½ pounds (110 kg) and under
Super heavyweight	
	275 pounds (125 kg) and under
Power lifting only	Unlimited

GENERAL RULES
Each competitor has the privilege of three trials for each scheduled event. In no case can a weight once tried be replaced by a lesser weight. The athletes themselves decide on the weight with which they will begin each event. The greatest amount in each event is then totaled, and the contestant with the highest total is the winner.

OLYMPIC LIFTS
Clean and jerk
Place the bar horizontally in front of the legs. Grip the bar with both hands and pull it up in a single, distinct motion from the ground to the shoulders while splitting or bending the legs. While resting the bar on the chest or arms, bring the feet back to the original position, that is, on the same line. Bend the legs, then extend the legs and the arms suddenly, thus jerking the bar to the arm's length above the head. The weight must be held int he final motionless position until the referee's signal to replace the bar on the platform.

Snatch
Place the bar horizontally in front of the legs. Grip the bar with both hands and pull it in one motion from the floor to the end of the arms vertically above the head, either splitting or bending the legs. The bar should pass with a continuous nonstop movement along the body, of which no part other than the feet may touch or graze the floor during execution of the movement. The lifted weight must be held in the final motionless position, arms and legs stretched and feet on the same line, until the referee gives the signal to lower the weight.

POWER LIFTS
Squat
Place the bar horizontally across the back of the shoulders. Assume an upright position with the hands gripping the bar and the feet flat on the platform. After the referee's signal, bend the knees and lower the body until the surface of the legs at the hip joint is lower than the tops of the knees. Then recover to the standing position.

Bench press
Assume a supine position on the bench, with the feet flat on the floor. The proper lift does not officially start until the bar is brought down and is absolutely motionless on the chest. The referee's signal is given, and the bar must be pressed vertically to arms' length.

Dead lift
Place the bar horizontally in front of the feet. Bend at the knees, grip the bar with both hands, and lift it upward with one continuous motion, with the arms remaining extended until standing erect with the knees locked and shoulders thrust back.

TEACHING CONSIDERATIONS

1. The decision to include weight training or circuit weight training in a program should be based in part on the availability of equipment in relation to the number of students involved. Unless a vigorous workout at least three times a week for a minimum of 6 weeks can be provided for each student, training effects are likely to be minimal.

2. For a school program, consider circuit weight training because of the total body effect. For units with specialized training goals, teach students the principles and possible effects of both weight training and circuit weight training.

3. Individual pretesting to assist with individual programs should be conducted before a full program is begun. Students can design their own programs if they are taught the principles of program design and if the teacher checks the programs before the students begin. Goal setting should be part of each program with periodic checks or progress in relation to goals.

4. Use exercises for which sufficient equipment is available to maintain the aerobic nature of the program.

5. Partner work is almost a necessity for many exercises.

6. Do not allow students to perform exercises incorrectly at any time. Insist on proper form and safety.

7. If students are kept off the equipment when they aren't using it for exercising, accidents are less likely to occur.

CREDITS

The Circulatory System

p.17-18, from HEART FACTS, RISKO, American Heart Association, 1988.

p.21, from Thibodeau, G: STRUCTURE AND FUNCTION, ed. 9, St. Louis, MO, 1992, Mosby-Year Book, Inc.,

The Respiratory System

p.33-36, from Thibodeau, G: STRUCTURE AND FUNCTION, ed. 9, St. Louis, MO, 1992, Mosby-Year Book, Inc.

The Digestive System

p.40-41, from Thibodeau, G: STRUCTURE AND FUNCTION, ed. 9, St. Louis, MO, 1992, Mosby-Year Book, Inc.

Nutrition and Weight Control

p.47-54, from McKenzie, J. and McKenzie, B: STUDENT STUDY GUIDE TO ACCOMPANY Payne/Hahn: UNDERSTANDING YOUR HEALTH, ed. 3, St. Louis, MO, 1992, Mosby-Year Book, Inc.

Calisthenic Exercise, Circuit Training, and Weight Training

p.60-61, from Thibodeau, G: STRUCTURE AND FUNCTION, ed. 9, St. Louis, MO, 1992, Mosby-Year Book, Inc.

p.62-67, from Prentice, W.E: FITNESS FOR COLLEGE AND LIFE, ed. 3, St. Louis, MO, 1991, Mosby-Year Book, Inc.

Human Sexuality

p.75, modified from Hatcher, R.A., et al: CONTRACEPTIVE TECHNOLOGY: 1986-1987, ed. 13, New York, NY 1986, Irvington Publishers, Inc.

p.77-78, from Haas, K. and Haas, A: UNDERSTANDING SEXUALITY, ed. 2, St. Louis, MO, 1990, Mosby-Year Book, Inc.

p.80-86, from Payne, W. and Hahn, D: UNDERSTANDING YOUR HEALTH, ed. 3, St. Louis, MO, 1992, Mosby-Year Book, Inc.

p.87, quiz from THE JOY OF BEING SINGLE, by Janice Haraycha, Copyright ©1986 by Janice Harayda, used with permission of Doubleday, a division of Bantam Doubleday, Dill Publishing Group, Inc.

p.90, from Denney, N. and Quadagno, D: HUMAN SEXUALITY, ed. 2, St. Louis, MO 1992, Mosby-Year Book, Inc.

Stress

p.99-101, from Seyle, H: STRESS WITHOUT DISTRESS, New York, NY, 1975, The New American Library

p.103-104, modified from an inventory developed by Rosellen Bonlen, University of Sranton.

p.105-108, from Payne, W. and Hahn, D: UNDERSTANDING YOUR HEALTH, ed. 3, St. Louis, MO, 1992, Mosby-Year Book, Inc.

Drug and Alcohol Use and Abuse

p.113-122, from Payne, W. and Hahn, D: UNDERSTANDING YOUR HEALTH, ed. 3, St. Louis, MO, 1992, Mosby-Year Book, Inc.

Mental Health

p.125-131, Payne, W. and Hahn, D, and Lipnickey, S: INSTRUCTOR'S MANUAL TO ACCOMPANY UNDERSTANDING YOUR HEALTH, ed. 3, St. Louis, MO, 1992, Mosby-Year Book, Inc.

p.133-134, from McKenzie, J. and McKenzie, B: STUDENT STUDY GUIDE TO ACCOMPANY UNDERSTANDING YOUR HEALTH, ed. 3, St. Louis, MO, 1992, Mosby-Year Book, Inc.

p.139-140, from STUDY GUIDE AND PERSONAL EXPLORATIONS FOR PSYCHOLOGY APPLIED TO MODERN LIFE: ADJUSTMENT IN THE 80's, by Wayne Weiten. Copyright ©1983 by Wadsworth, Inc.

Cancer
p.145-147, from Payne, W. and Hahn, D: UNDERSTANDING YOUR HEALTH, ed. 3, St. Louis, MO, 1992, Mosby-Year Book, Inc.
p.149, from Payne, W. and Hahn, D. and Lipnickey, S: INSTRUCTOR'S MANUAL TO ACCOMPANY UNDERSTANDING YOUR HEALTH, ed. 3, St. Louis, MO, 1992, Mosby-Year Book, Inc.

Aging
p.153, from Payne, W. and Hahn, D. and Lipnickey, S: INSTRUCTOR'S MANUAL TO ACCOMPANY UNDERSTANDING YOUR HEALTH, ed. 3, St. Louis, MO, 1992, Mosby-Year Book, Inc.
p.155, from Payne, W. and Hahn, D: UNDERSTANDING YOUR HEALTH, ed. 3, St. Louis, MO, 1992, Mosby-Year Book, Inc.

Death and Dying
p.159-160, reprinted with permission of Choice In Dying, Inc., 200 Varick Street, New York, NY 10014
p.161-162, from Payne, W. and Hahn, D: UNDERSTANDING YOUR HEALTH, ed. 3, St. Louis, MO, 1992, Mosby-Year Book, Inc.
p.163-165, from Payne, W. and Hahn, D. and Lipnickey, S: INSTRUCTOR'S MANUAL TO ACCOMPANY UNDERSTANDING YOUR HEALTH, ed. 3, St. Louis, MO, 1992, Mosby-Year Book, Inc.
p.167, from Payne, W. and Hahn, D: UNDERSTANDING YOUR HEALTH, ed. 3, St. Louis, MO, 1992, Mosby-Year Book, Inc.

Aerobic Dance, p.169-176, from Mood, D. and Musker, F. and Rink, J: SPORTS AND RECREATIONAL ACTIVITIES FOR MEN AND WOMEN, ed. 10, St. Louis, MO, 1991, Mosby-Year Book, Inc.

Jogging, p.177-184, from Mood, D. and Musker, F. and Rink, J: SPORTS AND RECREATIONAL ACTIVITIES FOR MEN AND WOMEN, ed. 10, St. Louis, MO, 1991, Mosby-Year Book, Inc.

Archery, p.185-192, from Mood, D. and Musker, F. and Rink, J: SPORTS AND RECREATIONAL ACTIVITIES FOR MEN AND WOMEN, ed. 10, St. Louis, MO, 1991, Mosby-Year Book, Inc.

Golf, p.193-202, from Mood, D. and Musker, F. and Rink, J: SPORTS AND RECREATIONAL ACTIVITIES FOR MEN AND WOMEN, ed. 10, St. Louis, MO, 1991, Mosby-Year Book, Inc.

Tennis, p.203-214, from Mood, D. and Musker, F. and Rink, J: SPORTS AND RECREATIONAL ACTIVITIES FOR MEN AND WOMEN, ed. 10, St. Louis, MO, 1991, Mosby-Year Book, Inc.

Badminton, p.215-224, from Mood, D. and Musker, F. and Rink, J: SPORTS AND RECREATIONAL ACTIVITIES FOR MEN AND WOMEN, ed. 10, St. Louis, MO, 1991, Mosby-Year Book, Inc.

Swimming, p.225-238, from Mood, D. and Musker, F. and Rink, J: SPORTS AND RECREATIONAL ACTIVITIES FOR MEN AND WOMEN, ed. 10, St. Louis, MO, 1991, Mosby-Year Book, Inc.

Volleyball, p.239-246, from Mood, D. and Musker, F. and Rink, J: SPORTS AND RECREATIONAL ACTIVITIES FOR MEN AND WOMEN, ed. 10, St. Louis, MO, 1991, Mosby-Year Book, Inc.

Weight Training, Circuit Weight Training, and Weight Lifting, p.246-253, from Mood, D. and Musker, F. and Rink, J: SPORTS AND RECREATIONAL ACTIVITIES FOR MEN AND WOMEN, ed. 10, St. Louis, MO, 1991, Mosby-Year Book, Inc.